Mometrix TEST PREPARATION

I0866898

TerraNova® NEXT

Grade 7 Mathematics Test Prep Guide

Written and edited by the Mometrix Test Preparation Team
Printed in the United States of America

TABLE OF CONTENTS

Introduction

Thank you for purchasing this resource! You have made the choice to prepare yourself for a test that could have a huge impact on your future, and this guide is designed to help you be fully ready for test day. Obviously, it's important to have a solid understanding of the test material, but you also need to be prepared for the unique environment and stressors of the test, so that you can perform to the best of your abilities.

For this purpose, the first section that appears in this guide is the **Success Strategies**. We've devoted countless hours to meticulously researching what works and what doesn't, and we've boiled down our findings to the most impactful steps you can take to improve your performance on the test. We start at the beginning with study planning and move through the preparation process, all the way to the testing strategies that will help you get the most out of what you know when you're finally sitting in front of the test.

We recommend that you start preparing for your test as far in advance as possible. However, if you've bought this guide as a last-minute study resource and only have a few days before your test, we recommend that you skip over the first two Success Strategies since they address a long-term study plan.

If you struggle with **test anxiety**, we strongly encourage you to check out our recommendations for how you can overcome it. Test anxiety is a formidable foe, but it can be beaten, and we want to make sure you have the tools you need to defeat it.

Strategy #1 – Plan Big, Study Small

There's a lot riding on your performance. If you want to ace this test, you're going to need to keep your skills sharp and the material fresh in your mind. You need a plan that lets you review everything you need to know while still fitting in your schedule. We'll break this strategy down into three categories.

Information Organization

Start with the information you already have: the official test outline. From this, you can make a complete list of all the concepts you need to cover before the test. Organize these concepts into groups that can be studied together, and create a list of any related vocabulary you need to learn so you can brush up on any difficult terms. You'll want to keep this vocabulary list handy once you actually start studying since you may need to add to it along the way.

Time Management

Once you have your set of study concepts, decide how to spread them out over the time you have left before the test. Break your study plan into small, clear goals so you have a manageable task for each day and know exactly what you're doing. Then just focus on one small step at a time. When you manage your time this way, you don't need to spend hours at a time studying. Studying a small block of content for a short period each day helps you retain information better and avoid stressing over how much you have left to do. You can relax knowing that you have a plan to cover everything in time. In order for this strategy to be effective though, you have to start studying early and stick to your schedule. Avoid the exhaustion and futility that comes from last-minute cramming!

Study Environment

The environment you study in has a big impact on your learning. Studying in a coffee shop, while probably more enjoyable, is not likely to be as fruitful as studying in a quiet room. It's important to keep distractions to a minimum. You're only planning to study for a short block of time, so make the most of it. Don't pause to check your phone or get up to find a snack. It's also important to **avoid multitasking**. Research has consistently shown that multitasking will make your studying dramatically less effective. Your study area should also be comfortable and well-lit so you don't have the distraction of straining your eyes or sitting on an uncomfortable chair.

The time of day you study is also important. You want to be rested and alert. Don't wait until just before bedtime. Study when you'll be most likely to comprehend and remember. Even better, if you know what time of day your test will be, set that time aside for study. That way your brain will be used to working on that subject at that specific time and you'll have a better chance of recalling information.

Finally, it can be helpful to team up with others who are studying for the same test. Your actual studying should be done in as isolated an environment as possible, but the work of organizing the information and setting up the study plan can be divided up. In between study sessions, you can discuss with your teammates the concepts that you're all studying and quiz each other on the details. Just be sure that your teammates are as serious about the test as you are. If you find that your study time is being replaced with social time, you might need to find a new team.

Strategy #2 – Make Your Studying Count

You're devoting a lot of time and effort to preparing for this test, so you want to be absolutely certain it will pay off. This means doing more than just reading the content and hoping you can remember it on test day. It's important to make every minute of study count. There are two main areas you can focus on to make your studying count.

Retention

It doesn't matter how much time you study if you can't remember the material. You need to make sure you are retaining the concepts. To check your retention of the information you're learning, try recalling it at later times with minimal prompting. Try carrying around flashcards and glance at one or two from time to time or ask a friend who's also studying for the test to quiz you.

To enhance your retention, look for ways to put the information into practice so that you can apply it rather than simply recalling it. If you're using the information in practical ways, it will be much easier to remember. Similarly, it helps to solidify a concept in your mind if you're not only reading it to yourself but also explaining it to someone else. Ask a friend to let you teach them about a concept you're a little shaky on (or speak aloud to an imaginary audience if necessary). As you try to summarize, define, give examples, and answer your friend's questions, you'll understand the concepts better and they will stay with you longer. Finally, step back for a big picture view and ask yourself how each piece of information fits with the whole subject. When you link the different concepts together and see them working together as a whole, it's easier to remember the individual components.

Finally, practice showing your work on any multi-step problems, even if you're just studying. Writing out each step you take to solve a problem will help solidify the process in your mind, and you'll be more likely to remember it during the test.

Modality

Modality simply refers to the means or method by which you study. Choosing a study modality that fits your own individual learning style is crucial. No two people learn best in exactly the same way, so it's important to know your strengths and use them to your advantage.

For example, if you learn best by visualization, focus on visualizing a concept in your mind and draw an image or a diagram. Try color-coding your notes, illustrating them, or creating symbols that will trigger your mind to recall a learned concept. If you learn best by hearing or discussing information, find a study partner who learns the same way or read aloud to yourself. Think about how to put the information in your own words. Imagine that you are giving a lecture on the topic and record yourself so you can listen to it later.

For any learning style, flashcards can be helpful. Organize the information so you can take advantage of spare moments to review. Underline key words or phrases. Use different colors for different categories. Mnemonic devices (such as creating a short list in which every item starts with the same letter) can also help with retention. Find what works best for you and use it to store the information in your mind most effectively and easily.

Strategy #3 – Practice the Right Way

Your success on test day depends not only on how many hours you put into preparing, but also on whether you prepared the right way. It's good to check along the way to see if your studying is paying off. One of the most effective ways to do this is by taking practice tests to evaluate your progress. Practice tests are useful because they show exactly where you need to improve. Every time you take a practice test, pay special attention to these three groups of questions:

- The questions you got wrong
- The questions you had to guess on, even if you guessed right
- The questions you found difficult or slow to work through

This will show you exactly what your weak areas are, and where you need to devote more study time. Ask yourself why each of these questions gave you trouble. Was it because you didn't understand the material? Was it because you didn't remember the vocabulary? Do you need more repetitions on this type of question to build speed and confidence? Dig into those questions and figure out how you can strengthen your weak areas as you go back to review the material.

Additionally, many practice tests have a section explaining the answer choices. It can be tempting to read the explanation and think that you now have a good understanding of the concept. However, an explanation likely only covers part of the question's broader context. Even if the explanation makes perfect sense, **go back and investigate** every concept related to the question until you're positive you have a thorough understanding.

As you go along, keep in mind that the practice test is just that: practice. Memorizing these questions and answers will not be very helpful on the actual test because it is unlikely to have any of the same exact questions. If you only know the right answers to the sample questions, you won't be prepared for the real thing. **Study the concepts** until you understand them fully, and then you'll be able to answer any question that shows up on the test.

It's important to wait on the practice tests until you're ready. If you take a test on your first day of study, you may be overwhelmed by the amount of material covered and how much you need to learn. Work up to it gradually.

On test day, you'll need to be prepared for answering questions, managing your time, and using the test-taking strategies you've learned. It's a lot to balance, like a mental marathon that will have a big impact on your future. Like training for a marathon, you'll need to start slowly and work your way up. When test day arrives, you'll be ready.

Start with the strategies you've read in the first two Success Strategies—plan your course and study in the way that works best for you. If you have time, consider using multiple study resources to get different approaches to the same concepts. It can be helpful to see difficult concepts from more than one angle. Then find a good source for practice tests. Many times, the test website will suggest potential study resources or provide sample tests.

Practice Test Strategy

If you're able to find at least three practice tests, we recommend this strategy:

UNTIMED AND OPEN-BOOK PRACTICE

Take the first test with no time constraints and with your notes and study guide handy. Take your time and focus on applying the strategies you've learned.

TIMED AND OPEN-BOOK PRACTICE

Take the second practice test open-book as well, but set a timer and practice pacing yourself to finish in time.

TIMED AND CLOSED-BOOK PRACTICE

Take any other practice tests as if it were test day. Set a timer and put away your study materials. Sit at a table or desk in a quiet room, imagine yourself at the testing center, and answer questions as quickly and accurately as possible.

Keep repeating timed and closed-book tests on a regular basis until you run out of practice tests or it's time for the actual test. Your mind will be ready for the schedule and stress of test day, and you'll be able to focus on recalling the material you've learned.

Strategy #4 – Pace Yourself

Once you're fully prepared for the material on the test, your biggest challenge on test day will be managing your time. Just knowing that the clock is ticking can make you panic even if you have plenty of time left. Work on pacing yourself so you can build confidence against the time constraints of the exam. Pacing is a difficult skill to master, especially in a high-pressure environment, so **practice is vital**.

Set time expectations for your pace based on how much time is available. For example, if a section has 60 questions and the time limit is 30 minutes, you know you have to average 30 seconds or less per question in order to answer them all. Although 30 seconds is the hard limit, set 25 seconds per question as your goal, so you reserve extra time to spend on harder questions. When you budget extra time for the harder questions, you no longer have any reason to stress when those questions take longer to answer.

Don't let this time expectation distract you from working through the test at a calm, steady pace, but keep it in mind so you don't spend too much time on any one question. Recognize that taking extra time on one question you don't understand may keep you from answering two that you do understand later in the test. If your time limit for a question is up and you're still not sure of the answer, mark it and move on, and come back to it later if the time and the test format allow. If the testing format doesn't allow you to return to earlier questions, just make an educated guess; then put it out of your mind and move on.

On the easier questions, be careful not to rush. It may seem wise to hurry through them so you have more time for the challenging ones, but it's not worth missing one if you know the concept and just didn't take the time to read the question fully. Work efficiently but make sure you understand the question and have looked at all of the answer choices, since more than one may seem right at first.

Even if you're paying attention to the time, you may find yourself a little behind at some point. You should speed up to get back on track, but do so wisely. Don't panic; just take a few seconds less on each question until you're caught up. Don't guess without thinking, but do look through the answer choices and eliminate any you know are wrong. If you can get down to two choices, it is often worthwhile to guess from those. Once you've chosen an answer, move on and don't dwell on any that you skipped or had to hurry through. If a question was taking too long, chances are it was one of the harder ones, so you weren't as likely to get it right anyway.

On the other hand, if you find yourself getting ahead of schedule, it may be beneficial to slow down a little. The more quickly you work, the more likely you are to make a careless mistake that will affect your score. You've budgeted time for each question, so don't be afraid to spend that time. Practice an efficient but careful pace to get the most out of the time you have.

Test-Taking Strategies

This section contains a list of test-taking strategies that you may find helpful as you work through the test. By taking what you know and applying logical thought, you can maximize your chances of answering any question correctly!

It is very important to realize that every question is different and every person is different: no single strategy will work on every question, and no single strategy will work for every person. That's why we've included all of them here, so you can try them out and determine which ones work best for different types of questions and which ones work best for you.

Question Strategies

✓ Read Carefully

Read the question and the answer choices carefully. Don't miss the question because you misread the terms. You have plenty of time to read each question thoroughly and make sure you understand what is being asked. Yet a happy medium must be attained, so don't waste too much time. You must read carefully and efficiently.

✓ Contextual Clues

Look for contextual clues. If the question includes a word you are not familiar with, look at the immediate context for some indication of what the word might mean. Contextual clues can often give you all the information you need to decipher the meaning of an unfamiliar word. Even if you can't determine the meaning, you may be able to narrow down the possibilities enough to make a solid guess at the answer to the question.

✓ Prefixes

If you're having trouble with a word in the question or answer choices, try dissecting it. Take advantage of every clue that the word might include. Prefixes can be a huge help. Usually, they allow you to determine a basic meaning. *Pre-* means before, *post-* means after, *pro-* is positive, *de-* is negative. From prefixes, you can get an idea of the general meaning of the word and try to put it into context.

✓ Hedge Words

Watch out for critical hedge words, such as *likely, may, can, often, almost, mostly, usually, generally, rarely,* and *sometimes.* Question writers insert these hedge phrases to cover every possibility. Often an answer choice will be wrong simply because it leaves no room for exception. Be on guard for answer choices that have definitive words such as *exactly* and *always.*

✓ Switchback Words

Stay alert for *switchbacks.* These are the words and phrases frequently used to alert you to shifts in thought. The most common switchback words are *but, although,* and *however.* Others include *nevertheless, on the other hand, even though, while, in spite of, despite,* and *regardless of.* Switchback words are important to catch because they can change the direction of the question or an answer choice.

✓ Face Value

When in doubt, use common sense. Accept the situation in the problem at face value. Don't read too much into it. These problems will not require you to make wild assumptions. If you have to go beyond creativity and warp time or space in order to have an answer choice fit the question, then you should move on and consider the other answer choices. These are normal problems rooted in reality. The applicable relationship or explanation may not be readily apparent, but it is there for you to figure out. Use your common sense to interpret anything that isn't clear.

Answer Choice Strategies

✓ ANSWER SELECTION

The most thorough way to pick an answer choice is to identify and eliminate wrong answers until only one is left, then confirm it is the correct answer. Sometimes an answer choice may immediately seem right, but be careful. The test writers will usually put more than one reasonable answer choice on each question, so take a second to read all of them and make sure that the other choices are not equally obvious. As long as you have time left, it is better to read every answer choice than to pick the first one that looks right without checking the others.

✓ ANSWER CHOICE FAMILIES

An answer choice family consists of two (in rare cases, three) answer choices that are very similar in construction and cannot all be true at the same time. If you see two answer choices that are direct opposites or parallels, one of them is usually the correct answer. For instance, if one answer choice says that quantity *x* increases and another either says that quantity *x* decreases (opposite) or says that quantity *y* increases (parallel), then those answer choices would fall into the same family. An answer choice that doesn't match the construction of the answer choice family is more likely to be incorrect. Most questions will not have answer choice families, but when they do appear, you should be prepared to recognize them.

✓ ELIMINATE ANSWERS

Eliminate answer choices as soon as you realize they are wrong, but make sure you consider all possibilities. If you are eliminating answer choices and realize that the last one you are left with is also wrong, don't panic. Start over and consider each choice again. There may be something you missed the first time that you will realize on the second pass.

✓ AVOID FACT TRAPS

Don't be distracted by an answer choice that is factually true but doesn't answer the question. You are looking for the choice that answers the question. Stay focused on what the question is asking for so you don't accidentally pick an answer that is true but incorrect. Always go back to the question and make sure the answer choice you've selected actually answers the question and is not merely a true statement.

✓ EXTREME STATEMENTS

In general, you should avoid answers that put forth extreme actions as standard practice or proclaim controversial ideas as established fact. An answer choice that states the "process should be used in certain situations, if..." is much more likely to be correct than one that states the "process should be discontinued completely." The first is a calm rational statement and doesn't even make a definitive, uncompromising stance, using a hedge word *if* to provide wiggle room, whereas the second choice is far more extreme.

✓ BENCHMARK

As you read through the answer choices and you come across one that seems to answer the question well, mentally select that answer choice. This is not your final answer, but it's the one that will help you evaluate the other answer choices. The one that you selected is your benchmark or standard for judging each of the other answer choices. Every other answer choice must be compared to your benchmark. That choice is correct until proven otherwise by another answer choice beating it. If you find a better answer, then that one becomes your new benchmark. Once you've decided that no other choice answers the question as well as your benchmark, you have your final answer.

✓ PREDICT THE ANSWER

Before you even start looking at the answer choices, it is often best to try to predict the answer. When you come up with the answer on your own, it is easier to avoid distractions and traps because you will know exactly what to look for. The right answer choice is unlikely to be word-for-word what you came up with, but it should be a close match. Even if you are confident that you have the right answer, you should still take the time to read each option before moving on.

General Strategies

⊘ Tough Questions

If you are stumped on a problem or it appears too hard or too difficult, don't waste time. Move on! Remember though, if you can quickly check for obviously incorrect answer choices, your chances of guessing correctly are greatly improved. Before you completely give up, at least try to knock out a couple of possible answers. Eliminate what you can and then guess at the remaining answer choices before moving on.

⊘ Check Your Work

Since you will probably not know every term listed and the answer to every question, it is important that you get credit for the ones that you do know. Don't miss any questions through careless mistakes. If at all possible, try to take a second to look back over your answer selection and make sure you've selected the correct answer choice and haven't made a costly careless mistake (such as marking an answer choice that you didn't mean to mark). This quick double check should more than pay for itself in caught mistakes for the time it costs.

⊘ Pace Yourself

It's easy to be overwhelmed when you're looking at a page full of questions; your mind is confused and full of random thoughts, and the clock is ticking down faster than you would like. Calm down and maintain the pace that you have set for yourself. Especially as you get down to the last few minutes of the test, don't let the small numbers on the clock make you panic. As long as you are on track by monitoring your pace, you are guaranteed to have time for each question.

⊘ Don't Rush

It is very easy to make errors when you are in a hurry. Maintaining a fast pace in answering questions is pointless if it makes you miss questions that you would have gotten right otherwise. Test writers like to include distracting information and wrong answers that seem right. Taking a little extra time to avoid careless mistakes can make all the difference in your test score. Find a pace that allows you to be confident in the answers that you select.

⊘ Keep Moving

Panicking will not help you pass the test, so do your best to stay calm and keep moving. Taking deep breaths and going through the answer elimination steps you practiced can help to break through a stress barrier and keep your pace.

Final Notes

The combination of a solid foundation of content knowledge and the confidence that comes from practicing your plan for applying that knowledge is the key to maximizing your performance on test day. As your foundation of content knowledge is built up and strengthened, you'll find that the strategies included in this chapter become more and more effective in helping you quickly sift through the distractions and traps of the test to isolate the correct answer.

Now that you're preparing to move forward into the test content chapters of this book, be sure to keep your goal in mind. As you read, think about how you will be able to apply this information on the test. If you've already seen sample questions for the test and you have an idea of the question format and style, try to come up with questions of your own that you can answer based on what you're reading. This will give you valuable practice applying your knowledge in the same ways you can expect to on test day.

Good luck and good studying!

Ratios and Proportional Relationships

Rates and Ratios

Rates and ratios are a way to express the relationship between units.

A **ratio** expresses the relationship between two values, often with similar units. A **rate** also expresses the relationship between two values, but usually these values have unlike units. Rates also describe the relationship between a dependent unit and an independent unit. Rates use the word "per" to compare the values. In a ratio, there is not one independent unit and one dependent unit. A few examples of ratios include comparing green paint to white paint, dogs to cats, or flour to sugar. Some common examples of rates include dollars per hour, miles per hour, and beats per second.

Rates and ratios are commonly expressed through words, symbols, and quotients.

Let's say that for every 2 cups of sugar, we need to add 3 cups of flour to a recipe. This is a comparison between sugar and flour for this recipe. You could say that the ratio of sugar to flour is 2 to 3, or the relationship between sugar and flour is $\frac{2}{3}$.

Review Video: Ratios
Visit mometrix.com/academy and enter code: 996914

Proportions

We can use proportions to solve problems with ratios and rates. A **proportion** is an equation with two equivalent comparisons. We use proportions to compare ratios and to solve ratio and rate problems.

For example, we can calculate that for every 4 cups of sugar, we would add 6 cups of flour because these ratios are equivalent. This can be described by the proportion.

$$\frac{\text{sugar}}{\text{flour}} = \frac{2}{3} = \frac{4}{6}$$

Each ratio is equivalent, so the relationship between sugar and flour remains proportional.

Review Video: Proportions
Visit mometrix.com/academy and enter code: 505355

Example

We are making cookies. The ratio of sugar to flour is 2 cups of sugar to every 3 cups of flour. We are increasing the recipe and using 8 cups of sugar. How many cups of flour will we need for the recipe?

We can use proportions to help us solve this problem where x is the number of cups of flour needed. Since the ratio of sugar to flour does not change, the proportion in the original recipe is equal to the proportion in the adjusted recipe.

$$\frac{2}{3} = \frac{8}{x}$$

Now, we can solve the proportion for the number of cups of flour needed for 8 cups of sugar by using cross multiplication.

$$\frac{2}{3} = \frac{8}{x}$$
$$2 \times x = 8 \times 3$$
$$2x = 24$$
$$\frac{2x}{2} = \frac{24}{2}$$
$$12 = x$$

So, if we are using 8 cups of sugar, we need 12 cups of flour.

$$\frac{2}{3} = \frac{8}{12}$$

These are equivalent ratios. Their equivalent values show that the comparison of flour to sugar remains proportional.

EXAMPLE

In a given week, a veterinarian sees 5 dogs in his office for every 3 cats that come in his office. The vet saw 18 cats this week. How many dogs did the vet see this week?

This problem can be solved using ratios. To find the number of dogs the vet saw this week, we can set up a proportion using x to represent the number of dogs, and solve.

$$\frac{\text{dogs}}{\text{cats}} = \frac{5}{3} = \frac{x}{18}$$

To solve the proportion, we will cross multiply to find the value of x.

$$\frac{5}{3} = \frac{x}{18}$$
$$5 \times 18 = 3x$$
$$90 = 3x$$
$$\frac{90}{3} = \frac{3x}{3}$$
$$30 = x$$

The vet saw 30 dogs this week.

EXAMPLE

A screen-printing shop prints 450 shirts every 3 hours. How many shirts do they print each hour if they print shirts at a constant rate?

This problem focuses on solving a rate problem. To solve this problem, we can set up a proportion to find the equivalent rate to find the number of shirts printed per hour.

$$\frac{\text{shirts}}{\text{hour}} = \frac{450}{3} = \frac{x}{1}$$

Now, we can cross multiply and solve.

$$\frac{450}{3} = \frac{x}{1}$$
$$450 = 3x$$
$$150 = x$$

The screen-printing shop prints 150 shirts each hour.

Representing Rates

Tables

Rates can be expressed through tables. If you make $12 per hour, you can create a table to express how much you would make after a certain number of hours.

Hours (x)	Dollars (y)
1	12
2	24
10	120
20	240

This table expresses the relationship, or comparison, of dollars and hours. For each hour, the value of dollars increases at a rate of 12.

Equations

Rates can be expressed algebraically using the equation $y = kx$, where k is the rate of change. If you make $12 per hour, the rate of pay could be described as $y = 12x$. This equation can also be determined from the table provided where x represents the number of hours and y represents the number of dollars. The rate of change is 12, so the value of dollars, y, is determined by the number of hours, x, multiplied by 12.

Graphs

Finally, rates can be expressed graphically. Combining the data found on the table and the given equation, $y = 12x$, the rate of $12 per hour can be expressed using a graph where the x values align with the number of hours and the y values align with the number of dollars.

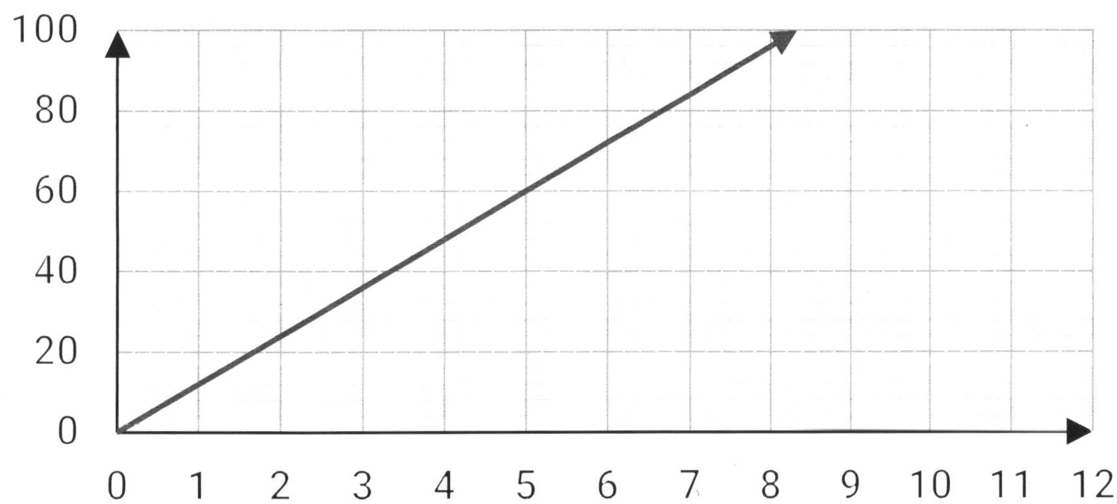

This graph represents the rate of pay if you make \$12 per hour and represents the equation $y = 12x$. To verify that a graph represents the rate, we can identify a point on the line and compare its x value and its y value. If the relationship between those values matches the rate, then we can reasonably conclude that the graph represents the rate. On the graph, a point on the line is (5,60), where $x = 5$ and $y = 60$. We know that $\frac{60}{5} = 12$, or the rate of $\frac{60 \text{ dollars}}{5 \text{ hours}} = \frac{12 \text{ dollars}}{1 \text{ hour}}$. The graph should also have a y-intercept of 0. This graph crosses the y-axis at (0,0), so it has a y-intercept of 0.

EXAMPLE

Apples cost \$1.30 per pound at the grocery store. Which equation represents the relationship between *d*, dollars, and *p*, pounds?

a. $p = 1.3d$
b. $p = d + 1.3$
c. $d = 1.3p$
d. $d = p + 1.3$

This problem focuses on representing rates using equations. The given rate is that apples cost \$1.30 per pound. We want to identify the equation that appropriately represents the relationship between d, dollars, and p, pounds.

If the rate of the cost of apples, or the relationship between dollars and pounds, is \$1.30 per pound, this means that the number of dollars the apples cost depends on the number of pounds of apples purchased. To find the number of dollars, you can take the number of pounds and multiply that value by 1.3. This can also be stated as dollars is equal to the number of pounds times 1.3, or $d = p \times 1.3$, which can also be written as $d = 1.3p$.

The correct answer is C.

EXAMPLE

Kim types at a rate of 45 words each minute. Which graph can be used to represent the relationship between w, words and m, minutes?

a.

$(y = 45x)$

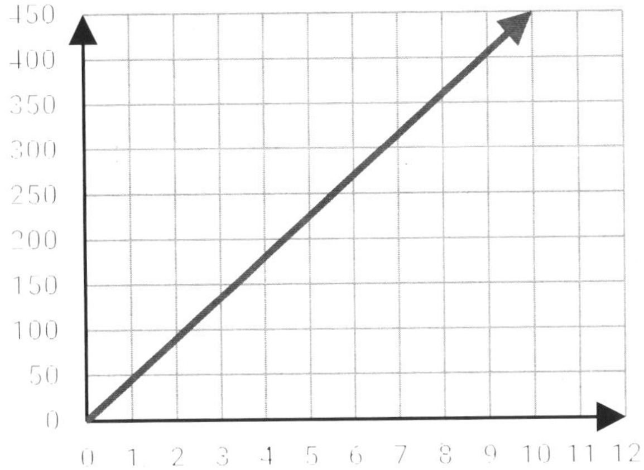

b.

$(y = 45x + 45)$

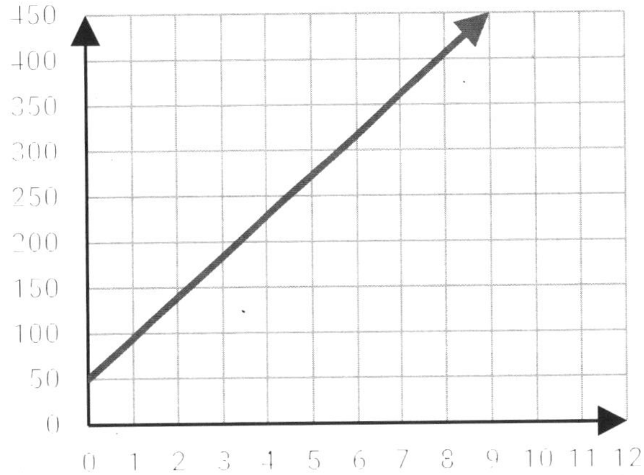

c.

$(y = 90x)$

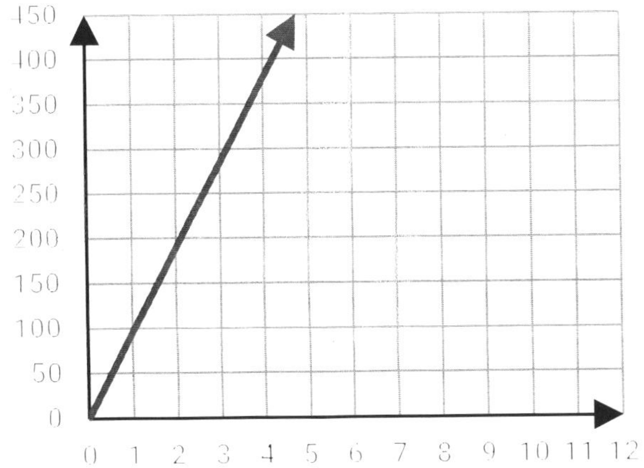

d.

$(y = 50x)$

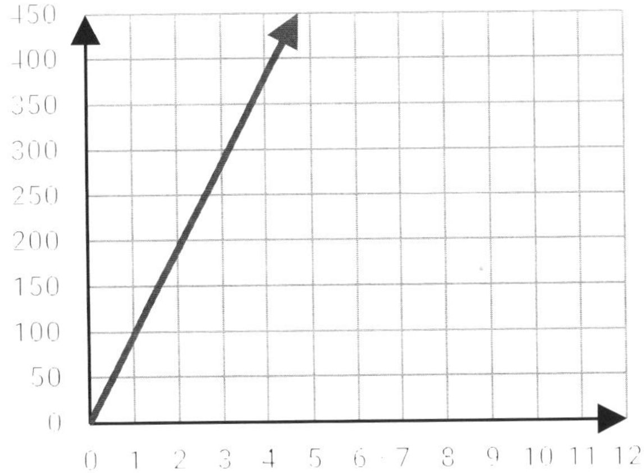

The given rate is that Kim types 45 words per minute. We want to identify the graph that appropriately represents the relationship between w, words, and m, minutes.

If Kim types at a rate of 45 words per minute, then the number of words typed is dependent on the Dnumber of minutes spent typing. For example, after 1 minute, Kim will type 45 words, and after 10 minutes, Kim will type 450 words. This information can be described in a table.

Minutes	1	2	5	10
Words	45	90	225	450

We can see that the value of words is 45 times the value of minutes, so we can say that the number of words is 45 times the number of minutes, $w = 45m$.

This information can be expressed graphically using x and y values. If the number of words is dependent on the number of minutes, words is going to be our y value, and minutes will be our x value. This means that $w = 45m$ can be graphed using the equation $y = 45x$. To express this rate graphically, we will need to find at least two points. The table can be used to find our points. The graphed line that represents the rate 45 words per minute will include the points (0,0) and (1,45).

The correct answer is A.

EXAMPLE

A car travels at a constant rate of 60 miles per hour. Which representation does NOT appropriately represent the relationship between distance and time?

a. $d = 60t$

b.

Hours	60	120	180	240
Miles	1	2	3	4

c.

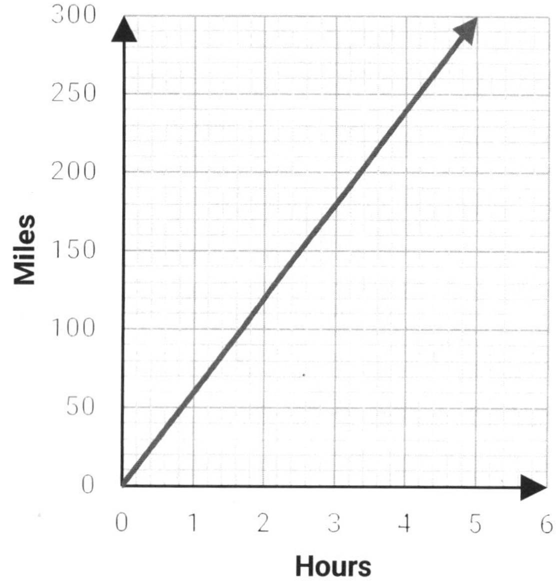

d.

Hours	Miles
2	120
4	240
9	360
8	480

This problem focuses on representations of rates. We know that the rate of travel is 60 miles per hour and we need to identify the representation that does NOT appropriately represent the relationship between distance and time.7

Algebraically, the relationship between distance and time is a special type of relationship. We know that constant rates can be described using a linear equation in the form $y = kx$, where k represents the rate. When traveling at a constant rate, the relationship can be described using the equation $d = rt$, where d represents distance, r represents the rate of travel, and t represents time.

Knowing this, we can describe the relationship between distance and time expressed in the problem. The car travels at a constant rate of 60 miles per hour. The distance is represented by miles, the time is represented by hours, and the rate is 60 miles per hour. This means that the equation that represents this rate is $d = 60t$, where the total distance in miles is 60 times the value of time in hours.

This information can also be described in a table.

Hours (t)	Miles (d)
1	60
2	120
5	300
10	600

The given rate can also be described using a graph. To graph the line that represents the rate, we need to identify two or more points that would lie on that line. To do that, we can input x values and identify the corresponding y values. Usually, $x = 0, x = 1$, and $x = 2$ are great choices to identify points along a line. Since constant rates can also be expressed using the form $y = kx$ as well as $d = rt$, these values can be input into the formula $y = 60x$.

$$y = 60x$$
$$y = 60(0)$$
$$0 = 60(0)$$

The line will begin at the origin, (0,0).

$$y = 60x$$
$$y = 60(1)$$
$$60 = 60(1)$$

Another point on the line is (1,60).

$$y = 60x$$
$$y = 60(2)$$
$$120 = 60(2)$$

And another point on the line is (2,120).

Now, we can graph these points on a plane.

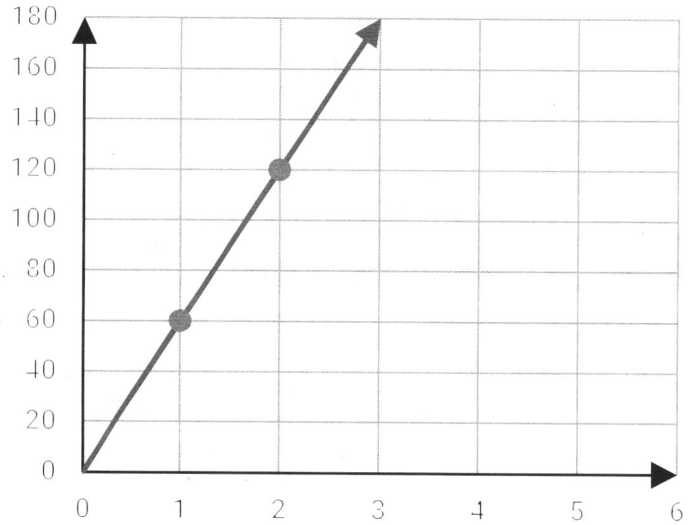

Now that we have three representations, we can compare these representations to the given options.

Choice A represents the rate algebraically because it matches the equation we created. Choice C correctly represents the rate graphically because it includes the appropriate points. Choice D represents the rate using a table because the value of miles is 60 times the value of hours.

Choice B does not appropriately represent the rate because the relationship between miles and hours is NOT 60, it is $\frac{1}{60}$, where the value of hours is 60 times the value of miles.

The correct answer is B.

UNIT RATES

A rate describes the relationship between units. A **unit rate** is a rate written in simplest form, where one of the two units is one. Let's say you work as a dog trainer for 4 hours and make \$50. You are paid at a rate of \$50 per 4 hours. The unit rate would describe how much you make in 1 hour.

To find the unit rate, this rate can be written as a fraction, $\frac{50}{4}$ dollars per hour. By simplifying the fraction, we find the unit rate.

$$\frac{50}{4} = \frac{12.5}{1} = 12.5$$

So, you work for \$12.50 per hour.

Review Video: Rates and Unit Rates Visit mometrix.com/academy and enter code: 185363

EXPRESSING UNIT RATES

Rates can be expressed in two ways. For example, we can find the rate of dollars to 1 hour, and we can also find the rate of hours to 1 dollar.

If you work as dog trainer and earn $50 for 4 hours of work, you make $12.50 per hour. But how many hours do you have to work to make 1 dollar? We can use the same strategies as before to express the relationship between hours and dollars.

$$4 \text{ hours per } \$50 = \frac{4 \text{ hours}}{50 \text{ dollars}} = \frac{4}{50} \text{ hours per dollar}$$

Simplify the fraction and convert it to a decimal to find the unit rate.

$$\begin{aligned} &= \frac{4}{50} \\ &= \frac{1}{12.5} \\ &= 0.08 \end{aligned}$$

You work 0.08 hours to make 1 dollar.

We can also use a table.

Hours	Dollars
4	50
	1

We can find the unit rate of hours to dollars by dividing each value by 50 to find the rate of 0.08 hours per dollar, which means that you will make $1 for every 0.08 hours of work.

When working as a dog trainer, you made 12.5 dollars per hour and worked $\frac{1}{12.5}$ hours per dollar.

Hours	Dollars	$\frac{\text{hours}}{\text{dollars}}$	$\frac{\text{dollars}}{\text{hours}}$
4	50	$\frac{4}{50}$	$\frac{50}{4}$
1	12.5	$\frac{1}{12.5}$	$\frac{12.5}{1}$

Example

Trevor read 150 pages in 8 hours. At this rate, how many pages does Trevor read each hour? Write your answer in decimal form.

This problem focuses on finding the unit rate of pages to 1 hour. If Trevor read 150 pages in 8 hours, then how many pages did he read in 1 hour? To solve this problem, we can use equivalent fractions. Since the number of pages Trevor reads in 1 hour is unknown, we can represent it using the variable x.

$$\frac{150 \text{ pages}}{8 \text{ hours}} = \frac{x \text{ pages}}{1 \text{ hours}}$$

When solving for a variable using equivalent fractions, which may also be called a **proportion**, it is helpful to convert the fractions to non-fraction values. Remember that in an equation, if you multiply one side by a value, you must do the same to the other side. When you multiply a fraction by its denominator, the product will be equal to the numerator.

$$\frac{150}{8} \times 8 = 150$$

However, when we know that the denominator of both fractions will be canceled out by multiplying each numerator by the other fraction's denominator, we can skip these steps and rewrite the equation. One side of the new equation will show the numerator of one fraction multiplied by the denominator of the second fraction. This will be equal to the numerator of the second fraction multiplied by the denominator of the first fraction. This strategy is called **cross multiplication.**

$$8x = 150 \times 1$$

Then, solve for the variable by dividing both sides by 8.

$$8x = 150 \times 1$$
$$8x = 150$$
$$\frac{8x}{8} = \frac{150}{8}$$
$$x = 18.75$$

Trevor read at a rate of 18.75 pages per hour.

Constant Rates

A **rate** is a comparison of two values with different units. A **constant rate** means that the relationship between units remains the same. Some common examples are the comparison of dollars to hour, miles to hours, and beats to seconds. Rates can be expressed in a variety of ways, including using language, as quotients, using equivalent rates, algebraically, using tables, or graphically.

Rates can be expressed through language. Let's say you get your first job working at a store making $12 for every hour of work. This is a rate, a comparison between two unlike units, dollars and hours. This rate can be expressed through words. We use the word *per* when expressing rates. You could say that you make 12 dollars per hour.

Rates can be expressed as a fraction, or division. If you make 12 dollars per hour, you could express that as $12/hour. You could express the rate as $\frac{\text{12 dollars}}{\text{1 hour}}$. You could even say that the rate of dollars per hour is $\frac{12}{1}$.

Rates can be expressed using equivalent rates. $12/hour can be expressed as $24/2 hours. Or, if you work 20 hours per week, you could say you make $240/week. Regardless of the number of hours worked, the number of dollars made per hour remains constant, or the same.

Constant of Proportionality

A rate or unit rate describes the relationship between units. If the relationship between units is constant, then the relationship is proportional. If a car is traveling at a constant rate of 60 miles per hour, then it will travel 120 miles in 2 hours, and 180 miles in 3 hours.

Hours (x)	1	2	3	4	5
Miles (y)	60	120	180	240	300

Regardless of the value of hours or miles, the relationship between miles, y, and hours, x, remains constant. The relationship between miles and hours in this case is that miles is 60 times the number of hours. This can be described using the equation $y = 60x$.

When there is a constant relationship between units, the rate can be described algebraically using the equation $y = kx$, where k represents the **constant of proportionality,** or the value of the relationship between x and y.

EXAMPLE

A donut shop sells sets of donuts for a constant rate. The table below shows the cost for different amounts of donuts.

Number of Donuts	Cost
6	$4.50
12	$9.00
24	$18
50	$37.50

What is the constant of proportionality that relates the number of donuts, x, and the cost of the donuts, y?

This problem focuses on identifying the constant of proportionality from a situation. We know that the constant of proportionality is the value of the relationship between x and y, and this relationship can be modeled using the equation $y = kx$, where k represents the constant of proportionality.

Use the equation $k = \frac{y}{x}$ to solve for the constant of proportionality, k.

The y value is the cost of the donuts, and the x value is the number of donuts. We can choose any of the given pairs of x and y values.

$$k = \frac{y}{x}$$
$$k = \frac{4.5}{6}$$
$$k = 0.75$$

The constant of proportionality is 0.75.

Parts Compared to a Whole

Fractions, decimals, and **percentages** share a common function: they each compare a **part** to a **whole**. One example of a part of a whole is a quarter. A quarter is 25 cents, or $0.25. There are a few ways we could express the relationship between quarters and dollars. We could express this as a fraction. A quarter is $\frac{25}{100}$ of a dollar because it is 25 cents out of 100 cents. This could be simplified to $\frac{1}{4}$ of a dollar. We could express this as a decimal. A quarter is 0.25 of a dollar. And we could express this as a percent. A quarter is 25% of a dollar. Each of these representations show the same value of part compared to the whole.

SOLVING PROBLEMS INVOLVING PERCENTS

In problems involving percents, it may be important to use fractions, decimals, and percents interchangeably and understand how to convert between each representation. Fractions can be converted to decimals through division and decimals can be converted into percents by multiplying the value by 100. To find the percentage of a value, you will multiply the decimal form of the percentage by the total value to get the value of the percent.

Suppose you are at a restaurant and want to tip your waiter 20%. The total bill before you add the tip is $43. How much should you leave for a tip?

In this problem, we want to find 20% of $43. To find the value of a percentage, we need to multiply the total by the percent in decimal form.

Let's start by converting 20% to a decimal by dividing 20 by 100.

$$20 \div 100 = 0.20$$

Now, we can multiply 43 by 0.2.

$$\begin{array}{r} 43 \\ \times 0.2 \\ \hline 8.6 \end{array}$$

So, 20% of 43 is 8.6.

You will leave an $8.60 tip for your waiter.

Example

You have a business selling t-shirts. You buy the t-shirts for $3.50 each and resell them for 450% of the amount you pay for them. What is the price of a t-shirt to your customer?

This problem focuses on finding the percent of a total. We know the total cost of a t-shirt and we want to find the value of 450% of $3.50. To find the percent, we will multiply the decimal form of the percent by the total price.

$$450\% = 4.5$$
$$4.5 \times 3.5 = 15.75$$

450% of $3.50 is $15.75 which means that the price of a t-shirt to your customer is $15.75.

Percent Change

A percent change problem is a percentage problem where there is a percent increase or a percent decrease. To find a percent change, we find the value of the change and divide this by the starting value.

For example, suppose a store is having a sale on tablets. A tablet that originally cost $250 is on sale for $175. By what percentage was the price was reduced?

In this problem, we want to know by what percentage the cost was decreased. The price decreases from $250 to $175. To find a percent change, find the value of the change, and divide this by the starting value, $250.

The change is the difference between the beginning and ending value.

$$250 - 175 = 75$$

The change is $75. Now, we can divide this value, the part, by the starting value, the whole.

$$\frac{75}{250} = 0.3$$

This decimal can now be converted to a percent.

$$0.3 \times 100 = 30\%$$

The price of the tablet has decreased by 30%

Review Video: Percent Change
Visit mometrix.com/academy and enter code: 907890

EXAMPLE

The gas tank on a car contains 11.6 gallons of gas. At the end of the week, the gas tank has 2.9 gallons of gas. What is the percent decrease of gallons of gas in the tank from the beginning to the end of the week?

In this problem, the number of gallons of gas reduces from 11.6 to 2.9 through the week. To find the percent decrease, identify the value of the change, divide the change by the beginning value, and convert the quotient to a percent.

The change can be found through subtraction.

$$11.6 - 2.9 = 8.7$$

The change is 8.7 gallons.

Now, we can divide the change by the beginning value.

$$\frac{8.7}{11.6} = 0.75$$

Last, convert the decimal change to a percentage.

$$0.75 \times 100 = 75\%$$

The gas decreased by 75% through the week.

EXAMPLE

Last year, a middle school sold 187 tickets to their talent show. This year, the talent show sold 220 tickets. What was the percentage increase in the number of tickets sold from last year to this year?

In this problem, the number of tickets sold for a talent show increase from 187 tickets to 220 tickets. To find the percent increase, we will identify the value of the change, divide by the beginning value, and convert the decimal to percent.

$$220 - 187 = 33$$

$$33 \div 220 = 0.15$$

$$0.15 \times 100 = 15$$

The number of tickets sold increased by 15%.

The Number System

Rational Numbers

Rational numbers are all numbers that can be written as a fraction. **Rational numbers** include positive numbers, negative numbers, fractions, improper fractions, most decimals, and some repeating decimals. If it can be written as a fraction, it is rational. An example is 6, which can be written as $\frac{6}{1}$. Another example is 0.75, which can be written as $\frac{3}{4}$. A number that is not rational is called an irrational number. An example of an **irrational number** is π, or 3.1415963..., because it is a decimal that continues without a pattern and cannot be written as a fraction.

Rational numbers, **integers**, **whole numbers**, and **natural numbers** are four categories used to classify numbers. Rational numbers include all numbers that can be written as a fraction, and these numbers form the broadest category of the four. All integers, whole numbers, and natural numbers can be described as rational numbers.

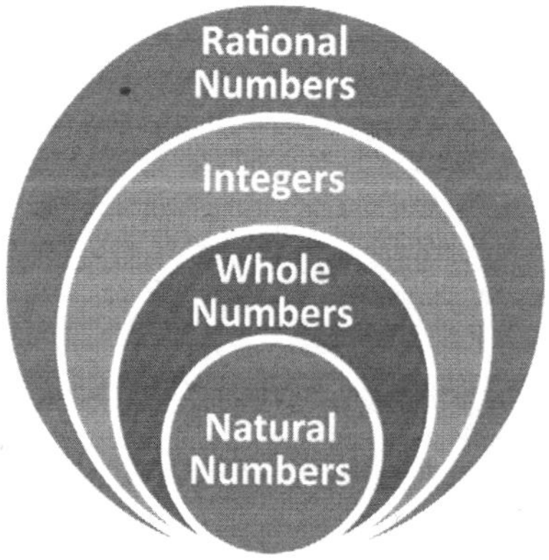

Review Video: Rational and Irrational Numbers
Visit mometrix.com/academy and enter code: 280645

Integers

Integers are a subset of rational numbers, and they include all positive and negative numbers that can be written without a fraction or decimal. Some examples include 7 and −56. All integers are rational numbers, as they can be written as a fraction.

Whole Numbers

Whole numbers are a subset of integers that include all the positive numbers that can be written without a fraction or decimal. 0, 1, 2, 3... to infinity are all whole numbers. All whole numbers can also be described as integers or rational numbers.

Natural Numbers

Natural numbers are a subset of whole numbers that include all whole numbers greater than zero. This means that zero is a whole number, but not a natural number. All natural numbers can also be described as whole numbers, integers, and rational numbers. Natural numbers form the most specific subset of the number categories.

Review Video: Classification of Numbers
Visit mometrix.com/academy and enter code: 461071

Converting Fractions and Decimals

To convert a fraction to a decimal, simply divide the numerator by the denominator in the fraction.

$$\frac{5}{8} = 0.625$$

$$\begin{array}{r} 0.625 \\ 8\overline{)\,5.000} \\ -\underline{0} \\ 5\,0 \\ -\underline{4\,8} \\ 20 \\ -\underline{16} \\ 40 \\ -\underline{40} \\ 0 \end{array}$$

When a rational number is converted to a decimal, it will either terminate or repeat. For example, $\frac{1}{3}$ and $\frac{5}{11}$ are both repeating decimals. When converted to decimals, they both have repeating sequences. $\frac{1}{3} = 0.33333333 \ldots = 0.\overline{3}$ and $\frac{5}{11} = 0.45454545 \ldots = 0.\overline{45}$. The bar across the top of the number indicated that the value is repeated indefinitely. On the other hand, $\frac{1}{2}$ and $\frac{1}{8}$ are both terminating decimals. When converted to decimals, they both terminate or stop. $\frac{1}{2} = 0.5$ and $\frac{1}{8} = 0.125$. Both values can have an infinite number of zeros added to the end of them without changing the value itself. Decimal values that do not repeat or terminate cannot be rational numbers.

To convert a decimal to a fraction, put the decimal in the numerator with 1 in the denominator. Multiply the numerator and denominator by tens until there are no more decimal places. Then simplify the fraction to lowest terms. For example, converting 0.24 to a fraction:

$$0.24 = \frac{0.24}{1} = \frac{0.24 \times 100}{1 \times 100} = \frac{24}{100} = \frac{6}{25}$$

Locating Rational Numbers on a Number Line

When locating the placement of integers and rational numbers on a number line, we use whole numbers and negative numbers as a guide. We can easily locate, compare, and order whole numbers like 0, 1, 2, 5, 9, and 258 on a number line. They lie in ascending order to the right of zero. Negative numbers lie on the number line to the left of zero in ascending order. An integer that is in the form of an improper fraction or square root, such as $\frac{12}{3}$ or $-\sqrt{49}$, should be converted into its whole number or negative number counterpart, so $\frac{12}{3}$ simplifies to 4, and $-\sqrt{49}$ simplifies to -7, and can now be placed appropriately on a number line.

Rational numbers can be slightly more complicated. When you are given a rational number, a number that can be written as a fraction, it is best to convert it to a number that is easy for you to use. Are you more familiar with the values of fractions or decimals? That is a decision only you can make. Regardless of which you choose, convert the rational number to a number that is easier to work with, and find its place on the number line.

Example

Place $-\frac{8}{3}$ on the number line.

There are three strategies to approach this task:

Strategy 1: Convert to a decimal using division.

$$\begin{array}{r} 2.6\overline{6} \\ 3\overline{)8.00} \\ \underline{6} \\ 2\,0 \\ \underline{1\,8} \\ 20 \\ \underline{18} \\ 2 \end{array}$$

$$-\frac{8}{3} = -2.\overline{6}$$

Given this value, we can determine that this number belongs to the left of the number line because it is less than zero. It is between −3 and −2. And we can divide the section between −3 and −2 into tenths, and estimate that this value is slightly to the right of −2.7.

Strategy 2: Convert to a mixed number.

Ask yourself, how many times will 3 go into 8 evenly, or how many $\frac{3}{3}$ are in $\frac{8}{3}$?

3 goes into 8 two times and has a remainder of 2.

In other words, there are two $\frac{3}{3}$ in $\frac{8}{3}$ with $\frac{2}{3}$ left over.

$$-\frac{8}{3} = -2\frac{2}{3}$$

Given this value, we can determine that this number is between −3 and −2. We can divide this section further into thirds, and count two to the left to place this value at $-2\frac{2}{3}$.

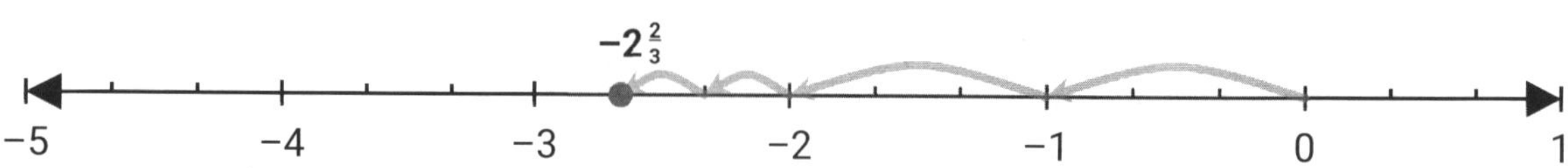

Strategy 3:

Place $-\frac{8}{3}$ on the number line using thirds.

Given this value, we can determine that this value is less than one and will be to the left of 0. We can also determine that each section between whole numbers should be divided into 3 sections to represent thirds.

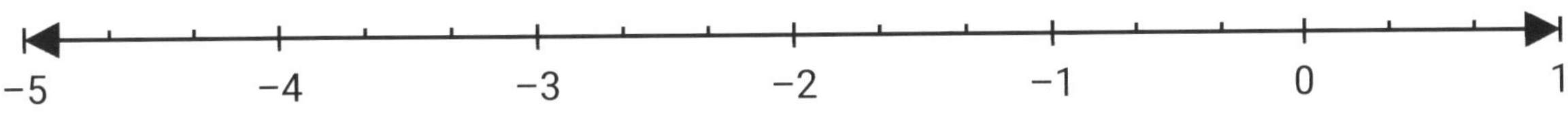

We can now count 8 thirds to the left because we are dealing with a negative fraction.

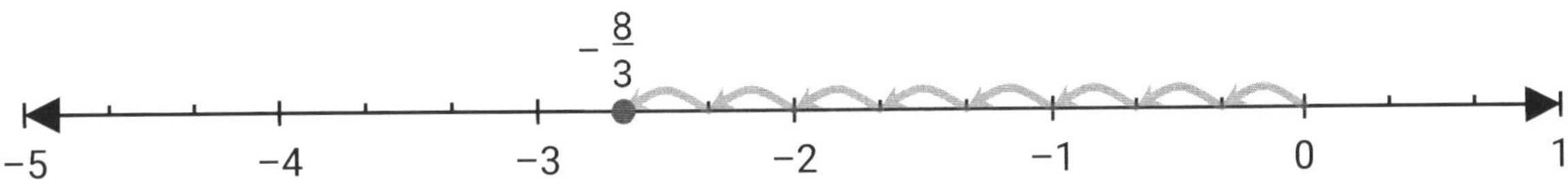

Each strategy will give you the same approximate placement on the number line. The strategy that is chosen is dependent on which type of value is the simplest for you. Each person has number preferences. Choose the best strategy for you based on your preferences. Which strategy was easier for you to follow? Which version of the same value (decimal, mixed number, or improper fraction) was simpler for you to estimate? You may choose more than one strategy!

Comparing and Ordering Rational Numbers

Comparing numbers involves making decisions about whether one number is greater than, less than, or equal to another. Ordering numbers involves making comparisons between more than two numbers to order them from least to greatest, or greatest to least. When you compare and order a set of rational numbers, it is important to first identify where you can make simple judgments. Can you identify the negative and positive numbers? That can help narrow down which numbers are greater and less than others. Can you identify a number that is much larger or much smaller than the rest of the set of numbers? Great! Use your knowledge of numbers to make some judgments and narrow down the set from there. Each set of numbers is different, and you will have to make observations and judgments based on the values given.

Once you have made preliminary judgments, next it is time to rewrite the remaining values as a representation that is easy to work with and convert them appropriately. The goal is to have forms that are easy to visualize so you may make comparisons between numbers. When you are given a list of fractions, it is often helpful to find a common denominator. When working with a mix of decimals and fractions, it is often helpful to convert the values to a common format: all fractions or all decimals. When you are given a rational number using an exponent or a square root, express these numbers in their integer form. Remember, place value is very important when comparing and ordering numbers, specifically integers and decimals.

Do not make the mistake of comparing numbers correctly but not ordering them the way the question is asked. Pay attention and double check if the question is asking for numbers to be ordered from greatest to least, or least to greatest.

Review Video: Ordering Rational Numbers
Visit mometrix.com/academy and enter code: 419578

Example

Order the values from greatest to least.

$$-3.48, -\frac{3}{5}, 4, \frac{17}{4}, -3\frac{1}{2}$$

Step 1: Start by making some judgments about the numbers in this list. We can see that there are some negative values and some positive values. Using this judgment, we can determine that 4 and $\frac{17}{4}$ are greater than the other values just by their signs alone. These two values will be first in our list because they are the greatest. Let's compare these values first to create the beginning of our list.

4 is a value that is easy to work with, but $\frac{17}{4}$ is a little tougher. This should be converted to a number that is easier to work with. You may choose to perform the division problem, $17 \div 4$, to find this value as a decimal. Or, you may choose to find the mixed number form of this improper fraction. Let's find both.

Converting to decimal:

```
    4.25
4 ) 17.00
    16
     1 0
       8
       20
       20
        0
```

So, $\frac{17}{4} = 4.25$.

Converting to mixed number:

To find the whole number, we can ask ourselves, how many times does 4 go into 17 evenly, or how many times does $\frac{4}{4}$ go into $\frac{17}{4}$? 4 times, so 4 is our whole number.

Now, to find the fractional part of this number, we can ask, what is left over. Since $\frac{4}{4} \times 4 = \frac{16}{4}$, we can subtract and find that $\frac{17}{4} - \frac{16}{4} = \frac{1}{4}$. So, 4 is our whole number, and $\frac{1}{4}$ is our fraction.

This means that $\frac{17}{4} = 4\frac{1}{4}$.

Step 2: Now that we have a decimal or mixed number, we can compare this value to 4. We make the judgment that $4 < \frac{17}{4}$.

Now we have our first two values. We are ordering numbers from greatest to least, so the greatest value is $\frac{17}{4}$ and the next greatest value is 4.

Step 3: Continue to make judgments about the remaining values. We can see that there are two values that include −3 as a whole number and then a negative proper fraction. Without doing any conversions, we can determine that the numbers that have −3 as a whole number are smaller than the negative proper fraction. This tells us that $-\frac{3}{5} > -3.47$ and $-\frac{3}{5} > 3\frac{1}{2}$.

We can now include this value to our list from greatest to least. So far, we know:

$$\frac{17}{4} > 4 > -\frac{3}{5}$$

Step 4: Compare the remaining values. We only have two values left, -3.48 and $-3\frac{1}{2}$. We can now make judgments on these values. To compare these numbers, we can convert them both to decimals, convert them both to fractions, or use our number sense. You may be able to look at these values and make an automatic judgment. Let's convert our values to decimals to make sure. I know that $\frac{1}{2}$ is equivalent to 0.5, so I can say that $-3\frac{1}{2} = -3.5$.

Now that our values are in similar forms, we can compare.

When dealing with negative numbers, remember the "larger" the number, the smaller the value. Given -3.48 and -3.5, we will start with the largest place value and compare. We can say that they each have a 3 in the ones place, so we will move to the tenths. The tenths are different. -3.48 has a 4 in the tenths place and -3.5 has a 5 in the tenths place. Because these are negative numbers, we can determine that $-3.48 > -3.5$, or $-3.5 < -3.48$.

Step 5: Review the order and rewrite the values.

We are asked to order this list from greatest to least and we have all the information needed to do this. We have found that $\frac{17}{4} > 4 > -\frac{3}{5} > -3.48 > -3.5$. We can now order these values from greatest to least.

$$\frac{17}{4}, 4, -\frac{3}{5}, -3.48, -3\frac{1}{2}$$

The Four Operations

It is important to be able to add, subtract, multiply, and divide rational numbers quickly and easily. This includes operations with whole numbers, integers, and rational numbers, including fractions and decimals. When you are solving operations with integers, a common way to get a question wrong is to mix up your signs. There are a few rules that you should remember and practice frequently so you can avoid sign errors.

Addition

When you add two positive numbers, your answer will be positive.

$$7 + 32 = 39$$

When you add two negative numbers, your answer will be negative.

$$-7 + (-32) = -39$$

When you add a negative number to a positive number, the total value will be less than the positive number. Adding a negative number is the same as subtracting the positive version of that negative number.

$$\begin{aligned} &= 25 + (-5) \\ &= 25 - 5 \\ &= 20 \end{aligned}$$

When you add a positive number to a negative number, the total value will be greater than the negative number. When adding a positive number to a negative number, use subtraction.

$$\begin{aligned} &= -6 + 36 \\ &= 36 + -6 \\ &= 36 - 6 \end{aligned}$$

$$= 30$$

Subtraction

When you subtract two positive numbers, and the first number is larger, your answer will be positive.

$$24 - 3 = 21$$

When you subtract two positive numbers, and the first number is smaller, your answer will be negative.

$$3 - 24 = -21$$

When you subtract two negative numbers, your answer will be greater than the starting value. Subtracting a negative number is equivalent to adding the number.

$$-16 - (-4) = -16 + 4 = -12$$
$$-4 - (-16) = -4 + 16 = 12$$

Example

What is the value of the expression $5\frac{1}{4} + (-12.42)$?

This problem focuses on adding and subtracting rational numbers. To solve this problem, we need to understand operations with positive and negative rational numbers and converting the given values to the same form.

In this problem, you could convert these values to fraction form or decimal form. Decimal form would give numbers that are easier to work with, so converting to decimals would be the best option.

$$5\frac{1}{4} + (-12.42) = 5.25 + (-12.42)$$

Adding a negative number is the same as subtracting its opposite.

$$5.25 + (-12.42) = 5.25 - 12.42$$

The final step is to subtract.

$$5.25 - 12.42 = -7.17$$

The correct answer is –7.17.

Multiplication and Division

When multiplying and dividing positive and negative rational numbers, it is important to remember and practice the rules for integer multiplication and division. Whether the answer will be negative or positive depends on the number of negative numbers in your problem. If the total number of negative signs is even, your answer will be positive. If you have an odd number of negative numbers, your answer will be negative.

When multiplying and dividing two positive numbers, the answer will be positive.

$$5 \cdot 6 = 30$$
$$72 \div 9 = 8$$

When multiplying and dividing two negative numbers, the answer will be positive.

$$-7 \cdot (-3) = 21$$
$$-16 \div (-4) = 4$$

When multiplying or dividing a negative number and a positive number, the answer will be negative.

$$-2 \cdot 8 = -16$$
$$-24 \div 6 = -4$$

Review Video: Mathematical Operations
Visit mometrix.com/academy and enter code: 208095

EXAMPLE

What is the value of the expression $\left(-2\frac{3}{4}\right)(30.2)$?

This problem focuses on multiplying rational numbers. To solve this problem, the first step is to convert these values so they are written in the same form. You may choose to convert these values to fractions or decimals. Your choice depends on which form you feel most comfortable working with.

Strategy 1:

If you choose to convert the values to fractions, converting values to improper fractions makes the numbers easier to multiply. To convert a mixed number to an improper fraction, begin by multiplying the whole number by the denominator of the fraction. Next, add the product to the numerator of the fraction. This value becomes the numerator for the improper fraction. The denominator used in the mixed number will be the denominator used in the improper fraction.

$$-2\frac{3}{4} = -\frac{11}{4}$$

$$30.2 = 30\frac{2}{10} = 30\frac{1}{5} = \frac{151}{5}$$

When multiplying fractions, multiply numerator by the other numerator and the denominator by the other denominator. That is, multiply straight across.

$$-\frac{11}{4} \times \frac{151}{5} = \frac{(-11 \times 151)}{(4 \times 5)} = \frac{-1{,}661}{20}$$

This can also be expressed as the mixed number $-83\frac{1}{20}$.

Strategy 2:

If you choose to convert the values to decimals, the expression $\left(-2\frac{3}{4}\right)(30.2)$ can be converted to $-2.75(30.2)$.

Now you can use multiplication to solve.

$$-2.75 \times 30.2 = -83.05$$

The correct answer is -83.05.

EXAMPLE

What is the value of the expression $36.75 \div \left(-7\frac{1}{2}\right)$?

This problem focuses on dividing rational numbers. To solve this problem, each value should be converted so they are written in the same form. You may choose to convert these values to fractions or decimals.

Strategy 1:

If you choose to convert the values to fractions, the conversion should be to improper fractions to make the numbers easier to divide.

$$36.75 = 36\frac{3}{4} = \frac{147}{4}$$

$$-7\frac{1}{2} = -\frac{15}{2}$$

When dividing fractions, find the reciprocal of the divisor and multiply.

$$\frac{147}{4} \div \left(-\frac{15}{2}\right) = \frac{147}{4} \times \left(-\frac{2}{15}\right) = \frac{(147 \times (-2))}{(4 \times 15)} = \frac{-294}{60} = -\frac{49}{10}$$

This can also be expressed as a mixed number: $-4\frac{9}{10}$.

Strategy 2:

If you choose to convert the values to decimals, the expression $36.75 \div \left(-7\frac{1}{2}\right)$ can be converted to $36.75 \div (-7.5)$.

Now you can use division to solve.

$$36.75 \div (-7.5) = -4.9$$

The correct answer is -4.9.

WORD PROBLEMS AND THE FOUR OPERATIONS

Solving problems using all operations might include answering word problems that involve more than one step or operation. When you encounter a problem that describes a situation, the best way to approach these problems is to identify the information that is known, identify the information that is unknown, and draw a picture.

EXAMPLE

Theresa is planning a family trip to an amusement park. The total cost of admission is \$88.25. There are 3 adults and 7 children going to the amusement park. Children's tickets cost \$7.25 each. What is the price of 1 adult ticket?

The first step to solve this problem is by identifying the known and the unknowns. Let's start with what is known. We know that there are 3 adults and 7 children going to the amusement park, we know that children's tickets cost \$7.25 each, and we know that the total cost is \$88.25.

Now, what is the unknown? In this problem, the unknown is the price of 1 adult's ticket. This is what we need to find. We do not have all the information needed to quickly determine the cost of adult tickets, so there might be a "hidden" unknown.

A picture can be helpful to find out other missing pieces.

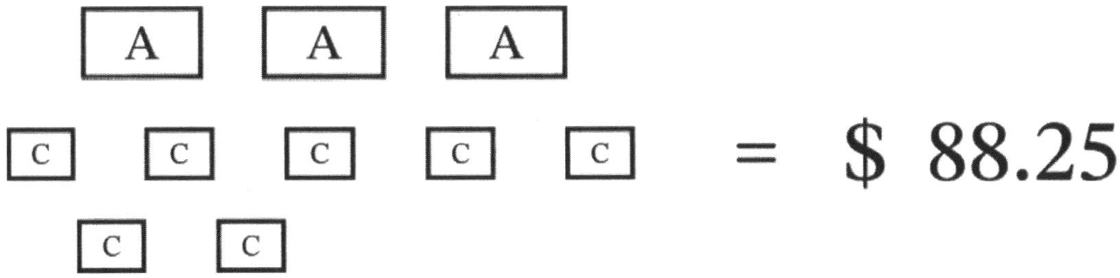

Now, we can see that there are two parts that make the total cost: the total cost of adults' tickets and the total cost of children's tickets. If we can find the total cost of children tickets, we can find the total cost of adult tickets. The total cost of children's tickets is the "hidden" unknown. We have the information to find this value. We know that there are 7 children going and that each child's ticket costs $7.25 and we can use multiplication to find the total cost.

$$\$7.25 \times 7 = \$50.75$$

If the children's tickets cost a total of $50.75, then we can use this value to find the total cost of adult's tickets. The total cost of adult's tickets is the difference between the total ticket cost and the total children's ticket cost.

$$\$88.25 - \$50.75 = \$37.50$$

Now we know that the total cost of adult's tickets is $37.50, but we need to find the cost of 1 adult's ticket. We now have all the information we need. We know the total cost of adult's tickets is $37.50 and there are 3 adults going to the amusement park. We can use division to solve.

$$\$37.50 \div 3 = \$12.50$$

The cost of 1 adult's ticket is $12.50.

This problem took multiple steps to complete, but by starting with the knowns and unknowns and drawing a picture, we were able to work through the problem using logical steps.

EXAMPLE

The middle school student council sold cupcakes to raise money. They sold 345 cupcakes.

- $\frac{2}{5}$ of the cupcakes sold were chocolate.
- $\frac{1}{3}$ of the cupcakes sold were red velvet.
- The rest of the cupcakes sold were vanilla.
- Cupcakes were sold for $3.

How much money did the student council collect by selling vanilla cupcakes?

To solve this problem, we will start with identifying the knowns, identifying the unknowns, and making a table.

We know the total number of cupcakes, we know the fraction of cupcakes that were chocolate and the fraction that were red velvet, and we know that cupcakes were sold for $3. We want to know how much money was collected from vanilla cupcakes.

$\frac{2}{5}$ chocolate	$\frac{1}{3}$ red velvet	? vanilla

From the table we can see that the hidden unknowns are the number of cupcakes of each flavor that were sold.

There are a couple of ways to approach this problem. One way would be to start by identifying the number of cupcakes in each flavor.

To find the number of chocolate cupcakes, we can multiply the fraction by the total.

$$345 \times \frac{2}{5} = \frac{345}{1} \times \frac{2}{5} = \frac{690}{5} = 690 \div 5 = 138$$

There were 138 chocolate cupcakes sold.

We can use the same strategy to find the number of red velvet cupcakes sold.

$$345 \times \frac{1}{3} = \frac{345}{1} \times \frac{1}{3} = \frac{345}{3} = 115$$

There were 115 red velvet cupcakes sold.

To find the number of vanilla cupcakes sold, we can subtract the number of chocolate and red velvet cupcakes sold from the total number of cupcakes sold.

$$138 + 115 = 253$$

$$345 - 253 = 92$$

There were 92 vanilla cupcakes sold.

Now, we can multiply this value by \$3 to find the total amount of money collected from selling vanilla cupcakes.

$$92 \times \$3 = \$276$$

The middle school student council collected \$276 selling vanilla cupcakes.

Properties of Operations

Using the Inverse Property

The **inverse property of addition** states that the sum of a number and its opposite is always equal to 0. Remember, the opposite of a number is a number that is opposite on the number line from zero, or the same number with the opposite sign. For example, −4 is opposite to 4, and 1,726.9 is opposite to −1,726.9. So, the inverse property of addition states that if you add opposite numbers, their sum is zero. For example, $5 + (-5) = 0$ and $-5 + 5 = 0$.

The **inverse property of multiplication** states that a number multiplied by its reciprocal is always equal to 1. The **reciprocal** of a number is its "flipped" fraction. For example, the reciprocal of 5 is $\frac{1}{5}$, or the reciprocal of $\frac{2}{3}$ is $\frac{3}{2}$. The inverse property of multiplication can be applied for these values, $5 \times \frac{1}{5} = 1$ and $\frac{2}{3} \times \frac{3}{2} = 1$. This is because when you multiply across, you get a fraction that is equal to 1.

$$\frac{2}{3} \times \frac{3}{2} = \frac{6}{6} = 1$$

Examples

Equivalent expressions can be generated using these inverse properties. There is an endless number of possibilities. Let's look at a few examples.

Given the expression $12 \times 0 + (4 - 6)$, we can use the inverse property of addition to generate equivalent expressions.

Using the inverse property of addition, we can say that $12 \times 0 + (4 - 6)$ is equivalent to $12(3 + -3) + (4 - 6)$. Alternatively, the expression $12 \times 0 + (4 - 6)$ is also equivalent to $12(-36 + 36) + (4 - 6)$.

We can do this because the sum of opposite numbers is equal to 0. In this example, we used $(3 + -3)$ and $(36 + -36)$ as equivalent expressions to 0. We could replace the 0 in the original expression with any expression that is equivalent to 0.

Given the expression $1 + (4 - 6)$, we can use the inverse property of multiplication to generate equivalent expressions. Using the inverse property of multiplication, we can say that $1 + (4 - 6)$ is equivalent to $\left(2 \times \frac{1}{2}\right) + (4 - 6)$, or $\left(\frac{5}{4} \times \frac{4}{5}\right) + (4 - 6)$. We can do this because when we multiply a number and its reciprocal, we get 1.

Using the Identity Property

The **identity property of multiplication** states that when a number is multiplied by 1, you get the same number. That is, anything multiplied by 1 is itself. For example, $2 \times 1 = 2$, or $1 \times -36 = -36$. Using the identity property of multiplication, we can identify and generate equivalent expressions. Let's say that we are given the expression $15 - (3 \times 4)$. We can generate equivalent expressions using the identity property. One equivalent expression example would be $(15 \times 1) - (3 \times 4)$. Another example would be $15 - (1 \times 3 \times 4)$. We can say these expressions are equivalent because the identity property of multiplication states that we can multiply any portion of an expression by 1 to get the same value.

The **identity property of addition** states that when 0 is added to a number, you get the same number. For example, $2 + 0 = 2$, or $0 + -3 = -3$. We can also use this property to identify and generate equivalent expressions. For example, if we are given the expression $2 \times (1 + 2)$, we could write the equivalent expressions $2 \times (0 + 1 + 2)$ or $(2 + 0) \times (1 + 2)$.

Using the Commutative Property

The commutative property applies to addition and multiplication and states that these operations can be completed in any order. The **commutative property of addition** states that numbers and terms can be added together in any order to still get the same value. For example, $3 + 4 = 7$ and $4 + 3 = 7$. Also, we can use the commutative property of addition to show that $3x + 4 + 2^2$ is equivalent to $4 + 3x + 2^2$ and $2^2 + 4 + 3x$. When adding terms, you can add in any order and get the same value.

The **commutative property of multiplication** states that numbers and terms can be multiplied in any order to get the same value. For example, 12×3 is equivalent to 3×12. Additionally, we can use the commutative property of multiplication to assume that $(5 + 3) \times (36 - 6)$ is equivalent to $(36 - 6) \times (5 + 3)$. You can multiply terms in any order and still get the same value.

Using the Associative Property

The **associative property of addition** states that if three or more terms are being added together, the value is the same regardless of the groupings.

For example, given the expression $3 + 4 + 6$, these terms can be grouped and added in any form. $3 + 4 + 6$ is equivalent to $(3 + 4) + 6$ and is also equivalent to $3 + (4 + 6)$. This can be applied to write equivalent expressions in a variety of ways.

For example, suppose we are given the expression $5 + (y + 2) + 4$. We can generate equivalent expressions knowing the associative property. Knowing that when three or more terms are added, the grouping is irrelevant, we can say that this expression is equivalent to $5 + y + (2 + 4)$, and it is equivalent to $(5 + y) + (2 + 4)$. It is even equivalent to $5 + y + 2 + 4$.

The **associative property of multiplication** states that if three or more terms are being multiplied together, the value is the same regardless of the grouping. We can use this property to identify and generate equivalent expressions.

For example, given the expression $2 \times 7 \times 3$, these terms can be grouped in any way and still get the same value. $2 \times 7 \times 3$ is equivalent to $(2 \times 7) \times 3$ or $2 \times (7 \times 3)$.

We can use this information to generate and identify equivalent expressions. Knowing that terms can be grouped in any way when dealing with multiplication, we can find equivalent expressions by regrouping terms.

An example would be given the expression $5 \times (2 \times y) \times 4$. Using the associative property of multiplication, we know that when three or more terms are multiplied, we can group them in any way, so $5 \times (2 \times y) \times 4$ is equivalent to $(5 \times 2) \times (y \times 4)$. It is also equivalent to $(5 \times 2) \times y \times 4$ and $5 \times 2 \times (y \times 4)$. It is even equivalent to $(5 \times 2 \times y) \times 4$ and $5 \times (2 \times y \times 4)$.

Using the Distributive Property

The distributive property is one of the most used properties when generating equivalent expressions. This concept is tested very often, so it is important to be able to use this property effectively. The **distributive property** states that when the sum of two or more terms is multiplied by a number, it is the same as adding the product of each term multiplied by that number. Let's look at the expression $4(3 + 2)$. With the distributive property, we can say that this expression is equivalent to $(4 \times 3) + (4 \times 2)$. This also applies to more simplified multiplication problems. For example, 6×87 can be expressed as $6(80 + 7)$ which is equivalent to $(6 \times 80) + (6 \times 7)$. This is very useful when simplifying expressions, especially when generating or identifying equivalent expressions.

Review Video: Commutative, Associative, and Distributive Properties
Visit mometrix.com/academy and enter code: 483176

Example

Use the **distributive property** to identify an equivalent expression.

Which of the following is equivalent to the expression $2(y + 5) - 3$?

a. $2 + y + 2 + 5 - 3$
b. $2 \times y \times 2 \times 5 - 3$
c. $2 \times y + 2 \times 5 - 3$
d. $2 \times y \times 2 + 5 - 3$

We can approach this problem in a few ways. For this example, let's expand the given expression using the distributive property to identify an equivalent expression from the choices.

In the expression $2(y + 5) - 3$, we have the term $y + 5$ being multiplied by 2. This means that each term can be multiplied by 2 to give the same value.

So, $2(y + 5)$ is equivalent to $(2 \times y) + (2 \times 5)$.

Now, we have one operation left in our expression, -3. In this expression, $2(y + 5) - 3$, the entire expression $2(y + 5)$ has 3 subtracted by it. This comes at the end of the simplification, so we can place this at the end of our expression.

So, we can say that $2(y + 5) - 3$ is equivalent to $(2 \times y) + (2 \times 5) - 3$.

Review the answer choices. It looks like our options do not have parenthesis. Let's look at what we have so far: $(2 \times y) + (2 \times 5) - 3$.

Knowing order of operations and the fact that the multiplication operation is done before the addition and subtraction operation, we can rewrite this expression without parentheses.

This means $(2 \times y) + (2 \times 5) - 3$ is equivalent to $2 \times y + 2 \times 5 - 3$.

Review our choices. Choice C is the expression that is equivalent to the given expression.

Opposites and Absolute Value

A number's **opposite** is the number that is opposite to it on a number line or has an opposite sign. The opposite of −53 is 53. The opposite of 187 is −187. The opposite of a number can be found by multiplying the number by −1. They both have the same distance from zero on a number line, just in different directions. Opposite numbers have the same **absolute value**.

The **absolute value** of a number is its distance from zero. Absolute value is notated by placing a vertical line on each side of a number. For instance, $|-46|$ means the absolute value of −46. We know the names of numbers based on their distance from zero. Numbers and their opposite have the same distance from zero. −2 and 2 have a distance of 2 from zero. So, the absolute value of −2 is 2, or $|-2| = 2$. Also, the absolute value of 2 is 2, or $|2| = 2$. This may be noted by words, or with symbols. You may see something like "$|-89| = 89$," or "the absolute value of $|543|$ is 543," or "find the absolute value of $-\frac{1}{3}$ on a number line." In the last case, you would select $\frac{1}{3}$ on a number line.

Zero is its own opposite. The absolute value of zero is zero.

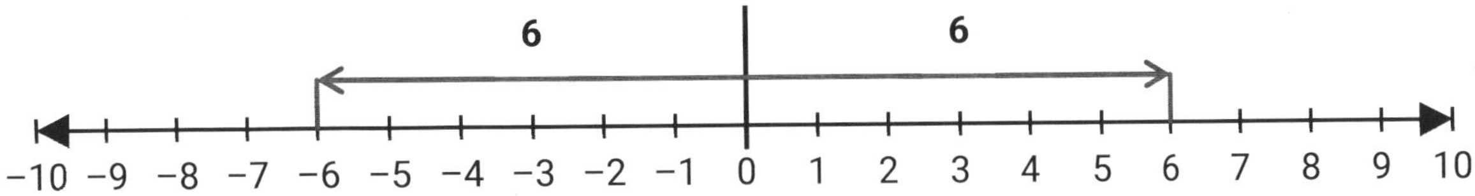

Review Video: Absolute Value
Visit mometrix.com/academy and enter code: 314669

Expressions and Equations

Expressions Versus Equations

An **expression** includes numbers, variables, or numbers and variables separated with operation signs. Anything that stands alone or could belong on one side of an equal sign, is an expression. $3x + 4$ is an example of an expression. It contains numbers, a variable, and an operation. A single number is also considered an expression. Often, expressions are simplified. $2x + 4x - 1x$ is an example of an expression because there is no equal sign. It cannot be solved; you cannot solve for x in an expression, but it can be simplified. The expression below is simplified.

$$2x + 4x - 1x$$
$$6x - 1x$$
$$5x$$

Each step gives a more simplified version of the same expression. Each step in the simplification gives an equivalent expression.

Generating Equivalent Expressions

Identify Equivalent Expressions with Variables

A **variable** is any unknown value represented by a letter or symbol, most commonly x. A **term** is a number or a number multiplied by a variable, like 3, or $3x$. Numerical expressions will include variable terms, and you may be required to identify or generate equivalent expressions that include these variable terms. When you encounter variables, it is important to remember that with each variable, any repetition of that variable is a **like term**. For example, x and y are not like terms because they are different unknown values. Also, x and 4 are not like terms because 4 is a whole number and x is an unknown term. However, x and $3x$ are like terms because they share the same variable. When encountering an expression with like terms, you may be required to simplify or expand the expression to find equivalent expressions.

Simplify the expression $4x + 2x + 7$.

Given the expression $4x + 2x + 7$, you have two like terms. We simplify these terms to find an equivalent expression. We can combine $4x + 2x$ to $6x$ because they are like terms.

So, $4x + 2x + 7$ is equivalent to $6x + 7$.

Expand the expression $4x + 2x + 7$.

Given the same expression $4x + 2x + 7$, we can expand the variable terms to find an equivalent expression. For example, $4x$ can be expanded to $(x + x + x + x)$, and $2x$ can be expanded to $(x + x)$.

So, $4x + 2x + 7$ is equivalent to $(x + x + x + x) + (x + x) + 7$.

When identifying equivalent expressions with variables, like terms can be combined, simplified, or expanded to generate an equivalent expression.

Using the Order of Operations

An **equivalent expression** is part of a set of expressions that have an equivalent value. The order of operations is essential to finding and identifying equivalent expressions. Finding equivalent expressions may require you to simplify or expand an expression. You may simplify the whole expression, or just part of the expression. For example, you may be required to simplify or identify an equivalent expression like $3(2 + 4) - 5$. There are many equivalent expressions that can be generated by this example. These are just a few possibilities.

Simplification

$3(6) - 5$ is an equivalent expression. The part of the expression in parentheses was simplified.

$18 - 5$ is an equivalent expression. The parentheses and multiplication parts of the expression were simplified.

13 is an equivalent expression. All components of the expression have been simplified.

Expansion

$3(2 + 2^2) - 5$ is an equivalent expression. The term 4 has been expanded to include an exponent.

$3(2 + 4) - (5 \times 1)$ is an equivalent expression. The term 5 has been expanded as 5×1.

There are many variations of the same expression. You may be required to simplify or expand an expression to identify equivalence.

Using Exponents

An **exponent** is used to identify a multiple of the same factor. The symbol for an exponent is a small number to the top right of a whole number. The small number shows how many times the whole number should be multiplied by itself. For example, 2^3 is equivalent to $2 \times 2 \times 2$, or 8. When identifying equivalent expressions using exponents, you may be required to simplify exponents, expand exponents, or generate exponents.

Simplification

Given the expression $4^2 + 2 - 3$, you may find an equivalent expression by simplifying the exponent. In this case, the exponential expression is 4^2. This can be simplified by finding the value of 4^2, which is 16. So, an equivalent expression to $4^2 + 2 - 3$ is $16 + 2 - 3$.

Expansion

You may be required to expand an expression including an exponent. Given the expression 4×2^3, you may expand this exponent. In this case, the exponential expression is 2^3. This can be expanded to $2 \times 2 \times 2$. So, an equivalent expression to 4×2^3 is $4 \times (2 \times 2 \times 2)$.

Generate Exponents

You may be required to generate an exponent to identify an equivalent expression. Given the expression $8 + 4 + 36$, you may convert each of these values to an exponential expression. 8 can be rewritten as 2^3, 4 can be rewritten as 2^2, and 36 can be rewritten as 6^2. So, an equivalent expression to $8 + 4 + 36$ is $2^3 + 2^2 + 6^2$.

When identifying equivalent expressions with exponents, these values can be simplified, expanded, or generated to identify equivalent expressions.

Review Video: Exponents
Visit mometrix.com/academy and enter code: 600998

Linear Relationships

A **linear relationship** is a relationship between x and y values where the relationship is constant. Linear relationships are expressed using the equation $y = mx + b$, where m represents the **slope** of the line and b represents the ***y*-intercept**, or the point where the line passes the y-axis.

Linear relationships can be described verbally or using tables, graphs, and equations.

Let's look at the equation $y = 2x + 5$.

This is a linear relationship between x and y values. In the equation $y = 2x + 5$, we can see that the slope of the line this equation describes is 2, and the y-intercept to this line is 5.

This equation can be described using a table or a graph.

Representing Linear Equations in Tables

To describe this relationship using a table, we can use the equation and input various x-values to identify the corresponding y-values.

x	y
-5	
5	
10	

This table gives the x-values –5, 5 and 10. We can substitute these values into the equation to find the matching y values in this linear relationship.

Let's start with $x = -5$.

$$y = 2x + 5$$
$$y = 2(-5) + 5$$
$$y = -10 + 5$$
$$y = -5$$

Now, find y when $x = 5$.

$$y = 2x + 5$$
$$y = 2(5) + 5$$
$$y = 10 + 5$$
$$y = 15$$

And finally, $x = 10$.

$$y = 2x + 5$$
$$y = 2(10) + 5$$
$$y = 20 + 5$$
$$y = 25$$

Now the table can be completed.

x	y
-5	-5
5	15
10	25

This table can be used to describe the linear relationship between x and y values represented in the equation $y = 2x + 5$. It can also be used to graph the line that is represented by the equation.

Representing Linear Equations on Graphs

Linear relationships form straight lines on a graph. We can graph the linear equation in the form $y = mx + b$ in two ways.

Let's look at the equation $y = 2x + 5$. This is a linear equation in the form $y = mx + b$ where m, the slope, is 2 and b, the y-intercept, is 5.

We can use a table to identify 2 or more points along the line and connect the points, or we can use the y-intercept and the slope to graph the line.

The table represents three x and y value sets.

x	y
–5	–5
5	15
10	25

This table gives three coordinate pairs: $(-5,-5)$, $(5,15)$, and $(10,25)$.

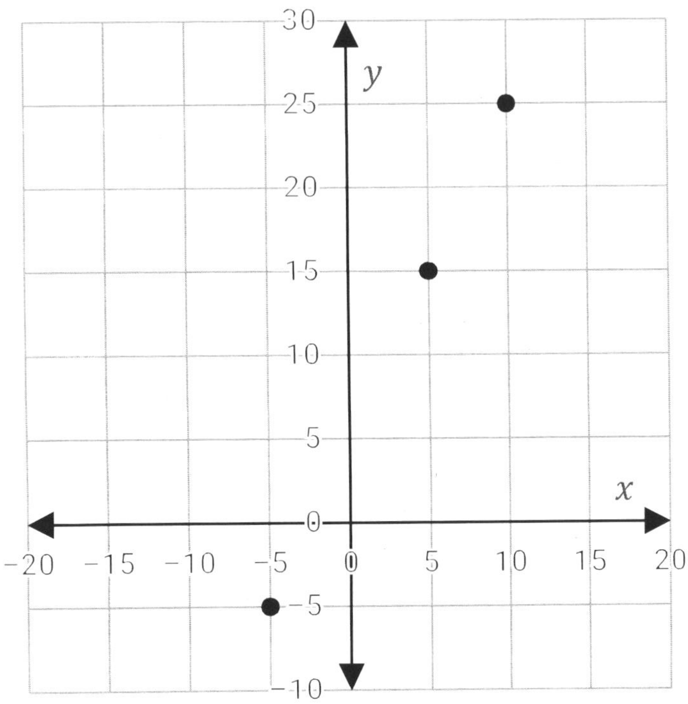

When these points are connected, they form the line $y = 2x + 5$.

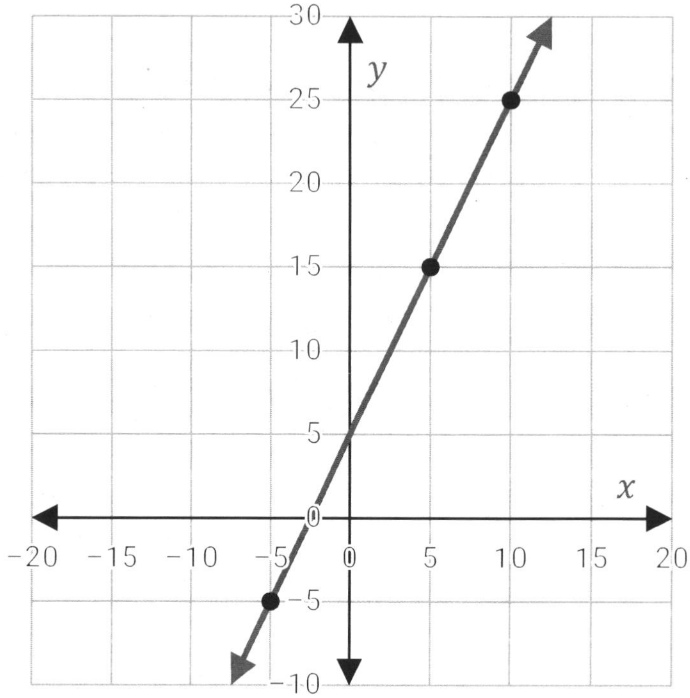

The other way we can graph a line in the form $y = mx + b$ is by identifying the slope and the y-intercept and graphing these attributes.

In the equation $y = 2x + 5$, the y-intercept is 5. This means that the point where the line crosses the y-axis has a y value of 5.

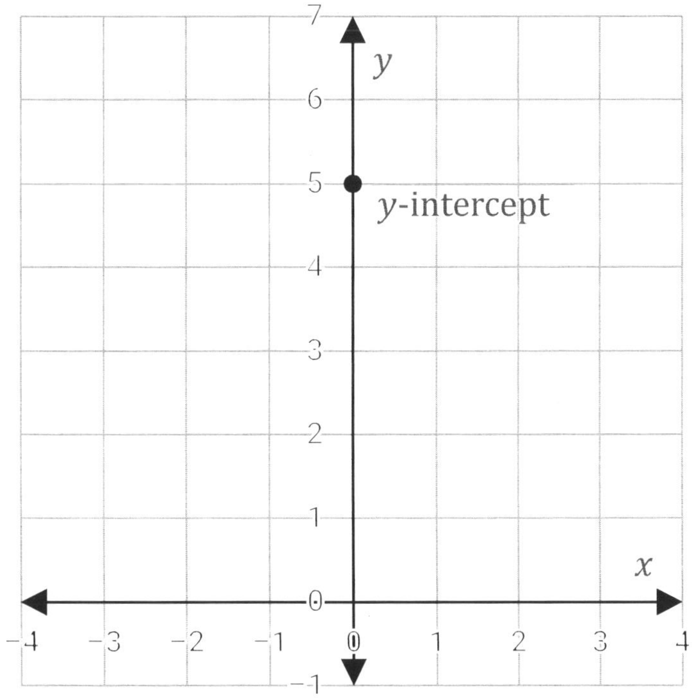

We also know that the slope of the line is 2. The slope of the line running between two points can be found by using the formula $m = \frac{y_2 - y_1}{x_2 - x_1}$. The slope is usually expressed as a fraction. The numerator is the change in y-values, also called the **rise**, and the denominator is the change in x-values, also called the **run**. The slope will be simplified to a whole number if the change in x-values is 1.

We can use the two points, (5,15) and (−5, −5), to find the slope. Let's say that (5,15) will give us x_1 and y_1 and (−5, −5) will give us x_2 and y_2.

$$m = \frac{y_2 - y_1}{x_2 - x_1}$$

$$m = \frac{-5 - 15}{-5 - 5}$$

$$m = \frac{-20}{-10}$$

$$m = 2$$

The slope of this line is 2, which means that the coordinate points on this line can be found by starting at a known point, moving up 2 y-values, then moving 1 x-value to the right.

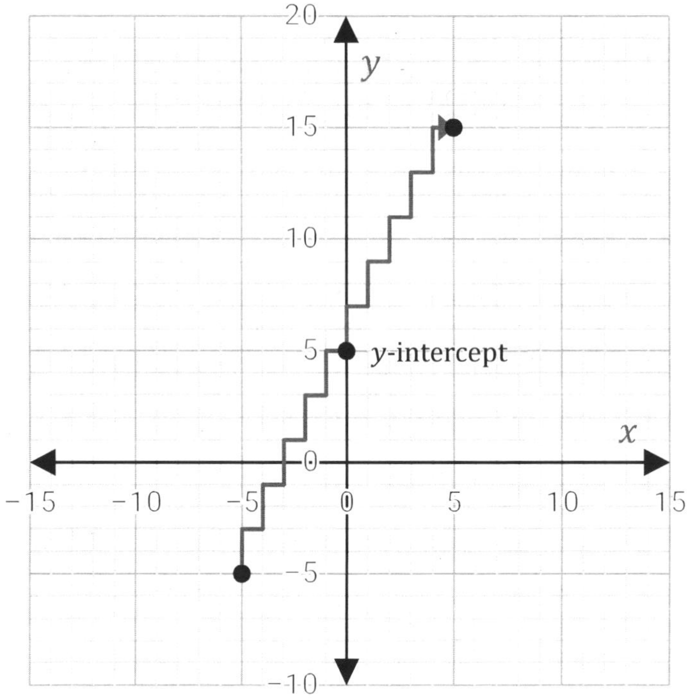

Now we can form a line.

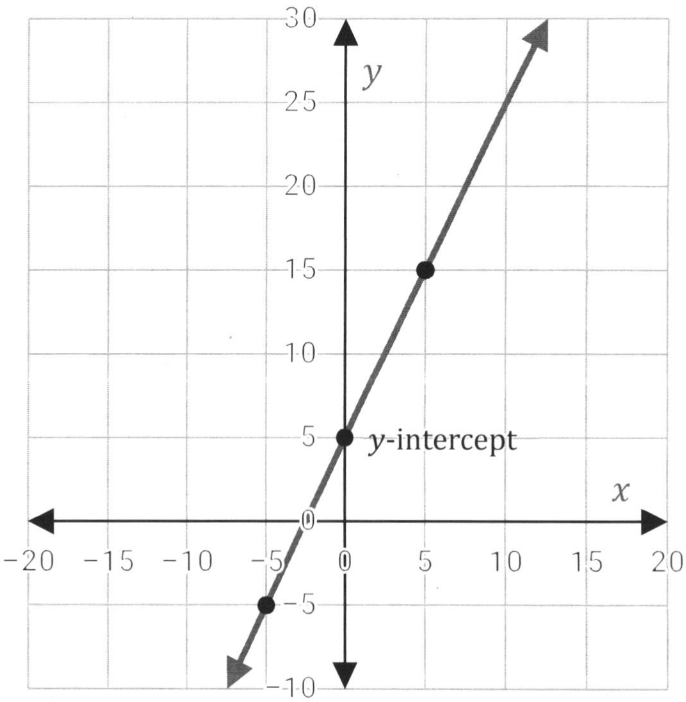

Both graphs created represent the same equation, $y = 2x + 5$. Both graphs include a line that intersects the y-axis at (0,5) and have a slope of 2.

Review Video: Graphing Linear Equations
Visit mometrix.com/academy and enter code: 479576

EXAMPLE

What equation best represents the relationship between x and y in the graph?

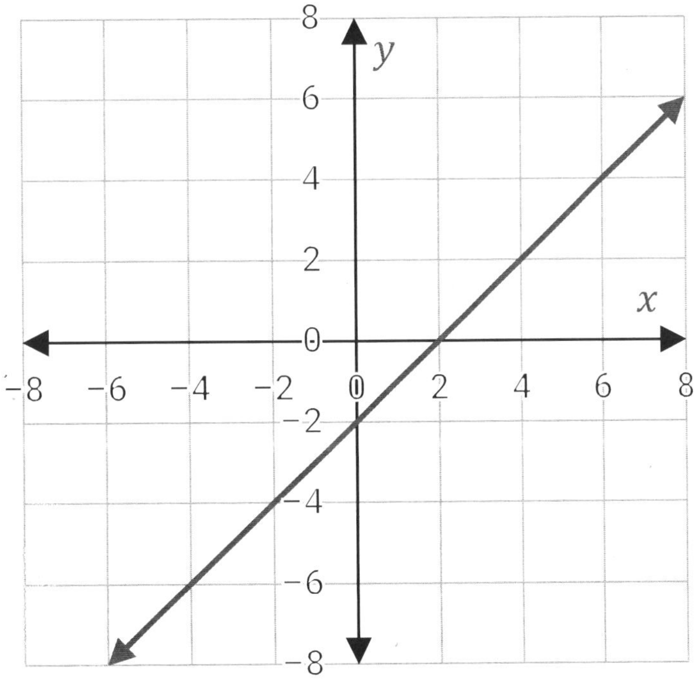

This is a line, so the equation will be in the form $y = mx + b$.

Based on the graph, we can see that the y-intercept is –2 because the point where the line crosses the y-axis is at $(0, -2)$. This means that $b = -2$ in our equation.

Next, we can identify the slope of the line. The slope of the line can be found by using the formula $m = \frac{y_2 - y_1}{x_2 - x_1}$. To find the slope, identify two points and plug their x and y-values into the formula.

Let's use the x-intercept, (0,2), and the y-intercept, (−2,0). The x-intercept gives us x_1 and y_1 and the y-intercept gives us x_2 and y_2.

$$m = \frac{y_2 - y_1}{x_2 - x_1}$$

$$m = \frac{0 - 2}{-2 - 0}$$

$$m = \frac{-2}{-2}$$

$$m = 1$$

Or we can use a graph.

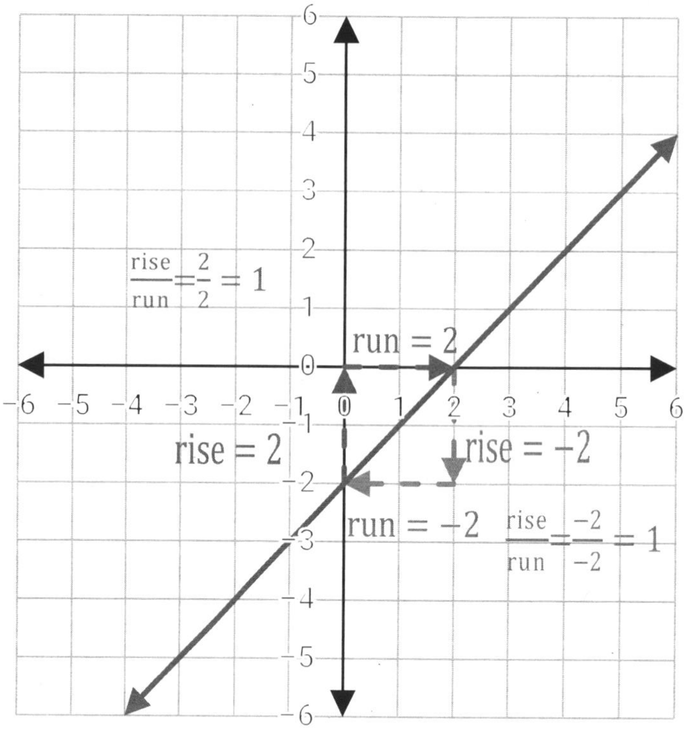

So, now we know that the y-intercept is –2 and the slope is 1. We can use these values to write the equation of the line.

$$y = mx + b$$

$$y = 1x + -2$$

$$y = x - 2$$

The equation that best represents the relationship between x and y is $y = x - 2$.

EXAMPLE

What equation best represents the relationship between x and y in the graph?

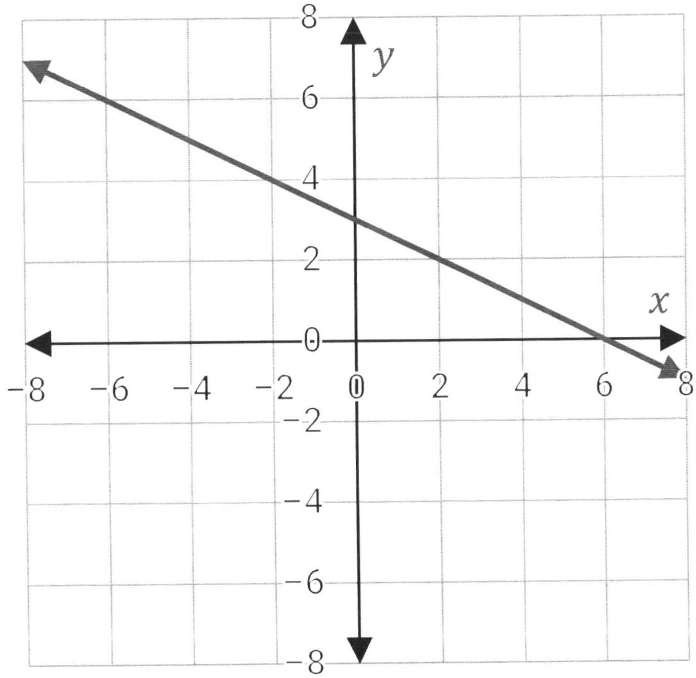

The relationship between x and y in the graph is linear, so the equation will be in the form $y = mx + b$.

Based on the graph, we can see that the y-intercept is 3 because the point where the line crosses the y-axis is at (0,3). This means that $b = 3$ in our equation.

Next, we can identify the slope of the line. The slope of the line can be found by using the formula $m = \frac{y_2 - y_1}{x_2 - x_1}$.

Let's use the y-intercept, (0,3), and the x-intercept (6,0).

$$m = \frac{y_2 - y_1}{x_2 - x_1}$$

$$m = \frac{0 - 3}{6 - 0}$$

$$m = \frac{-3}{6}$$

$$m = -\frac{1}{2}$$

Or by using a graph.

$$\frac{\text{rise}}{\text{run}} = \frac{3}{-6} = -\frac{1}{2}$$

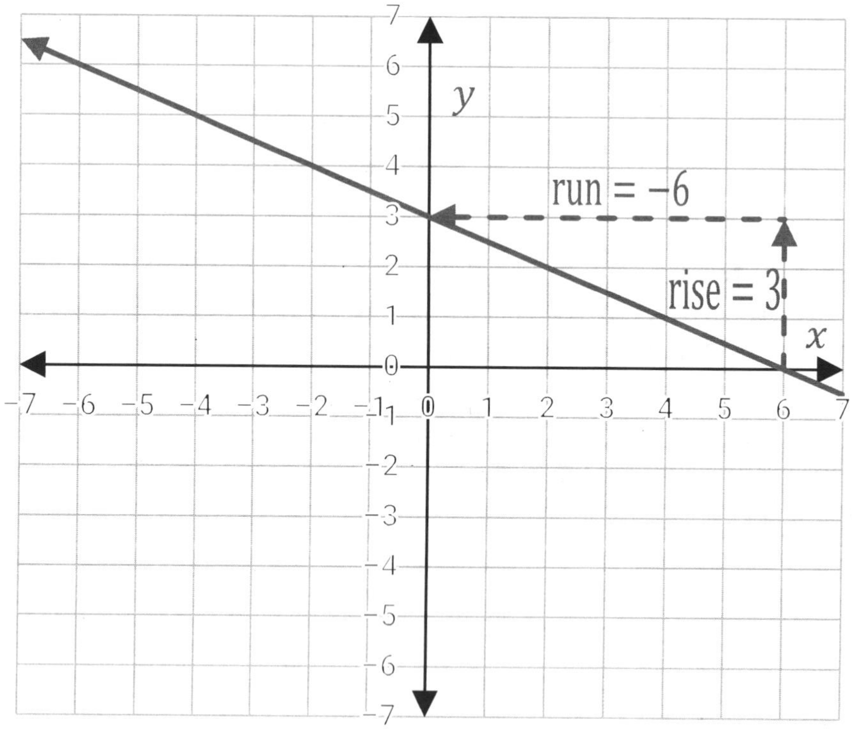

So, now that we know that the y-intercept is 3 and the slope is $-\frac{1}{2}$, we can substitute these values to write the equation of the line.

$$y = mx + b$$

$$y = -\frac{1}{2}x + 3$$

The equation that represents the relationship between x and y is $y = -\frac{1}{2}x + 3$.

Linear Relationships in Real-World Scenarios

Linear relationships often appear in real world situations.

Let's say you are saving up to buy your first car. You work every Saturday to make \$50 each week, and all this money goes into savings. This is a linear relationship because you are making money at a constant rate of \$50 per week. We can describe the rate that you make money using the equation $y = 50x$, where y represents the number of dollars you have saved and x represents the number of weeks you have worked. But what if you already have money in savings when you start?

Let's say you started with \$250 in your savings account and *then* you start saving \$50 each week. This is still a linear relationship because you are saving money at a constant rate, but you already had some money to start with, so if we use the equation $y = 50x$, y would not give an accurate number of dollars in savings. Instead, we would use the equation $y = 50x + 250$ because you are making \$50 each week and you started with \$250.

This equation could then be used to find out how much money you would have after 25 weeks by plugging in 25 for x and solving for y.

$$y = 50x + 250$$
$$y = 50(25) + 250$$
$$y = 1{,}250 + 250$$
$$y = 1{,}500$$

This means that you would have \$1,500 in your savings account after 25 weeks.

Example

This scenario can also be described using a table. If you have \$250 in savings and save \$50 each week, after zero weeks, you would have \$250. After 1 week, you would have $\$250 + 50 = \$300$.

A table describing how much money you would have saved after a given number of weeks can be created by inputting the appropriate x-value, number of weeks, into the equation $y = 50x + 250$.

Weeks (x)	0	1	2	5	10	15	30
Total \$ (y)	250	300	350	500	750	1,000	1,750

The relationship between x and y values is $y = 50x + 250$.

When $x = 0, y = 50(0) + 250 = 250$

When $x = 1, y = 50(1) + 250 = 50 + 250 = 300$

When $x = 2, y = 50(2) + 250 = 100 + 250 = 350$

When $x = 5, y = 50(5) + 250 = 250 + 250 = 500$

When $x = 10, y = 50(10) + 250 = 500 + 250 = 750$

When $x = 15, y = 50(15) + 250 = 750 + 250 + 1{,}000$

When $x = 30, y = 50(30) + 250 = 1{,}500 + 250 = 1{,}750$

This table, as well as the equation $y = 50x + 250$, can be used to express this linear relationship graphically. To represent this relationship graphically, we need to use the point on the graphic plane when $x = 0$ and at least one other point. Based on the table, we can see that when $x = 0, y = 250$, so the starting point is (0,250).

We can choose any x-value to find another point that lies on the line. We can use $x = 2$, and when $x = 2$, $y = 350$, so we can use (2,350) as the other point.

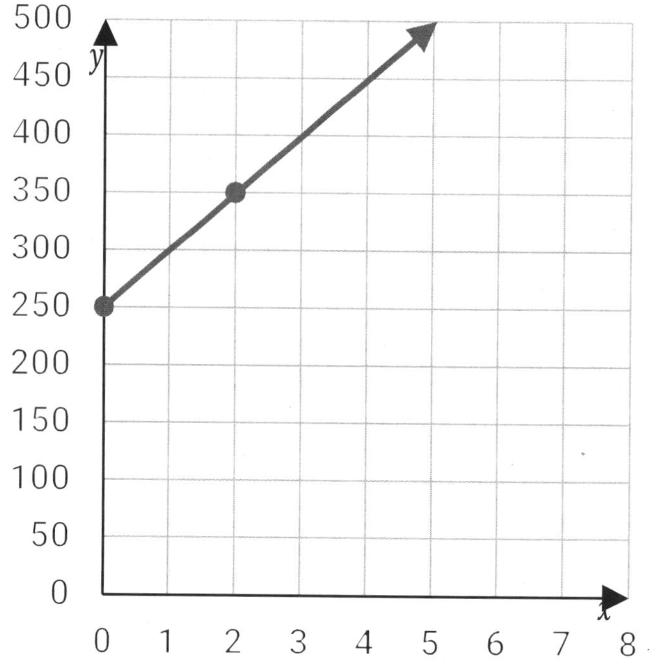

Now we have two points that lie on the line that represents the linear relationship. We can plot the points (0,250) and (2,350) on a coordinate plane and connect them with a line.

You started with $250, which is evident by the fact that the y-intercept, the point that lies along the y-axis, is 250. Then, you saved $50 each week, which is evident by the slope of the line, or relationship between x and y-values, where each week, the total cost along the line increases by 50.

EXAMPLE

You adopt a new puppy that weighs 6 pounds at its first vet visit. The puppy's weight increases by 2.5 pounds each week. What equation can be used to find *y*, the total weight of the puppy after *x* number of weeks?

In this case, we are given a new puppy's weight at the first vet visit and the rate that the puppy's weight increases.

The puppy's weight increases at a constant rate of 2.5 pounds per week, and because it increases at a constant rate, we know that this is a linear relationship.

In this example, we know that the total weight of the puppy is represented by y and the number of weeks is represented by x. We also know that the puppy's weight increases at a rate of 2.5 pounds per week, so the total weight should include $2.5x$. Additionally, we know that the puppy weighed 6 pounds at its first visit, so the starting weight is 6 pounds.

The puppy's total weight is equal to 6 pounds plus 2.5 times the number of weeks that have passed since the first vet visit.

This means that to calculate the puppy's weight, we can use the equation $y = 2.5x + 6$.

EXAMPLE

The table shows a linear relationship between x and y.

x	y
-3	-2
-1	1
1	4

Based on the information in the table, what graph can be used to model the relationship between x and y?

We can see there are three coordinate pairs provided in the table: $(-3,-2)$, $(-1,1)$, and $(1,4)$. When these points are plotted on a coordinate plane, they will form a line that represents the relationship between x and y.

The first step to creating a graph that represents the relationship between x and y given in the table is to plot the coordinate pairs. Then, these points can be connected by a line.

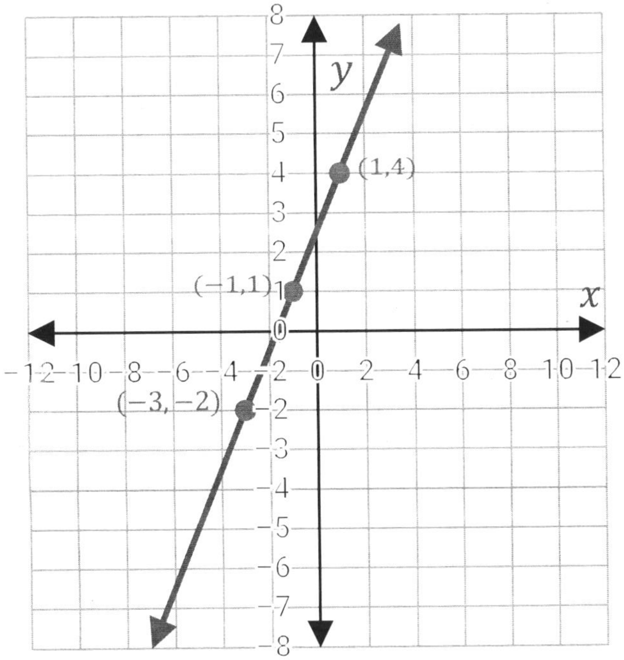

Remember, if the relationship between x and y is linear, the relationship can be represented by a line on a coordinate plane. If the points do not form a straight line, the relationship is not linear.

Equations

WRITING EQUATIONS TO REPRESENT SCENARIOS

An **equation** is a set of expressions separated by an equal sign. In an equation, each **expression** is **equal** to the other. We can use equations to represent real-world scenarios. When we write equations from problems, we need to understand the given values and the unknown values. If we can see what we know, and identify what we need to find, we can use numbers and symbols to illustrate the problem. When we write equations, we use variables to stand for the unknown values. You will have to write an appropriate equation for a given situation using different math operations.

Let's say you are given this situation: You get paid \$250 every week from your new job and received a one-time \$500 bonus once you finished your first week of work. You have made a total of \$6,500 at your job so far. How many weeks have you been working?

In this problem, we know how much money you get per week, we know that you were given a bonus, and we know how much money you have now.

What do we not know? We do not know how many weeks you have been working. The unknown in a problem is usually going to be part of the question and what you want to find. We are trying to find out how many weeks you had to have worked at your job to make \$6,500.

If we know an end total, this can usually go on one side of our equal sign.

$$\$6{,}500 =$$

Now we have 1 side of our equation. How will we get to \$6,500? You make \$250 for a number of weeks. We do not know how many weeks you work, so we can use x to represent the number of weeks. Any letter can be used as a variable to represent an unknown value, but x is commonly used. If you make \$250 per week, then we can say you make \$250 times the number of weeks, or $250x$.

$$\$6{,}500 = 250x +$$

Now, you worked x number of weeks and made \$250 each week, and you got a one-time \$500 bonus.

$$\$6{,}500 = 250x + 500$$

When writing an equation, it is important to identify what you know and what you don't know. Then you can start understanding what the problem is saying. Every problem has a starting point, something that happens, and an ending point. When you can identify these things, you can build an equation.

EXAMPLE

You are dividing 245 inches of ribbon into sections. Each section is 5 inches long. You have cut 23 sections so far. Which of the following equations can be used to find s, the number of sections you have left to cut?

a. $\frac{245}{s} - 23 = 5$
b. $\frac{245}{5} - 23 = s$
c. $5s + 23 = 245$
d. $23 \cdot 5 \cdot s = 245$

We know that the ribbon is 245 inches long, we know that each section is 5 inches, and we know that you have cut 23 sections so far.

We do not know how many sections you have left to cut.

This story can be read as a division and subtraction problem. We have 245 inches divided into 5-inch sections with 23 sections cut so far where s represents the number of sections left to cut.

245 inches divided into 5-inch sections can be written as:

$$\frac{245}{5}$$

245 inches divided into 5-inch sections with 23 sections already cut could be written as:

$$\frac{245}{5} - 23 = s$$

The answer is B.

Writing Scenarios for Equations

Situations can be expressed through equations. You can write an equation to match a situation or write a situation to match an equation. It is important to understand what is going on in an equation so that you can choose a situation that makes sense. An addition equation will include adding a value to an existing value and ending with a total. A subtraction equation will include a starting value, ending value, and a value being taken away. A multiplication equation will usually have a certain number of groups of a value, or a value being replicated a certain number of times, with an ending value. And a division equation will usually have a starting value that is broken into segments or groups a certain number of times.

A variable is an important part of an equation and represents an unknown value. A situation may include an unknown number that is added, subtracted, multiplied, or divided by a value. A situation may include two of these actions, which would be expressed by a two-step equation.

Once you identify what is happening in an equation, you can match a situation to the problem and vice versa.

Example

Let's say we are given the equation $3x + 12 = 45$. We can write a situation to match the equation after understanding what is happening in the equation.

The expression $3x$ represents an unknown value multiplied by 3. We can describe this using words and real-world examples: 3 apples per tree, 3 words per second, 3 houses per block.

The expression $3x + 12$ describes an unknown value multiplied by 3 and added to 12. The other side of the equation is 45. This represents the total. The total could be anything: total number of apples picked, total number of words read, or total number of houses passed.

Now, we can put this all together to form some situations that represent the equation.

1. You go to an orchard to pick apples. You collected 12 apples off of the ground and then picked 3 apples per tree. At the end of the trip, you have 45 apples. How many trees did you pick apples from?
2. You read at a rate of 3 words per second. You have already read 12 words. At the end of a number of seconds, you have read 45 words. For how many seconds did you read?
3. You are riding your bike and notice that there are 3 houses on each block. You have already passed 12 houses. At the end of your ride, you have passed 45 houses. How many additional blocks did you travel?

Each situation can be expressed by the same equation. You have 12 of something. There is a rate of 3 per unit. At the end, you have a total of 45. $3x + 12 = 45$.

Then, you could use the equation to solve for the missing value, whether it is the number of trees you picked from, the number of seconds you spent reading, or the number of blocks you rode.

EXAMPLE

Which situation can be represented by this equation?

$25x - 15 = 110$

a. You went shopping and bought x shirts for $25 each. You had a coupon for $15 off of the total price. You paid a total of $110. How many shirts did you buy?
b. You went shopping and bought 25 pencils that cost x dollars each. You also got a pencil case that cost $15. The total you paid is $110. How much did each pencil cost?
c. You went to the store with $110 and spent this money on x hats that cost $15 each and a jersey that cost $25. How many hats did you buy?
d. You had a budget of $110 dollars. You bought 25 boxes that cost x dollars each and then had $15 left over. How much did each box cost?

To solve this problem, we need to analyze the equation to determine what is happening in this problem.

The first part of the equation contains the expression $25x$, which means that 25 is being multiplied by an unknown value, or an unknown value is being multiplied by 25.

The next part of the equation is represented by −15. This means that 15 is being subtracted from the product of 25 and the unknown value.

The last part of the equation is $= 110$, which means that 15 subtracted from the product of 25 and the unknown value is 110.

Choice A describes x shirts that cost $25 each and a coupon for $15 off of the total price. The cost after the coupon is $110. This can be expressed by the equation $25x - 15 = 110$. This matches the equation. Choice A is correct.

Choice B describes 25 pencils that cost x dollars and a pencil case that cost $15. The cost of the pencils and the pencil case is $110. This can be expressed by the equation $25x + 15 = 110$. Choice B is incorrect, as this equation does not match the equation given.

Choice C describes going to the store with $110 and spending it on x hats that cost $15 each and a jersey that cost $25 dollars. This can be expressed using the equation $15x + 25 = 110$. This does not match the equation, so choice C is wrong.

Choice D describes a budget of $110, buying 25 boxes that cost x dollars, and having $15 left over. This story describes an ending value of 15. This can be expressed using the equation $110 - 25x = 15$. This does not match the equation given. Choice D is incorrect.

The correct answer is A.

SOLVE EQUATIONS

The solution to an equation is the value of the variable. We can solve equations by performing inverse operations to isolate the variable. Isolating the variable means to get the variable by itself on one side of the equal sign.

Let's say we are given the equation $2x + 4 = 12$. This equation can be solved by performing operations to isolate x.

$$2x + 4 = 12$$
$$2x + 4 - 4 = 12 - 4$$
$$2x = 8$$
$$\frac{2x}{2} = \frac{8}{2}$$
$$x = 4$$

The solution to the equation is $x = 4$.

EXAMPLE

The model represents an equation.

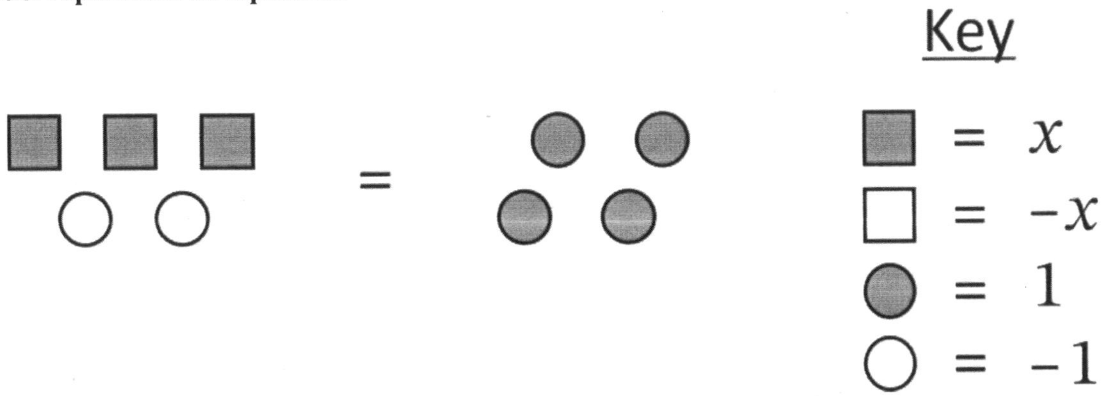

What is the solution to the equation?

This problem can be solved by identifying the equation that is being represented by the model and then performing inverse operations to isolate the variable.

The model identifies two expressions that are equal to each other, and a key is provided to identify what value each shape represents. The left side of the equation models the expression $3x - 2$ because there are three grey boxes that each represent x and two white circles that each represent −1. The right side of the equation models 4 because there are four grey circles that each represent 1. The modeled equation is:

$$3x - 2 = 4$$

To find the solution for the equation, solve for the value of x. To do that, we will perform inverse operations to get x by itself on one side of the equal sign.

The first step to solve the equation is to add 2 to both sides.

$$3x - 2 + 2 = 4 + 2$$

$$3x = 6$$

The next step is to divide both sides by 3.

$$\frac{3x}{3} = \frac{6}{3}$$

$$x = 2$$

The solution to the equation $3x - 2 = 4$ is $x = 2$.

EXAMPLE

What is the solution to the following equation?

$9 = 7 + 8x$

The solution to this equation will be the value of x that makes this sentence true. Perform inverse operations to isolate x.

The first step to solve the equation is to subtract 7 from each side.

$$9 - 7 = 7 + 8x - 7$$

$$2 = 8x$$

The next step is to divide each side by 8.

$$\frac{2}{8} = \frac{8x}{8}$$

$$\frac{2}{8} = x$$

Simplify the fraction.

$$\frac{1}{4} = x$$

The solution to this equation is $x = \frac{1}{4}$ or 0.25.

DETERMINING IF A VALUE MAKES AN EQUATION TRUE

The solution to an equation is the value of a variable that makes the sentence true. To identify if a given value makes an equation true, replace the variable with the given value and simplify. If both expressions, or both sides of the equal sign, are equal, then the equation is true. If the expressions are not equal, the given value is not a solution.

Let's say we are given an equation and two solution possibilities.

$$3x - 12 = -21$$

The two possible solutions are $x = 11$ and $x = -3$.

To identify which value is the solution, we can replace x with each of the given values and simplify the expression. If the simplified expression is a true statement, the given value is a solution.

We can start with 11.

$$3x - 12 = -21$$

$$3(11) - 12 = -21$$

$$33 - 12 = -21$$

$$21 \neq -21$$

Since 21 does NOT equal -21, so $x = 11$ is NOT a solution.

Now we can try $x = -3$.

$$3x - 12 = -21$$

$$3(-3) - 12 = -21$$

$$-9 - 12 = -21$$

$$-21 = -21$$

This number sentence is true, so $x = -3$ is a solution to the equation.

EXAMPLE

If $x = 2.5$, which equation is true?

a. $2(x - 2.5) = 2$
b. $4(x - 3) = -2$
c. $2(5 + x) = 14$
d. $4x - 3 = -2$

To solve this problem, replace the x value in each equation with 2.5 and solve to see if it makes the equation true.

We will start with the equation in choice A.

$$2(x - 2.5) = 2$$

$$2(2.5 - 2.5) = 2$$

$$2(0) = 2$$

$$0 = 2$$

This number sentence is not true, so this equation is not true if $x = 2.5$. Choice A is incorrect

Next, we will simplify equation B.

$$4(x - 3) = -2$$
$$4(2.5 - 3) = -2$$
$$4(-0.5) = -2$$
$$-2 = -2$$

This number sentence is true, so this equation is true if $x = 2.5$. Choice B is correct.

Next, we can check equation C.

$$\begin{aligned} 2(5 + x) &= 14 \\ 2(5 + 2.5) &= 14 \\ 2(7.5) &= 14 \\ 15 &= 14 \end{aligned}$$

This number sentence is not true, so this equation is not true if $x = 2.5$. Choice C is incorrect.

Last, we can check equation D.

$$\begin{aligned} 4x - 3 &= -2 \\ 4(2.5) - 3 &= -2 \\ 10 - 3 &= -2 \\ 7 &= -2 \end{aligned}$$

This sentence is not true, so this equation is not true if $x = 2.5$. Choice D is incorrect.

Equation B is the only equation that is true when $x = 2.5$.

The correct answer is B.

Example

Which equation is true if $w = -10$?

a. $\frac{w}{5} + 20 = 22$
b. $-45 + 4w = -5$
c. $\frac{50}{w} + 15 = 10$
d. $2(w + 5) = -30$

To find the equation that is true if $w = -10$, we will replace w with –10 in each equation and simplify to see if the result is a true statement.

We will start with equation A.

$$\begin{aligned} \frac{w}{5} + 20 &= 22 \\ \frac{-10}{5} + 20 &= 22 \\ -2 + 20 &= 22 \\ 18 &= 22 \end{aligned}$$

This statement is not true, so this equation is not true if $x = -10$.

Next, we will simplify equation B.

$$-45 + 4w = -5$$

$$
\begin{aligned}
-45 + 4(-10) &= -5 \\
-45 + \ -40 &= -5 \\
-45 - 40 &= -5 \\
-85 &= -5
\end{aligned}
$$

This statement is not true, so this equation is not true if $x = -10$.

Next, we will try equation C.

$$
\begin{aligned}
\frac{50}{w} + 15 &= 10 \\
\frac{50}{-10} + 15 &= 10 \\
-5 + 15 &= 10 \\
10 &= 10
\end{aligned}
$$

This statement is true, so this equation is true if $x = -10$. The correct answer is C.

Last, we can try equation D.

$$
\begin{aligned}
2(w + 5) &= -30 \\
2(-10 + 5) &= -30 \\
2(-5) &= -30 \\
-10 &= -30
\end{aligned}
$$

This statement is not true, so this equation is not true if $x = -10$.

Equation C is the only equation that is true if $x = -10$.

The correct answer is C.

Inequalities

Writing Inequalities to Represent Scenarios

An **inequality** is a math sentence that connects two expressions with a comparison. These expressions are compared using a **greater than**, $>$, **less than**, $<$, **greater than or equal to**, $\geq$, or **less than or equal to**, $\leq$, sign.

There are some situations that can be illustrated by inequalities. In these scenarios, we need to identify what we know, what we don't know, and what the comparison is.

For example, imagine you go to the grocery store to buy avocados and one bag of tortillas. Avocados are $0.70 each, and a bag of tortillas costs $1.50. You only brought 5 dollars. An inequality can be used to illustrate how many avocados you can buy.

We know that avocados are $0.70 each and a bag of tortillas is $1.50. We know that you can't spend more than $5. We know that you want to buy a number of avocados and a bag of tortillas, but we don't know how many avocados we can get. That must be the unknown.

We can write an inequality using a for avocados.

We can't go over \$5, but the total cost can be equal to \$5. The cost of the avocados and the bag of tortillas has to be less than or exactly \$5.

$$\text{total cost} \leq 5$$

Now, we want avocados, and each one is \$0.70, so the other side of our inequality will have to include \$0.70 times the number of avocados.

$$0.70a \leq 5$$

We also want to get a bag of tortillas which cost \$1.50. This must be added to the avocado side of the inequality.

$$0.70a + 1.5 \leq 5$$

Inequalities can be solved in a way similar to solving equations, using inverse operations. Solving this inequality would reveal number of avocados you could buy without spending more than \$5.

EXAMPLE

You have saved \$1,200 toward buying your first car. Each month, you will save an additional \$150. You need at least \$3,500. Which inequality can be used to find all the possible number of months, m, you need to save to meet, or exceed, your goal?

a. $1{,}200 + 150m > 3{,}500$
b. $1{,}200 + 150m \geq 3{,}500$
c. $3{,}500 > 1{,}200 + 150m$
d. $3{,}500 \geq 1{,}200 + 150m$

In this problem, you have a goal of \$3,500, you have \$1,200, and you save an additional \$150 each month.

If the goal is \$3,500, that means that you need to have \$3,500 or more to meet your goal. That means that your total after you find the number of months needs to be greater than or equal to 3,500.

$$\text{your total} \geq 3{,}500$$

You started with \$1,200 and then save an additional \$150 each month, or $1{,}200 + 150m$.

$$1{,}200 + 150m \geq 3{,}500$$

The correct answer is B.

EXAMPLE

A bathtub holds 42 gallons of water. A faucet fills the bathtub at a rate of 3.5 gallons per minute. There are 5 gallons of water in the bathtub so far. Which inequality can be used to represent all possible number of m, minutes, the faucet can run before the bathtub overflows?

a. $42 \leq 3.5m + 5$
b. $42 \leq 5m + 3.5$
c. $42 \geq 3.5m + 5$
d. $42 \geq 5m + 3.5$

In this story, a bathtub holds 42 gallons of water. Water fills the bathtub at a rate of 3.5 gallons per minute and there are 5 gallons in the bathtub so far. We want to identify the inequality that represents all possible number of minutes the faucet can run before the bathtub overflows.

The bathtub fills at a rate of 3.5 gallons per minute, which can be represented by the expression $3.5m$, where m represents the number of minutes.

$$3.5m$$

There are 5 gallons in the bathtub already, which means we have started with 5 gallons. This can be represented by the expression $3.5m + 5$ because there are 5 gallons in the bathtub already and the water increases at a rate of 3.5 gallons per minute. This is one side of the inequality.

$$3.5m + 5$$

This expression represents the number of gallons in the bathtub after the faucet runs m number of minutes.

The bathtub holds 42 gallons of water. We need to know all number of minutes the faucet can run without the bathtub overflowing. This means that the expression $3.5m + 5$ must be less than or equal to 42 for the bathtub to not overflow.

$$3.5m + 5 \leq 42$$

This inequality can also be written as

$$42 \geq 3.5m + 5$$

The correct answer is C.

Writing Scenarios for Inequalities

Real-world scenarios can be expressed through inequalities, and we can also write situations based on an inequality. Inequalities usually use the language, “fewer than,” “more than,” “no more than,” “no less than,” “a maximum of,” “a minimum of,” etc. This language gives us clues that we are dealing with values that are greater than, less than, greater than or equal to, or less than or equal to a quantity.

If there is a number divided into some pieces, and there is no more than 5, that means the value is less than or equal to 5. If there is a value and some number is added and the total is more than 10, that means the value is greater than 10. If there is a value multiplied by a number and the total is at least 25, that means the value is greater than or equal to 25. If the value is less or more, you will use greater than or less than. If the value is less or more, but can also be that number, you will use less than or equal to, or greater than or equal to. It takes a little practice and logic to really think about what is happening in the situation.

Example

Which situation can be represented by this inequality?

$15y + 67 \geq 250$

a. You have 15 coins in your coin collection. You add 67 coins each year. How many years of collecting will result in a collection of at least 250 coins?
b. You have 15 coins in your coin collection. You add 67 coins each year. How many years of collecting will result in a collection of 250 coins, at most?
c. You have 67 coins in your coin collection. You add 15 coins each year. How many years of collecting will result in a collection of at least 250 coins?
d. You have 67 coins in your coin collection. You add 15 coins each year. How many years of collecting will result in a collection of 250 coins, at most?

To solve this problem, we can identify the inequality that describes each situation and match this to the given inequality.

Choice A describes having 15 coins and adding 67 coins each year. This means that you begin with 15 coins and add 67 each year for y years. So, after y years you will have $15 + 67y$ coins. The answer choice asks for the number of years it takes to collect *at least* 250 coins. If you want at least 250 coins, that means $15 + 67$ must be greater than or equal to 250. This situation can be represented by the inequality $15 + 67y \geq 250$.

Choice B describes having 15 coins and adding 67 coins each year. This means that you begin with 15 coins and add 67 each year for y years. The solution is every possible number of years that will result in at most 250 coins. If you want at most 250 coins, that means that the solution will give a total that is either 250 or less than 250. This story can be represented by the inequality $15 + 67y \leq 250$.

Choice C describes having 67 coins and adding 15 coins each year. This means that you begin with 67 coins and add 15 each year for y years. The solution is every possible number of years that will result in at least 250 coins. If you want at least 250 coins, that means that the solution will give a total that is either 250 or more than 250. This story can be represented by the inequality $67 + 15y \geq 250$.

Choice D describes having 67 coins and adding 15 coins each year. This means that you begin with 67 coins and add 15 each year for y years. The solution is every possible number of years that will result in at most 250 coins. If you want at least 250 coins, that means that the solution will give a total that is either 250 or less than 250. This story can be represented by the inequality $67 + 15y \leq 250$.

The only situation that gives an inequality that is equivalent to the given inequality is choice C. The correct answer is C.

Representing Inequalities on a Number Line

Inequalities can be represented on a number line. Inequalities are two expressions connected by a greater than, less than, greater than or equal to, or less than or equal to sign. We express solutions to these sentences using number lines and a series of arrows, open circles, and closed circles. You may be asked to draw or identify the number line that represents an inequality, including inequalities with variables.

When representing solutions to an inequality on a number line, we are identifying the number or group of numbers that makes the statement true.

We can represent the inequality $2x + 5 > 21$.

What are the possible values of x?

The first step to solving this inequality is to solve as you would solve an equation. Perform inverse operations to each side of the inequality to isolate x.

$$
\begin{aligned}
2x + 5 &> 21 \\
2x + 5 - 5 &> 21 - 5 \\
2x &> 16 \\
\frac{2x}{2} &> \frac{16}{2} \\
x &> 8
\end{aligned}
$$

This tells us that the value of x must be any value that is greater than 8.

The value must be greater than 8, but not exactly 8 because the symbol used is "greater than," not "greater than or equal to," so we will identify 8 on our number line with an **open circle** because the value cannot be 8. Open circles are used when the comparison is "greater than" or "less than" to show that the number that the circle identifies is not included in the possible values of x.

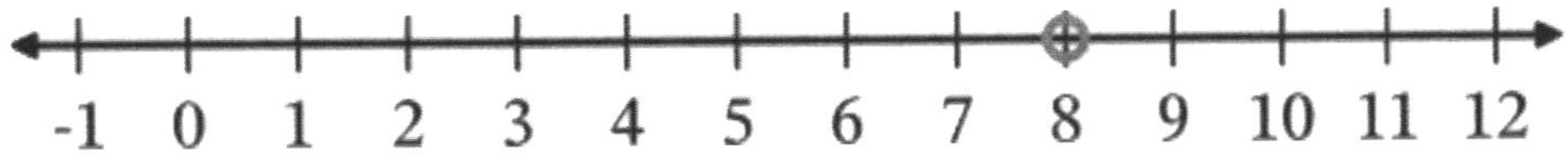

All numbers greater than 8 can be a solution, so we will place an arrow to the right to identify all numbers greater than 8.

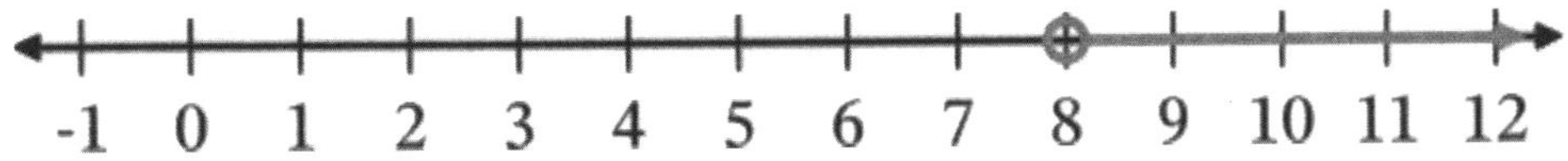

Let's look at another example. Consider the inequality $2x + 5 \leq 21$.

To solve this inequality, use inverse operations to isolate x.

$$2x + 5 \leq 21$$
$$2x + 5 - 5 \leq 21 - 5$$
$$2x \leq 16$$
$$\frac{2x}{2} \leq \frac{16}{2}$$
$$x \leq 8$$

This tells us that the value of x must be any value that is less than or equal to 8.

The value must be less than or equal to 8, so the value could be exactly 8. We will identify 8 on our number line with a **closed circle** because 8 is included as a solution to the inequality. Closed circles are used when the comparison is "greater than or equal to" or "less than or equal to" to show that the number that the circle identifies is included as a possible value of x.

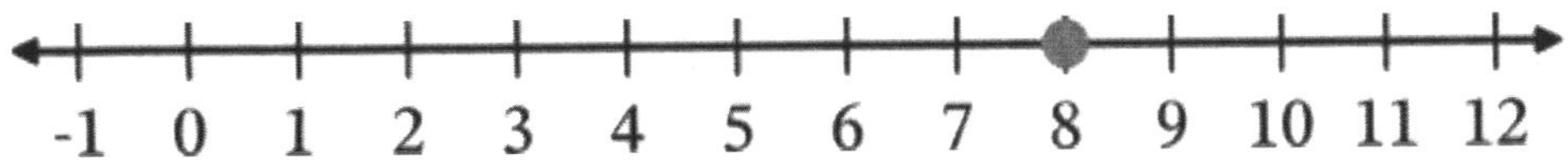

We know that the value of x is all values less than or equal to 8, so we can identify these values by placing an arrow to the left of 8 to identify all values less than 8, and the closed circle identifies 8 as one of the possible values.

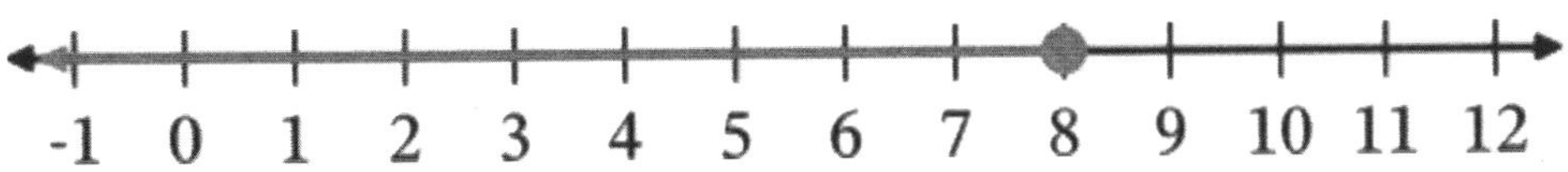

This number line appropriately represents all possible solutions to the inequality $2x + 5 \leq 21$.

Review Video: Solving Inequalities Using All 4 Basic Operations
Visit mometrix.com/academy and enter code: 401111

Review Video: Graphing Solutions to Inequalities
Visit mometrix.com/academy and enter code: 391281

EXAMPLE

Draw a number line that represents the solution to $42.5 \geq 9x - 2.5$.

To find all possible solutions to this inequality, we will solve the inequality by performing inverse operations to isolate x.

$$42.5 \geq 9x - 2.5$$
$$42.5 + 2.5 \geq 9x - 2.5 + 2.5$$
$$45 \geq 9x$$
$$\frac{45}{9} \geq \frac{9x}{9}$$
$$5 \geq x$$

This states that 5 is greater than or equal to x. This can also be read as $x \leq 5$, or the value of x is less than or equal to 5.

If the value of x is less than or equal to 5, then the solution to the inequality is all values less than 5 or exactly 5. If a possible solution is exactly 5, then we can notate 5 on the number line with a closed circle.

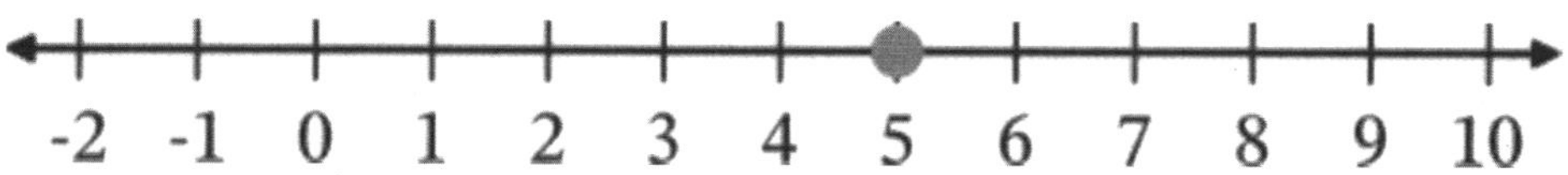

Now, the possible values of x are 5 and all values less 5. This means we can notate all possible solutions by drawing an arrow to the left of 5 to highlight all values less than 5.

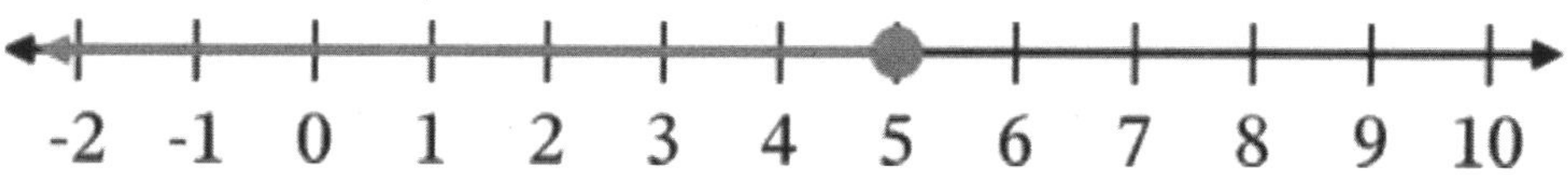

This number line appropriately represents all possible solutions to the inequality $42.5 \geq 9x - 2.5$.

EXAMPLE

Which number line represents the solution to the inequality $3.5x + 11.5 > 18.5$?

a.
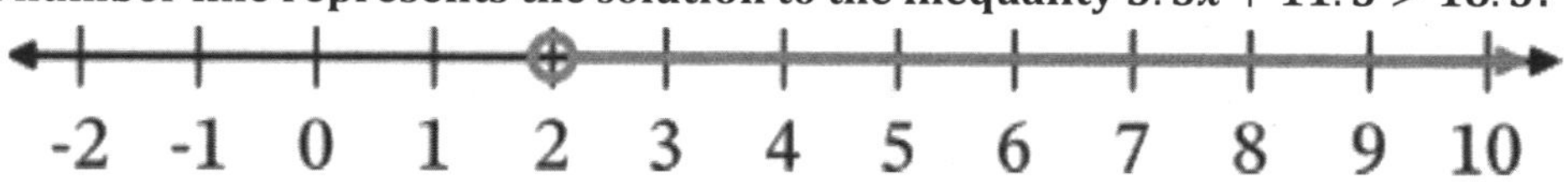

b.
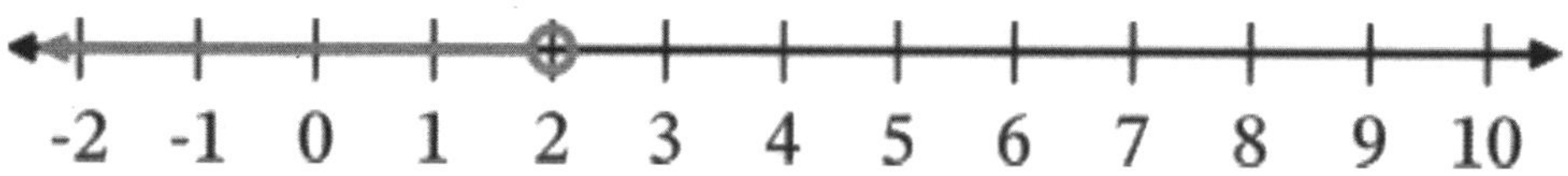

c.
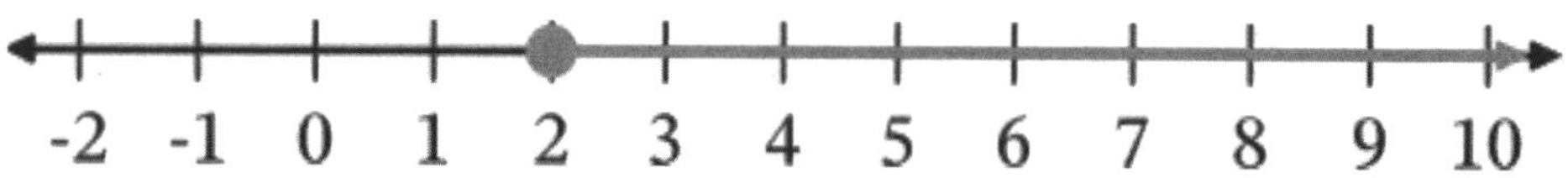

d.
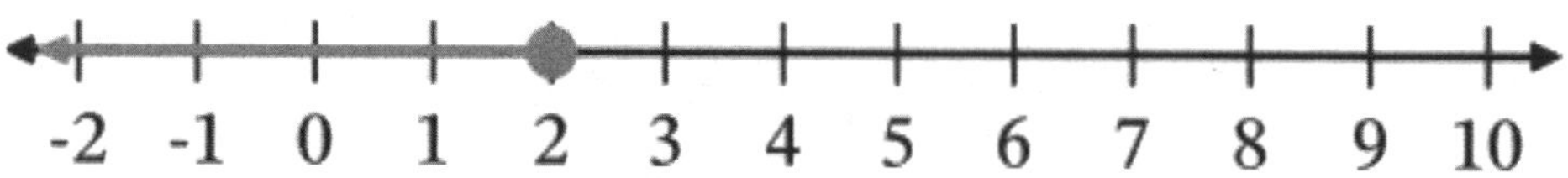

To identify the number line that represents all possible solutions to the inequality, we will perform inverse operations to isolate x.

$$3.5x + 11.5 > 18.5$$

$$3.5x + 11.5 - 11.5 > 18.5 - 11.5$$
$$3.5x > 7$$
$$\frac{3.5x}{3.5} > \frac{7}{3.5}$$
$$x > 2$$

This shows that the solution to the inequality is all values greater than 2.

This can be shown on a number line by notating 2 with an open circle and an arrow to the right of 2 because the solution is all values greater than 2, but not exactly 2.

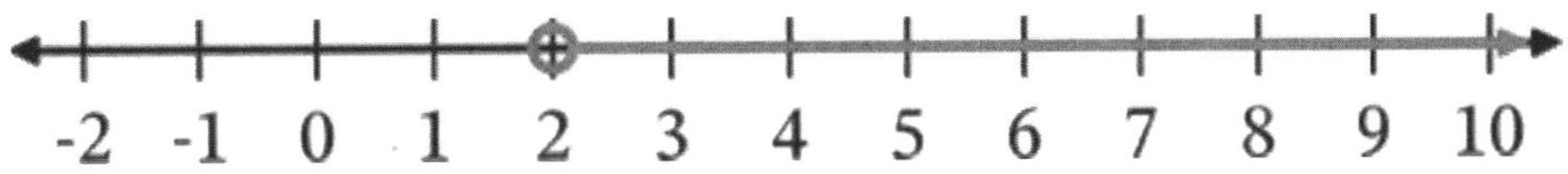

The correct answer is A.

Solving Inequalities

The solution to an inequality describes all possible values of a variable and is called a solution set. The solution is a set, or group, of solutions because there is more than one possible value that makes the inequality true. To find all possible solutions to an inequality, isolate the variable in an inequality. This can be done the same way as solving an equation: by performing inverse operations to get the variable alone on one side of the comparison.

Let's say we are given the inequality $15 > 2x + 4$. The solution set to this inequality can be found by performing inverse operations to isolate x.

$$15 > 2x + 4$$

The first step to solving the inequality is to subtract 4 from each side.

$$15 - 4 > 2x + 4 - 4$$

$$11 > 2x$$

The next step is to divide each side by 2.

$$\frac{11}{2} > \frac{2x}{2}$$

$$5.5 > x$$

The solution set to the inequality is $5.5 > x$, or $x < 5.5$, or the value of x is all values less than 5.5. The solution set is $x < 5.5$.

EXAMPLE

The model represents an inequality.

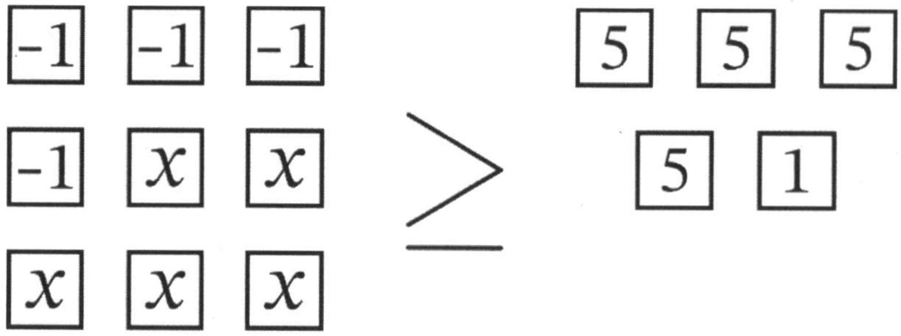

What is the solution set for the inequality?

To solve this problem, we will identify the inequality from the model and perform inverse operations to find the solution.

This model gives two expressions that are separated by a greater than or equal to sign. This means that the expression on the left is greater than or equal to the expression on the right. The model on the left represents the expression $5x - 4$ because there are five boxes that represent x and four boxes that each represent -1. The model on the right represents the expression 21 because there are four boxes that each represent 5 and one box that represents 1.

To find the solution set to the inequality, we can perform inverse operations to isolate x.

$$5x - 4 \geq 21$$

$$5x - 4 + 4 \geq 21 + 4$$

$$\frac{5x}{5} \geq \frac{25}{5}$$

$$x \geq 5$$

The solution set is $x \geq 5$, or the solution set is all values greater than or equal to 5.

EXAMPLE

What is the solution set for the inequality below?

$\mathbf{6 + 2x < 4}$

a. $x < 6$
b. $x < -6$
c. $x < 1$
d. $x < -1$

To find the solution set for the inequality, we can perform inverse operations to isolate the variable.

$$6 + 2x > 4$$

$$6 - 6 + 2x > 4 - 6$$

$$\frac{2x}{2} > \frac{-2}{2}$$

$$x > -1$$

The solution set is all values greater than -1, or $x > -1$.

The correct answer is D.

Solving Inequalities That Include Negative Numbers

The solution to an inequality can be found using a process similar to solving for an equation. However, there is an exception when you encounter negative numbers. When solving an inequality, and you must multiply or divide each side by a negative number, you must also flip, or reverse, the inequality symbol. This means that if you had a less than symbol and have to multiply or divide by a negative number, you will perform the operation AND change to a greater than symbol. Same if you had a greater than or equal symbol and must multiply or divide by a negative number, you will perform the operation and then change to a less than or equal to symbol.

Let's say you are given the inequality $-x + 8 \geq 15$ and you need to find the solution set.

First, solve the inequality like you would any other inequality or equation, by performing inverse operations to each side.

$$-x + 8 \geq 15$$

$$-x + 8 - 8 \geq 15 - 8$$

$$-x \geq 7$$

Now, the next step is to divide each side by -1 to remove the negative sign from the variable. Because we are dividing by a negative, we will also flip the inequality symbol.

$$\frac{-x}{-1} \geq \frac{7}{-1}$$

$$x \leq 7$$

We divided by -1 and flipped the symbol, so the solution set to the inequality is all values less than or equal to 7, or $x \leq 7$.

EXAMPLE

What is the solution set for this inequality?

$7 - 2x > 1$

a. $x > 3$
b. $x < -3$
c. $x < 3$
d. $x > -3$

To find the solution set for the inequality, we will perform inverse operations to isolate the variable.

$$7 - 2x > 1$$

$$7 - 7 - 2x > 1 - 7$$

$$-2x > -6$$

$$\frac{-2x}{-2} > \frac{-6}{-2}$$

Because we are dividing by a negative number, we will also flip the inequality symbol.

$$\frac{-2x}{-2} > \frac{-6}{-2}$$

$$x < 3$$

The solution set to the inequality is all values less than 3.

The correct answer is C.

EXAMPLE

What is the solution set for $-6x - 10 \leq 38$?

a. $x \leq 8$
b. $x \geq 8$
c. $x \leq -8$
d. $x \geq -8$

To find the solution set, we will perform inverse operations to isolate the variable. When dividing by a negative value, change the direction of the inequality symbol.

$$-6x - 10 \leq 38$$

$$-6x - 10 + 10 \leq 38 + 10$$

$$-6x \leq 48$$

$$\frac{-6x}{-6} \leq \frac{48}{-6}$$

$$x \geq -8$$

The solution set for the inequality is all values greater than or equal to -8.

The correct answer is D.

Determining If a Set of Values Makes an Inequality True

The solution set to an inequality is the set of values of a variable that make the simplified sentence true. To identify if a given set of values makes an inequality true, there are two main strategies. One strategy is like finding if a solution is true for an equation; replace each value with the variable and simplify to see if the simplified sentence is true. If the sentence is true, then the given value is a solution. If the sentence is not true, then the given value is NOT a solution.

Let's say we are given an inequality and a set of possible values.

$$3x - 12 \leq -21$$

The value set is $\{-10, -5, 0, 5, 10\}$.

One way to solve this problem is to replace x with each given value to see if they make the sentence true. Consider $x = -10$.

$$3x - 12 \leq -21$$

$$3(-10) - 12 \leq -21$$

$$-30 - 12 \leq -21$$

$$-42 \leq -21$$

This sentence is true, so $x = -10$ is one of the possible solutions.

Consider $x = -5$.

$$3x - 12 \leq -21$$
$$3(-5) - 12 \leq -21$$
$$-15 - 12 \leq -21$$
$$-27 \leq -21$$

This sentence is true, so $x = -5$ is another possible solution.

Consider $x = 0$.

$$3x - 12 \leq -21$$

$$3(0) - 12 \leq -21$$

$$0 - 12 \leq -21$$

$$-12 \leq -21$$

This sentence is not true, so $x = 0$ is not a possible solution.

Consider $x = 5$.

$$3x - 12 \leq -21$$

$$3(5) - 12 \leq -21$$

$$15 - 12 \leq -21$$

$$3 \leq -21$$

This sentence is not true, so $x = 5$ is not a possible solution.

Consider $x = 10$.

$$3x - 12 \leq -21$$

$$3(10) - 12 \leq -21$$

$$30 - 12 \leq -21$$

$$18 \leq -21$$

This sentence is not true, so $x = 10$ is not a possible solution.

This means that -10 and -5 are the only possible solutions from the given set of values.

EXAMPLE

In an inequality, there can by many solutions, so another strategy is to solve the inequality by finding the solution set and determining whether or not the given values fit in the solution set.

We are given an inequality and set of possible values.

$$3x - 12 \leq -21$$

The value set is $\{-10, -5, 0, 5, 10\}$.

We can solve the inequality and compare the solution to the value set. To solve the inequality, we will perform inverse operations to isolate the variable.

$$3x - 12 \le -21$$

$$3x - 12 + 12 \le -21 + 12$$

$$3x \le -9$$

$$\frac{3x}{3} \le \frac{-9}{3}$$

$$x \le -3$$

The solution to the inequality is $x \le -3$, or the solution is all values that are less than or equal to -3.

The given solution set is $\{-10, -5, 0, 5, 10\}$.

If all possible solutions are all values that are less than or equal to -3, this means that -10 and -5 are possible solutions because these are the given values that are less than or equal to -3.

Example

Which values from the set $\{-12, -8, -4, 0, 4, 8, 12\}$ are valid solutions to the following inequality?

$$\frac{x}{2} + 3 > -1$$

To solve this problem, there are two useful strategies. One is to substitute each value from the value set for x in the inequality and simplify to see if the sentence is true, and the other is to solve the inequality and compare the solution set to the value set. Solving the inequality and comparing is the quickest strategy, so this is the strategy we will practice.

To solve the inequality, we will perform inverse operations to isolate the variable.

$$\frac{x}{2} + 3 > -1$$

$$\frac{x}{2} + 3 - 3 > -1 - 3$$

$$\frac{x}{2} > -4$$

$$2 \cdot \frac{x}{2} > -4 \cdot 2$$

$$x > -8$$

The solution set to the inequality is $x > -8$, or all values greater than -8.

The given value set is $\{-12, -8, -4, 0, 4, 8, 12\}$, and the values in the set that are greater than -8 are -4, 0, 4, 8, and 12. These are valid solutions to the inequality.

EXAMPLE

Which values from the set satisfy the inequality $3 \leq -1 + 2x$?

$\{-6, -2, 0, 2, 4, 6\}$

a. 2, 4, and 6 only
b. 4 and 6 only
c. −6, −2, and 0 only
d. −6, and −2 only

To solve this problem, the quickest strategy is to solve the inequality and compare the solution set to the given value set.

To solve this inequality, we will perform inverse operations to isolate the x.

$$3 \leq -1 + 2x$$

$$3 + 1 \leq -1 + 1 + 2x$$

$$4 \leq 2x$$

$$\frac{4}{2} \leq \frac{2x}{2}$$

$$2 \leq x$$

The solution to this inequality is $2 \leq x$, which can also be written as $x \geq 2$. So, the solution is all values that are greater than or equal to 2. Out of the given value set, the values that are greater than or equal to 2 are $\{2, 4, \text{and } 6\}$.

The correct answer is A.

Modeling Equations and Inequalities

Equations and inequalities can be modeled using pictures and symbols. A model may have a key of labeled pictures or symbols and will express that each expression is either equal to, less than, greater than, less than or equal to, or greater than or equal to the other expression.

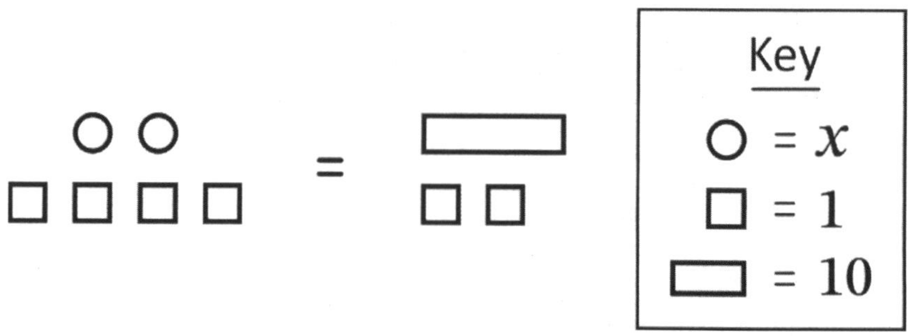

This model represents an equation. Both sides are equal because the equal sign separates each expression. The expression on the left side of the equal sign represents $2x + 4$ because there are two circles that represent x and four boxes that represent 1. The expression on the right side of the equal sign represents 12 because there is one rectangle that represents 10 and two boxes that represent 1. This model represents the equation $2x + 4 = 12$.

Geometry

Volume of Prisms

A **prism** is a three-dimensional shape with two equivalent bases, or faces, that are parallel. A rectangular prism has two equivalent rectangular (including square) bases that are parallel. A triangular prism has two equivalent triangular bases that are parallel.

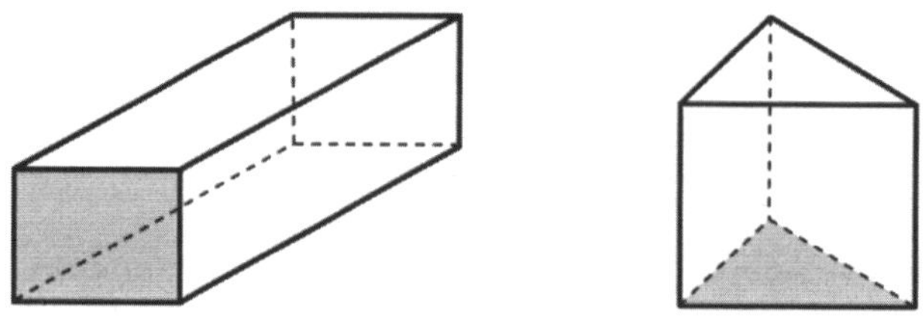

Rectangular prism Triangular prism

Volume refers to the total amount of space the object fills. To find the volume of a prism, V, we multiply the area of one base, B, by the height of the prism, h. This relationship is reflected by the formula $V = Bh$.

The "base" of a two-dimensional shape is represented by a lower case b, where the "base" of a three-dimensional shape is represented by an upper case B. The base of a three-dimensional shape is the two-dimensional area of the shape that forms the base.

Review Video: Volume and Surface Area of a Prism
Visit mometrix.com/academy and enter code: 420158

Example

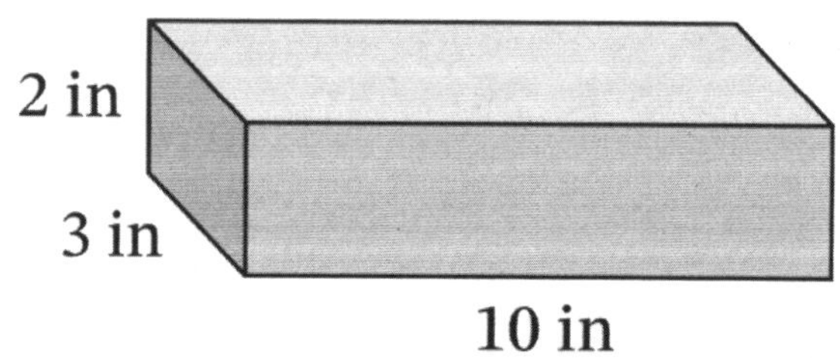

This rectangular prism has a base that measures 10 inches by 3 inches. These bases are connected by rectangles. The height of the prism is 2 inches. To find the volume we will use the formula $V = Bh$, where B represents the area of the base. The area of a rectangular base is found by multiplying the length and width of the base.

$$V = Bh$$
$$V = (10 \cdot 3) \cdot 2$$
$$V = 30 \cdot 2$$
$$V = 60$$

Because a prism is a three-dimensional figure and its units are multiplied three times to find the volume, the units for volume will be written in units cubed.

The volume of the rectangular prism is 60 cubic inches, or 60 in^3.

EXAMPLE

A triangular prism has two equivalent triangle bases. To find the volume of a triangular prism, we will use the prism volume formula: $V = Bh$.

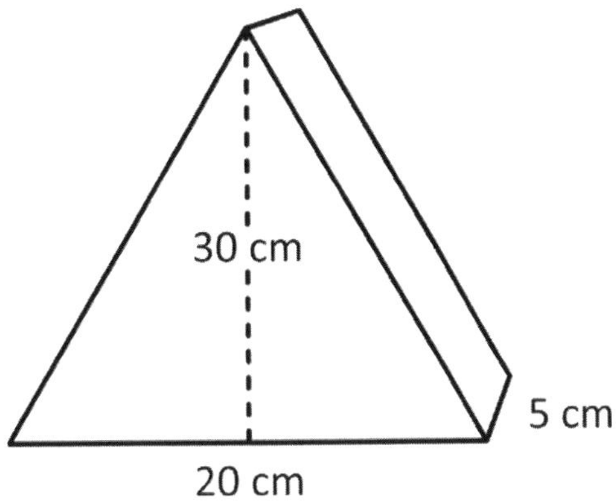

This triangular prism has two triangular bases which have a height of 30 centimeters and a base of 20 centimeters. The height of the prism is 5 centimeters. We can use the prism volume formula to find the volume of this prism.

The base of the prism is a triangle, and the area of a triangle can be solved using the formula $A = \frac{1}{2}bh$.

$$V = Bh$$
$$V = \left(\frac{1}{2} \cdot 30 \cdot 20\right) \cdot 5$$
$$V = \left(\frac{1}{2} \cdot 600\right) \cdot 5$$
$$V = (300) \cdot 5$$
$$V = 1{,}500$$

The volume of the triangular prism is 1,500 cubic centimeters, or 1,500 cm^3.

EXAMPLE

A suitcase is the shape of a rectangular prism. The height of the suitcase is 36 inches and the area of the base of the suitcase is 60 square inches. What is the volume of the suitcase in cubic inches?

We are told that the area of the base of the prism is 60 square inches and the height is 36 inches. We can use the prism volume formula to solve.

$$V = Bh$$
$$V = 60 \cdot 36$$
$$V = 2{,}160$$

The volume of the suitcase is 2,160 cubic inches.

EXAMPLE

The dimensions of a triangular prism are shown.

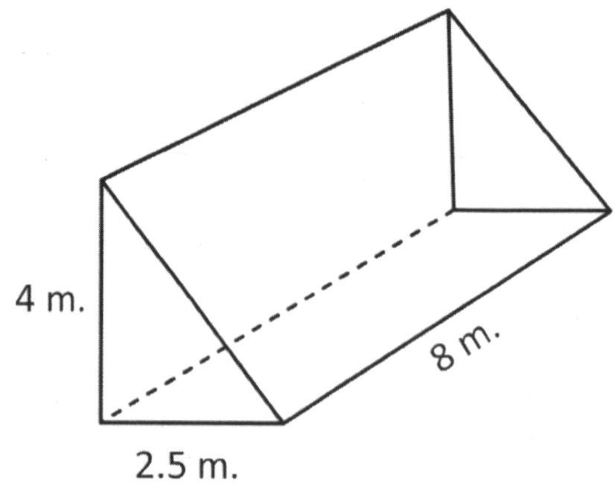

What is the volume of the triangular prism in cubic meters?

The base of the prism has a triangle shape. The height of the prism is 8 meters.

We can use the triangle area formula and volume formula to solve.

$$V = Bh$$
$$V = \left(\frac{1}{2} \times 2.5 \times 4\right) \cdot 8$$
$$V = \left(\frac{1}{2} \times 10\right) \cdot 8$$
$$V = 5 \times 8$$
$$V = 40$$

The volume of the triangular prism is 40 cubic meters, or 40 m^3.

Volume of Pyramids

A **pyramid** is a three-dimensional shape that is formed when a base has slanted sides that meet to form a point. A rectangular pyramid has a rectangular base that is connected to a point. A triangular pyramid has a triangular base that is connected to a point. The point of a pyramid where the sides connect is called the **apex**.

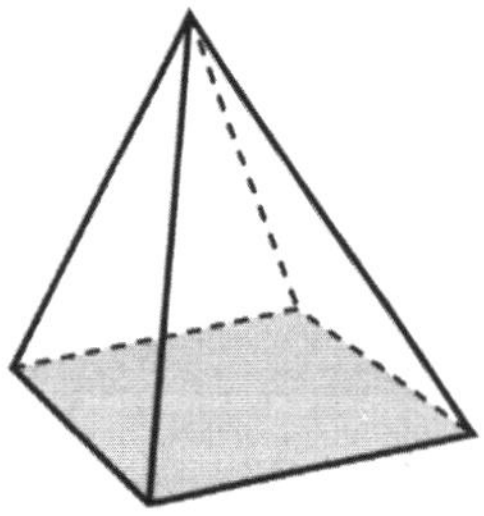

rectangular pyramid

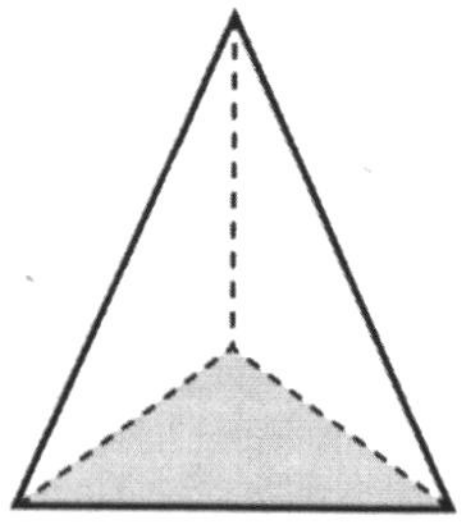

triangular pyramid

To find the volume of a pyramid, you will multiply the area of the base of the pyramid by the height of the pyramid and then multiply the product by one third. The formula that is used to find the volume of a pyramid is $V = \frac{1}{3}Bh$.

Review Video: Finding the Volume and Surface Area of a Pyramid
Visit mometrix.com/academy and enter code: 621932

EXAMPLE

A rectangular pyramid has a rectangular base that is connected to a point.

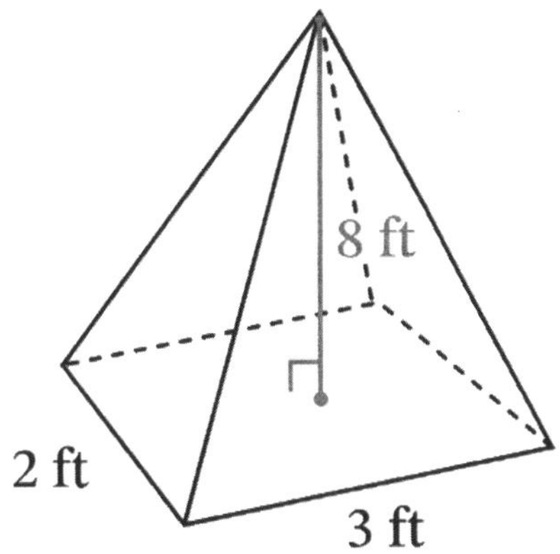

This rectangular pyramid has a rectangular base that measures 2 feet by 3 feet and has a height of 8 feet. We can find the volume by using the pyramid volume formula.

$$V = \frac{1}{3}Bh$$
$$V = \frac{1}{3}(2 \cdot 3) \cdot 8$$
$$V = \frac{1}{3}(6) \cdot 8$$
$$V = \frac{1}{3} \cdot 48$$
$$V = 48 \div 3$$
$$V = 16$$

The volume of a figure is written in cubic units, so the volume of the rectangular pyramid is 16 cubic feet, or 16 ft^3.

EXAMPLE

A triangular pyramid has a triangular base that connects to a point.

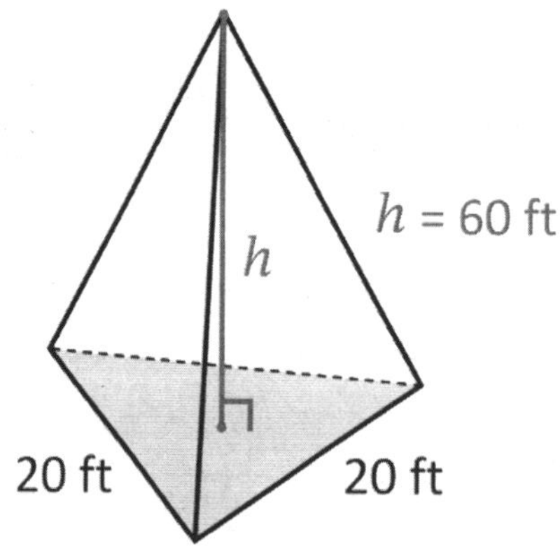

This triangular pyramid has a triangular base that has a base of 20 feet and height of 20 feet. The area of the base can be found using the triangle area formula, $A = \frac{1}{2}bh$.

The height of the pyramid is 60 feet. We can use the pyramid formula to find the volume.

$$V = \frac{1}{3}Bh$$
$$V = \frac{1}{3}\left(\frac{1}{2} \times 20 \times 20\right) \times 60$$
$$V = \frac{1}{3}(10 \times 20) \times 60$$
$$V = \frac{1}{3}(200) \times 60$$
$$V = \frac{1}{3}(12{,}000)$$
$$V = 4{,}000$$

The volume of the triangular pyramid is 4,000 cubic feet.

EXAMPLE

A rectangular pyramid's base has a base of 6 millimeters and a height of 8 millimeters. The height of the pyramid is 12 millimeters. What is the volume of the rectangular pyramid in cubic millimeters?

This question describes a pyramid with a rectangular base with a width of 6 millimeters and a length of 8 millimeters. The height of the pyramid is 12 millimeters. We can find the volume by using the pyramid volume formula.

$$V = \frac{1}{3}Bh$$
$$V = \frac{1}{3}(6 \cdot 8) \cdot 12$$
$$V = \frac{1}{3}(48) \cdot 12$$
$$V = \frac{1}{3} \cdot 576$$
$$V = 192$$

The volume of the rectangular pyramid is 192 cubic millimeters, or 192 mm^3.

EXAMPLE

A triangular pyramid has a base with an area of 16.5 square centimeters, and it has a height of 10 centimeters. What is the volume of the triangular pyramid in cubic centimeters?

We are given that the base of the pyramid has an area of 16.5 square centimeters and the height of the pyramid is 10 centimeters. We can use the pyramid volume formula to solve.

$$V = \frac{1}{3}Bh$$
$$V = \frac{1}{3} \times 16.5 \times 10$$
$$V = \frac{1}{3} \times 165$$
$$V = 55$$

The volume of the triangular pyramid is 55 cubic centimeters, or 55 cm^3.

Solving for Measurements of Circles

The relationships between the measurements of a circle are unique. A circle does not have any sides or angles. The perimeter of a circle is called the **circumference**, and the width of a circle is called the **diameter**. The **radius** of a circle is the length from the center to any point along the circumference. The radius is half of the diameter.

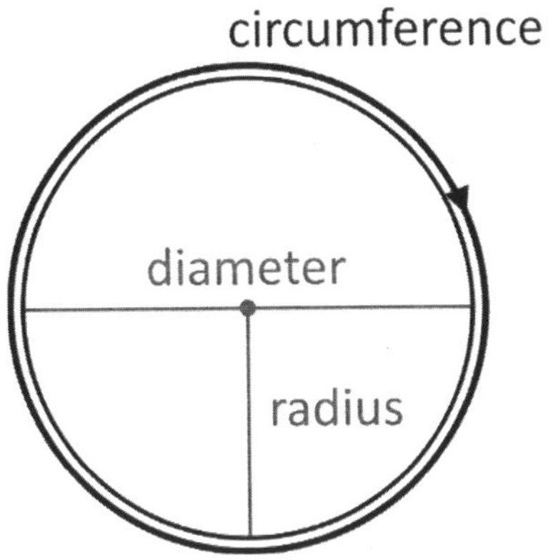

Pi, represented by the symbol π, is the constant for the proportional relationship between a circle's circumference and diameter. Pi is often rounded to 3.14. Formulas are used to find the circumference and area of circles and they all involve π.

CIRCUMFERENCE

The circumference of a circle can be found by multiplying the diameter by π. The formula to solve for the circumference of a circle is $C = \pi d$ where C represents the circumference and d represents the diameter.

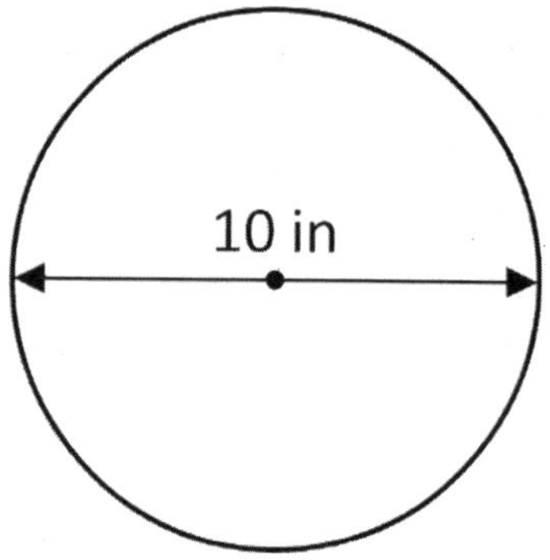

This circle has a diameter of 10 inches. We can use $C = \pi d$ to calculate the circumference.

$$C = \pi d$$
$$C = \pi \cdot 10$$
$$C = 10\pi$$

We could say that the circumference of the circle is 10π inches, or we can express the value as an approximate decimal.

$$C \approx 3.14 \cdot 10$$
$$C \approx 31.4$$

The circumference is about 31.4 inches. We say that it is about 31.4 inches because 3.14 is a rounded form of pi.

The diameter of a circle is twice the radius, so the circumference of a circle can also be found by multiplying the radius by 2 and π. An alternative circumference formula is $C = 2\pi r$, where r represents the radius.

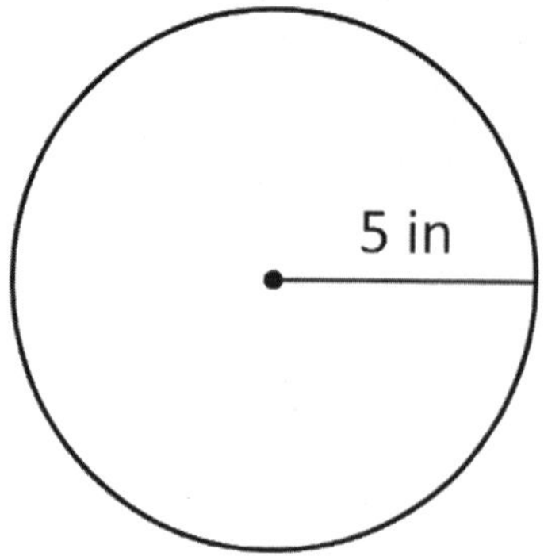

If a circle has a diameter of 10, then the radius is 5. We can use the radius to find the circumference of the circle.

$$C = 2\pi r$$
$$C = 2\pi(5)$$
$$C = 2 \cdot 5 \cdot \pi$$
$$C = 10\pi$$

$$C \approx 10 \cdot 3.14$$
$$C \approx 31.4$$

Both formulas find the circumference of the circle to be 10π inches or about 31.4 inches.

EXAMPLE

A circle has a radius of 6. Which measurement is closest to the circumference of the circle?

a. 113.04 cm
b. 37.68 cm
c. 452.16 cm
d. 18.84 cm

Each answer choice is a decimal, so we will substitute 3.14 for π in the circumference formula to solve.

$$C = 2\pi r$$
$$C \approx 2 \times 3.14 \times 6$$
$$C \approx 12 \times 3.14$$
$$C \approx 37.68$$

The circumference of the circle is about 37.68 centimeters. The correct answer is B.

AREA

The area of a circle can be found by multiplying π by the radius squared.

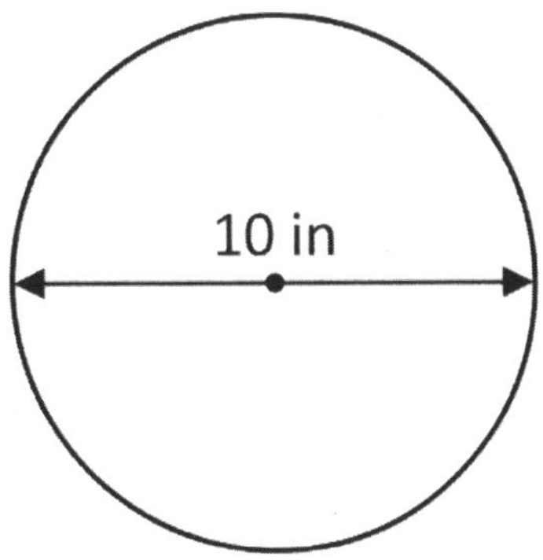

The diameter of this circle is 10 inches, so the radius of the circle is 5 inches. The formula for the area of a circle is $A = \pi r^2$.

$$A = \pi r^2$$
$$A = \pi \cdot 5^2$$
$$A = \pi \cdot 25$$
$$A = 25\pi$$

We can say that the area of the circle is 25π square inches, or we express the area as an approximate decimal by using 3.14 in place of π.

$$A \approx 25 \cdot 3.14$$
$$A \approx 78.5$$

The area of the circle is about 78.5 square inches.

EXAMPLE

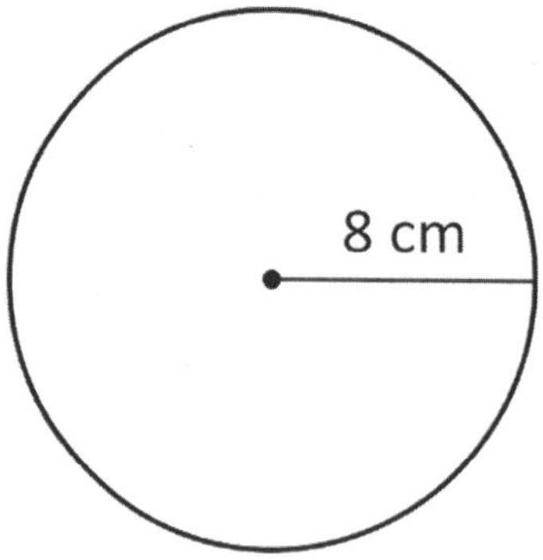

Which measurement is closest to the area of the circle?

a. 25.12 cm^2
b. 50.24 cm^2
c. 200.96 cm^2
d. 204.8 cm^2

Each answer choice is in decimal form, so we will substitute 3.14 for π in the circumference formula to solve.

$$A = \pi r^2$$
$$A \approx 3.14 \times 8^2$$
$$C \approx 3.14 \times 64$$
$$C \approx 200.96$$

The area of the circle is about 200.96 square centimeters. The correct answer is C.

EXAMPLE

Two circles are shown. Circle N has a radius of 5. Circle M has a radius of 3.

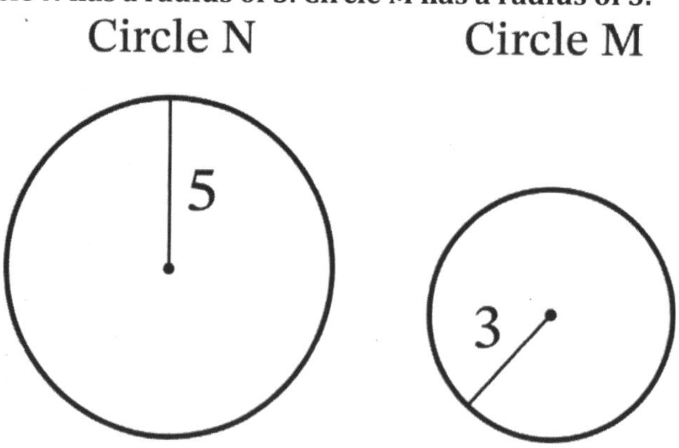

Which measurement is closest to the difference between the area of circle N and circle M, in square units?

a. 50.24 un^2
b. 20.41 un^2
c. 6.28 un^2
d. 12.56 un^2

To solve this problem, find the area of each circle and subtract to find the difference.

Circle M has a radius of 3. We can use the area formula to find the area.

$$A = \pi r^2$$
$$A \approx 3.14 \times 3^2$$
$$A \approx 3.14 \times 9$$
$$A \approx 28.26$$

The area of circle M is about 28.26 square units.

Circle N has a radius of 5.

$$A = \pi r^2$$
$$A \approx 3.14 \times 5^2$$
$$A \approx 3.14 \times 25$$
$$A \approx 78.5$$

The area of circle N is about 78.5 square units.

The difference in the areas of these circles is the difference between 78.5 and 28.26.

$$78.5 - 28.26 = 50.24$$

The difference between these two areas is 50.24 square units. The correct answer is A.

Review Video: Area and Circumference of a Circle
Visit mometrix.com/academy and enter code: 243015

Measurements of Circles

The proportional relationships found between figures and their measurements include the measurements of circles.

The perimeter of a circle is called the **circumference**, and the width of a circle is called the **diameter**.

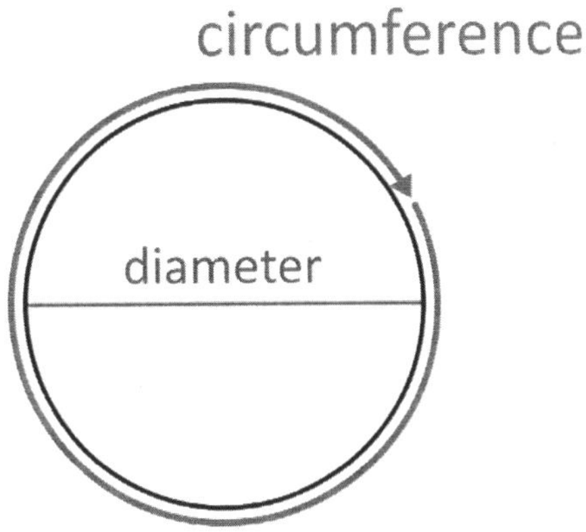

The relationship between a circle's circumference and diameter is proportional and can be described using a ratio $\frac{C}{d}$, where C represents the circumference and d represents the diameter. The value of this relationship, the quotient of the ratio $\frac{C}{d}$ is an infinite decimal that can be rounded to 3.14159, or 3.14, and is called pi. **Pi** is represented by the symbol .

$$\frac{\text{Circumference}}{\text{diameter}} = \frac{C}{d} = \pi$$

EXAMPLE

The circumference of a circle is about 10.99 feet and the diameter is 3.5 feet. Which expression best represents the value of π?

a. $\frac{3.5}{10.99}$
b. $\frac{7}{10.99}$
c. $\frac{10.99}{3.5}$
d. $\frac{10.99}{7}$

This problem focuses on identifying the relationship between circumference, diameter, and π.

We know the relationship between circumference and diameter is equal to the ratio $\frac{C}{d}$, and the value of this relationship is π. In this problem, the circumference is about 10.99 feet, and the diameter is 3.5 feet. This means that π is equal to 10.99 divided by 3.5, or the ratio $\frac{10.99}{3.5}$.

The correct answer is C.

Area of Composite Figures

The **area** is a measurement of the total space a two-dimensional figure occupies. Area is described using square units. Rectangles, squares, triangles, parallelograms, trapezoids, and circles are examples of shapes.

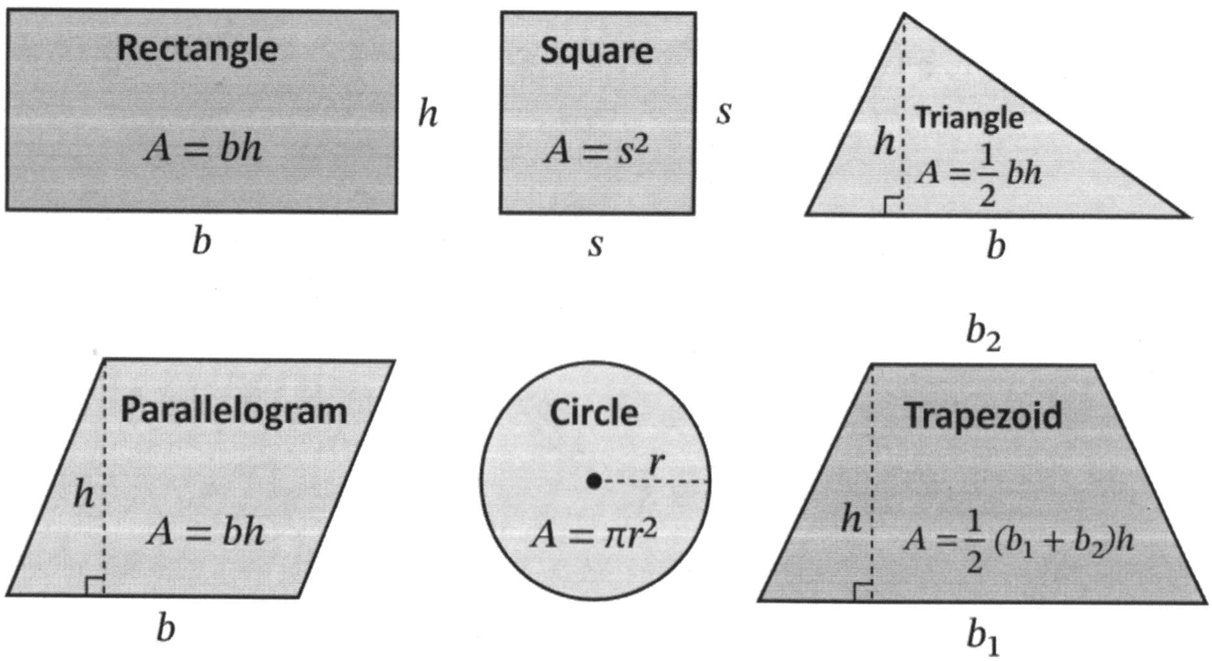

Figures that are made from a collection of shapes are called **composite figures**. Because composite figures are collections of shapes, we can find the areas of composite figures by combining known area formulas.

EXAMPLE

A window is comprised of a rectangle and a half circle.

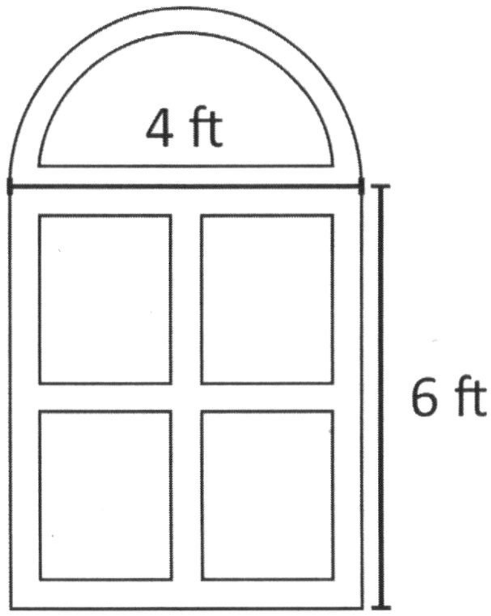

To find the area of the window, we can find the area of the rectangle and add this to the area of the half circle.

The formula for the area of a rectangle is $A = bh$. The base of the rectangle part of the window is 4 feet and the height is 6 feet.

$$A = bh$$
$$A = 4 \cdot 6$$
$$A = 24$$

The area of the rectangle part is 24 square feet, or 24 ft^2.

The formula for the area of a circle is $A = \pi r^2$. The window includes a half circle, so we can use the circle area formula and divide by 2 to find the area of the half circle. The diameter of the circle is 4 feet, which means that the radius is 2 feet.

$$A = \frac{\pi r^2}{2}$$
$$A = \frac{3.14 \cdot (2)^2}{2}$$
$$A = \frac{3.14 \cdot 4}{2}$$
$$A = \frac{12.56}{2}$$
$$A = 6.28$$

The area of the half circle is approximately 6.28 square feet, or 6.28 ft^2.

The area of the window is the sum of the two areas, $24 + 6.28 = 30.28$. So, the area of the window is approximately 30.28 square feet.

Review Video: Area of a Rectangle with a Semicircle
Visit mometrix.com/academy and enter code: 407216

Example

A parallelogram and two congruent triangles are used to form this figure.

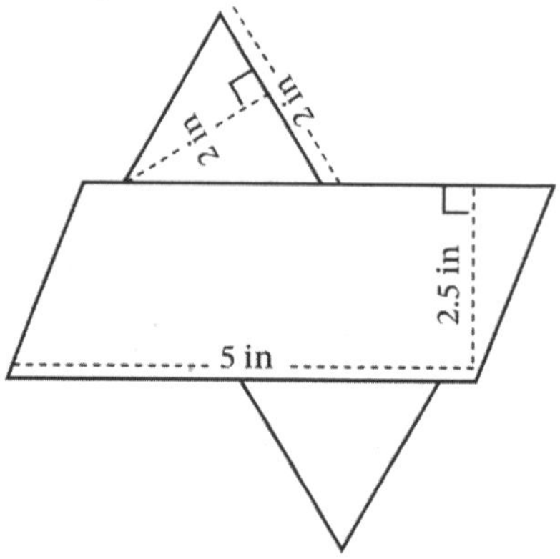

What is the area of the figure in square inches?

This composite figure is made of a parallelogram and two congruent triangles. The area of the figure can be found by finding the areas of the shapes and adding them together.

The formula for the area of a parallelogram is $A = bh$, where the base and height are perpendicular. The base of the parallelogram is 5 inches and the height is 2.5 inches.

$$A = bh$$
$$A = 5 \times 2.5$$
$$A = 12.5$$

The area of the parallelogram is 12.5 square centimeters.

The formula for the area of a triangle is $A = \frac{1}{2}bh$ where the base and height are perpendicular. The base of the triangles is 2 inches and the height is 2 inches.

$$A = \frac{1}{2}bh$$
$$A = \frac{1}{2} \cdot 2 \cdot 2$$
$$A = \frac{1}{2} \cdot 4$$
$$A = 2$$

The area of one of the triangles is 2 square inches.

The composite figure is formed by a parallelogram and two congruent triangles, so the total area is the sum of the areas of each shape, $12.5 + 2 + 2 = 16.5$. So, the area of the figure is 16.5 square inches.

EXAMPLE

A bathroom counter is a trapezoid with a circle cut out for a sink.

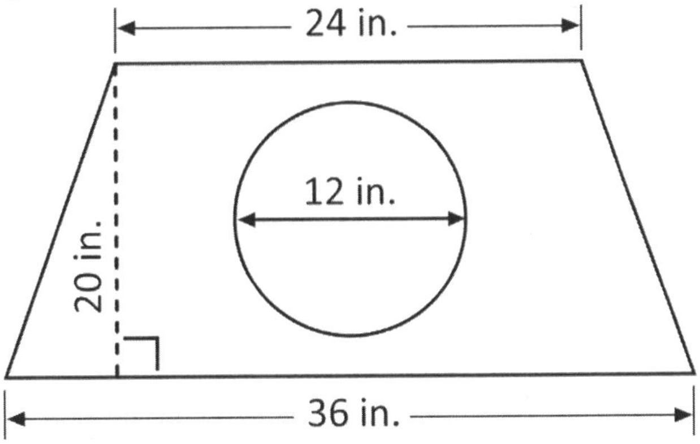

What is the best estimate of the area of the countertop that does not include the space for the sink?

This composite figure is made of a trapezoid with a circle removed. The area can be found by finding the area of the trapezoid and subtracting the area of the circle.

The formula to find the area of a trapezoid is $A = \frac{1}{2}(b_1 + b_2)h$. The trapezoid counter has two bases that measure 36 and 24 inches and a height of 20 inches.

$$A = \frac{1}{2}(b_1 + b_2) \cdot h$$
$$A = \frac{1}{2}(36 + 24) \cdot 20$$
$$A = \frac{1}{2}(60) \cdot 20$$
$$A = \frac{1}{2} \cdot 1{,}200$$
$$A = 600$$

The area of the trapezoid is 600 square inches.

The circle cut out of the trapezoid has a diameter of 12 inches, so it has a radius of 6 inches. The formula for the area of a circle is $A = \pi r^2$.

$$A = \pi r^2$$
$$A \approx 3.14 \times 6^2$$
$$A \approx 3.14 \times 36$$
$$A \approx 113.04$$

The area of the circle is about 113.04 square inches.

The area of the counter is the area of the trapezoid minus the area of the circle, $600 - 113.04 = 486.96$. So, the area of the counter is about 486.96 square inches.

Surface Area of Prisms and Pyramids

The **surface area** of a three-dimensional figure is the total two-dimensional area of the surface of the figure. We can find the surface area of a three-dimensional figure by adding the area of each face of the figure.

A **net** is an "unfolded" version of a three-dimensional figure. It is as if the figure is opened and laid flat. The net of a three-dimensional figure accurately identifies the polygon faces that make a three-dimensional figure.

EXAMPLE

The net of a rectangular prism is shown.

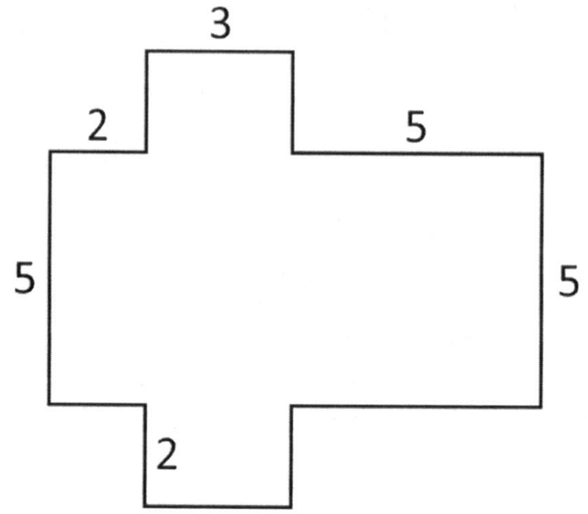

The total surface area of the rectangular prism can be found by finding the sum of the areas of each polygon in the figure. All "pieces" of the surface area of a rectangular prism are rectangles, so we can use the rectangle area formula to find the area of each rectangle.

There are many ways to divide the net of a rectangular prism into smaller rectangles. In this example, the net can be divided into one large rectangle, a small rectangle, and a square. It could also be divided into one large rectangle and two small rectangles, or it could be divided into five rectangles. The surface area is the same for every way it is divided.

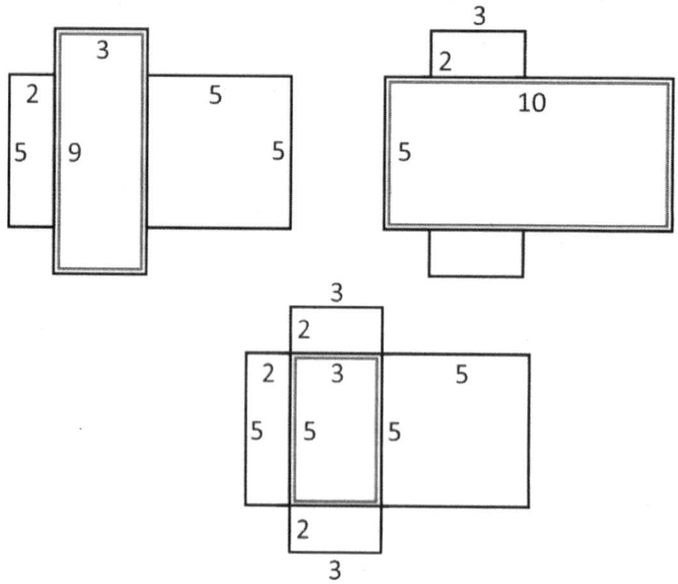

We will divide the net into one large rectangle and two small rectangles. The surface area of the rectangular prism is the sum of the areas of each rectangle. The areas of each rectangle can be found by multiplying the base and the height.

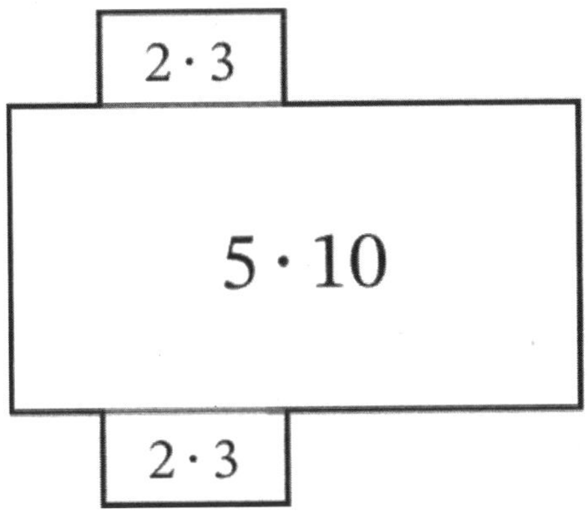

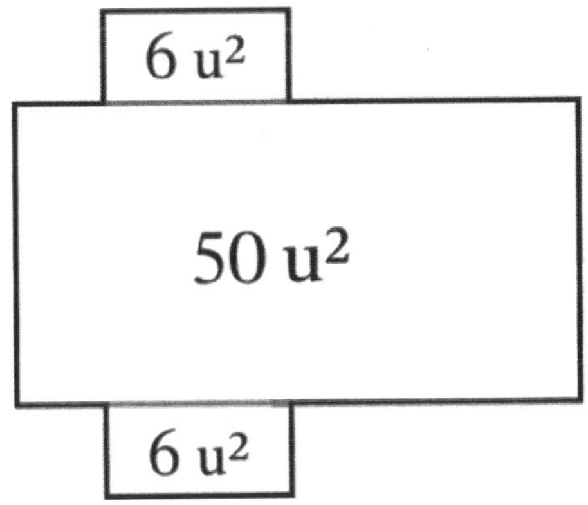

The surface area of the rectangular prism is the sum of the areas of each rectangle.

$$6 + 6 + 50 = 62$$

The surface area of the rectangular prism is 62 square units.

Example

A square pyramid is comprised of four congruent triangular faces and a rectangular base. The net of the rectangular pyramid is shown.

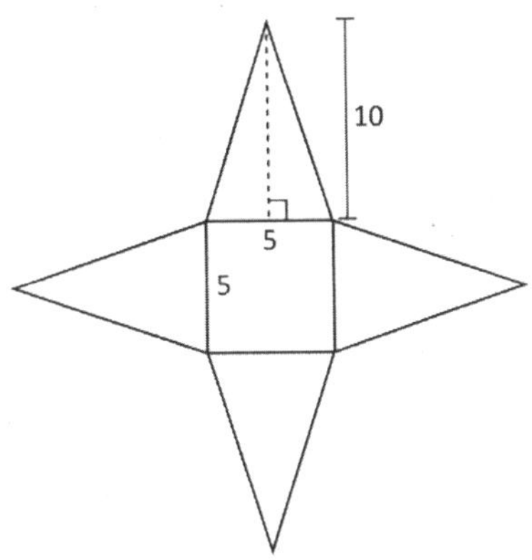

What is the surface area of the rectangular pyramid in square inches?

The surface area of the rectangular pyramid will be the sum of the areas of each shape included in the net. The net includes four triangles with a base of 5 inches and height of 10 inches.

$$A = \frac{1}{2}bh$$

$$A = \frac{1}{2} \cdot 5 \cdot 10$$

$$A = \frac{1}{2} \cdot 50$$

$$A = 25$$

The area of one triangle is 25 square inches.

The net also includes a rectangular base with a base of 5 inches and height of 5 inches. The area of the base can be found by using the area formula for rectangles.

$$A = bh$$
$$A = 5 \cdot 5$$
$$A = 25$$

The area of the rectangular base is 25 square inches.

There are four triangular faces and one rectangular base that form the net of the rectangular pyramid.

$$SA = (25 \cdot 4) + 25$$
$$SA = 100 + 25$$
$$SA = 125$$

The surface area of the rectangular pyramid is 125 square inches.

EXAMPLE

The net of a rectangular prism is shown.

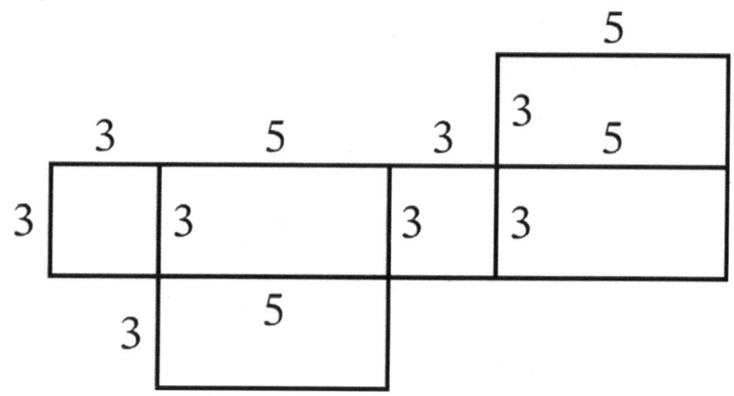

What is the surface area of the rectangular prism in square units?

The net of the rectangular prism shows that the surface area is comprised of four rectangles with a base of 5 units and a height of 3 units, and two squares with a base and height of 3 units. The surface area of the rectangular prism is the total areas of each of the six faces.

The area of each face can be found using the rectangle area formula: $A = bh$.

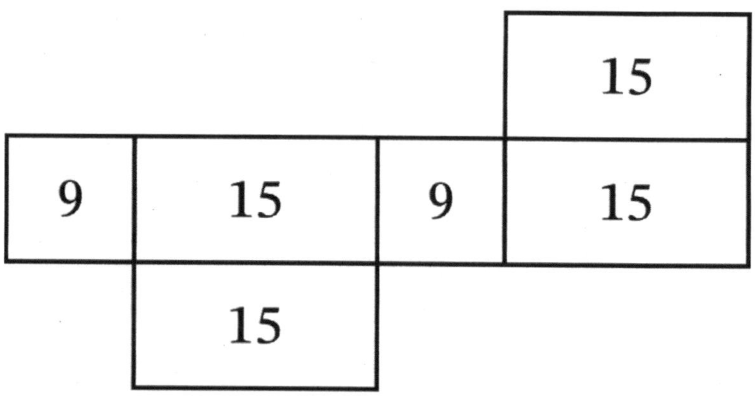

The surface area of the rectangular prism is the sum of the areas of the faces.

$$SA = (4 \cdot 15) + (2 \cdot 9)$$
$$SA = 60 + 18$$
$$SA = 78$$

The surface area of the rectangular prism is 78 square units.

Example

A triangular pyramid has a base with an area measure of 31.2 square inches. Each face has a base of 6 inches and height of 8.2 inches. What is the surface area of the triangular pyramid in square inches?

The triangular pyramid has a base with an area of 31.2 square inches, and each face has a base of 6 inches and a height of 8.2 inches.

A triangular pyramid has a triangular base and three triangular faces.

The area of one face of the pyramid can be found using the triangle area formula.

$$A = \frac{1}{2}bh$$
$$A = \frac{1}{2} \times 6 \times 8.2$$
$$A = \frac{1}{2} \times 49.2$$
$$A = 24.6$$

The area of one face is 24.6 square inches.

The area of the base of the pyramid is 31.2 square inches.

The surface area of the triangular pyramid can be found by finding the total area of the faces and base.

$$SA = (3 \times 24.6) + 31.2$$
$$SA = 73.8 + 31.2$$
$$SA = 105$$

The surface area of the triangular pyramid is 105 square inches.

Cross-Sections

A **cross-section** is a shape that results when a solid three-dimensional object is cut by a two-dimensional plane. For example, the cross-section is a circle when cutting a cylinder parallel to its bases. The cross-section is a rectangle when cutting a cylinder perpendicular to its bases.

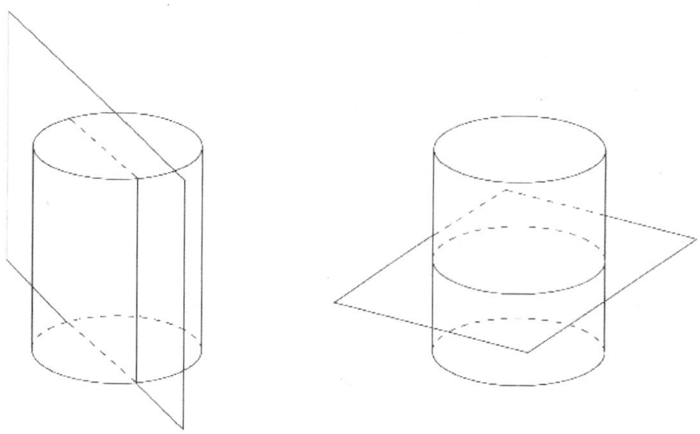

Consider finding cross sections both parallel and perpendicular to the base of a right rectangular prism. When a plane cuts a right rectangular prism parallel to its base (as seen in Figure 1), the resulting cross-section is a rectangle congruent to the prism's bases. When a plane cuts a right rectangular prism perpendicular to its base (as seen in Figures 2 and 3), the resulting cross section is also a rectangle; however, this rectangle is congruent to the lateral faces of the prism to which it is parallel. In Figure 2, the base of the cross-section is the long side of the base of the prism, and in Figure 3, the base of the cross-section is the short side of the base of the prism. This is because each cross-section is parallel to a different lateral face.

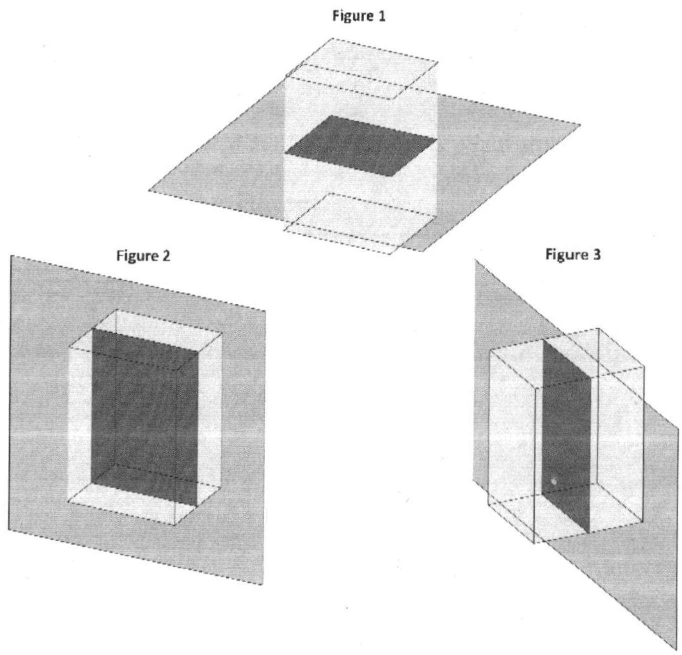

Depending on that plane's orientation, three different shapes result from cutting a right rectangular pyramid with a plane. When a right rectangular pyramid is cut by a plane parallel to its base, the resulting cross-section is a rectangle similar to the base but not congruent. These similar rectangle cross-sections are proportional to the base but do not have the same side lengths. When a plane cuts a right rectangular pyramid perpendicular to its base and through the apex, the result is a triangle with a base congruent to the parallel side of the rectangular base of the pyramid. If a perpendicular plane does not go through the apex, the resulting cross-section is a trapezoid with a base congruent to the parallel side of the rectangular base of the pyramid.

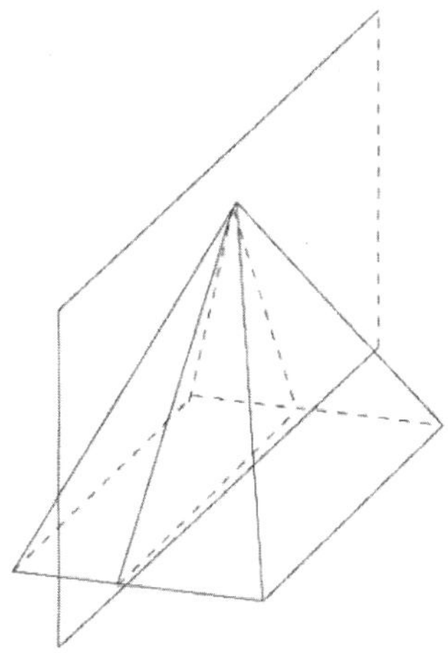

Perpendicular Cross Section through Apex

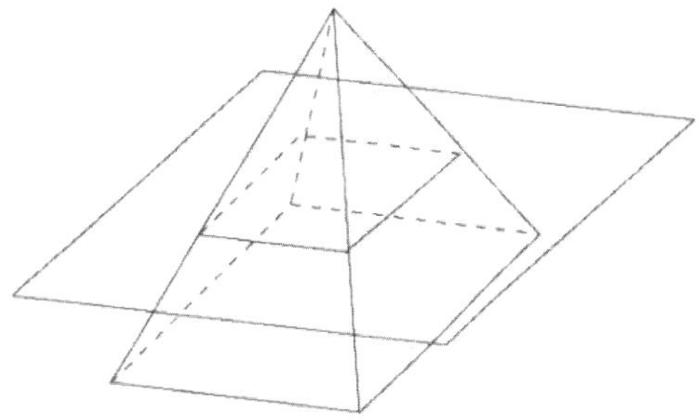

Parallel Cross Section

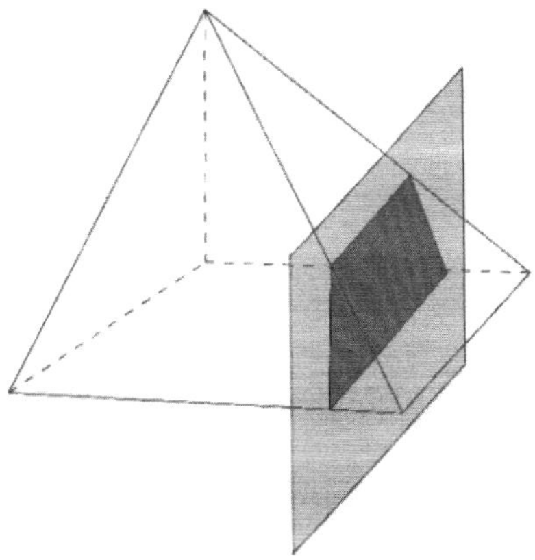

Perpendicular Cross Section not through Apex

Similar Figures

Similar figures are figures that have the same shape, but are different sizes. Similar figures have the same number of sides and angles. Their corresponding angles are congruent, and their sides are proportional.

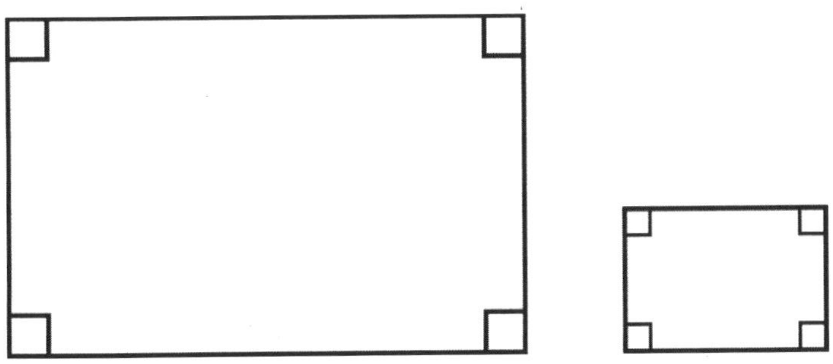

These two figures are rectangles. We know they are both rectangles because they each have four right angles and two sets of parallel sides. These rectangles are the same shape but are different sizes, which means these figures are similar.

The side lengths of similar figures are proportional. That means that when we compare the side lengths of these rectangles, the relationship will be constant.

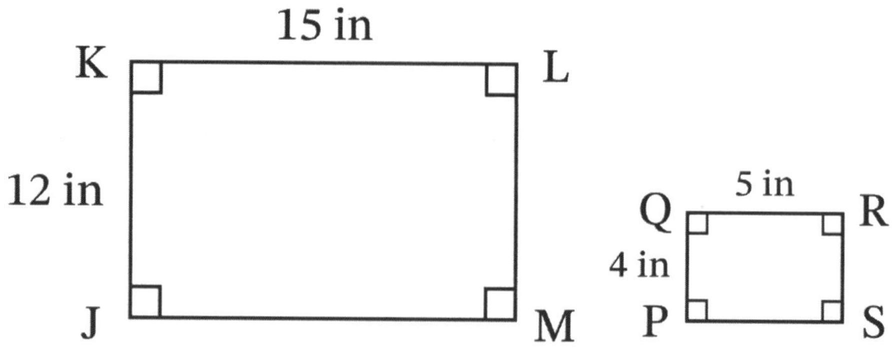

$$\frac{x}{y} = \frac{QP}{KJ} = \frac{4\text{ in}}{12\text{ in}} = \frac{1}{3}$$
$$\frac{x}{y} = \frac{QR}{KL} = \frac{5\text{ in}}{15\text{ in}} = \frac{1}{3}$$

The relationship between figure x and figure y is $\frac{1}{3}$.

This also means that $\frac{QP}{KJ} = \frac{QR}{KL}$. We can use cross multiplication to confirm.

$$\frac{4}{12} = \frac{5}{15}$$
$$4 \cdot 15 = 12 \cdot 5$$
$$60 = 60$$

This is also true if you compare the smaller rectangle to the larger rectangle.

$$\frac{y}{x} = \frac{KJ}{QP} = \frac{12\text{ in}}{4\text{ in}} = \frac{3}{1} = 3$$

$$\frac{y}{x} = \frac{KL}{QR} = \frac{15\text{ in}}{5\text{ in}} = \frac{3}{1} = 3$$

The relationship between figure y and figure x is 3.

This also means that $\frac{KJ}{QP} = \frac{KL}{QR}$. We can use cross multiplication to confirm.

$$\frac{12}{4} = \frac{15}{5}$$
$$12 \cdot 5 = 15 \cdot 4$$
$$60 = 60$$

EXAMPLE

We can use proportional relationships in similar figures to solve for missing side lengths.

Let's say we are given two triangles and told that these triangles are similar. This means that their side lengths are proportional.

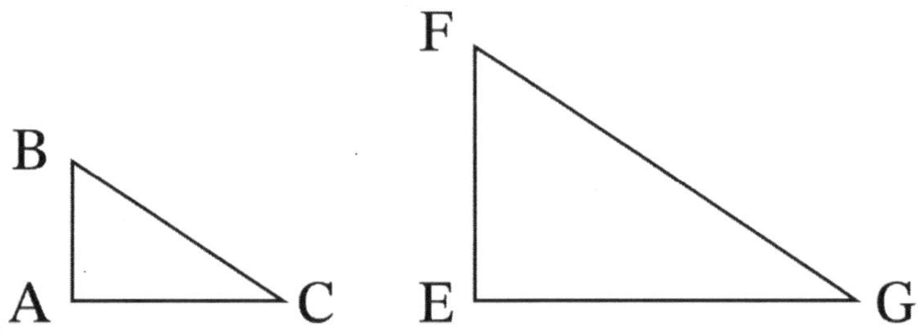

Since triangle ABC is similar to triangle EFG, their side lengths are proportional. Here are some true statements about these similar triangles.

$$\frac{AB}{EF} = \frac{AC}{EG}$$

$$\frac{BC}{FG} = \frac{AB}{EF}$$

$$\frac{AC}{EG} = \frac{BC}{FG}$$

Because these statements are true, we can use this information to find a missing side length. Since these triangles are similar, we can use proportions to solve for missing side lengths.

Triangle ABC and triangle EFG are pictured, but triangle EFG has a missing side length. What is the value of the missing side length?

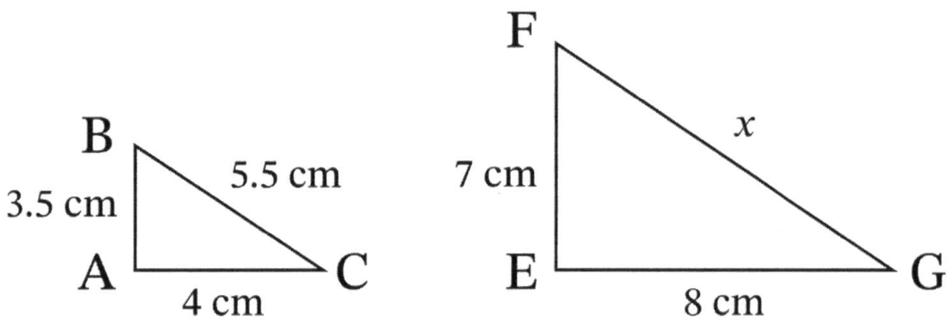

To find the value of the missing side length, we can use what we know about similar shapes. For example, we know that $\frac{AB}{EF} = \frac{BC}{FG}$. We can use this to solve for FG.

$$\frac{AB}{EF} = \frac{BC}{FG}$$
$$\frac{3.5}{7} = \frac{5.5}{x}$$
$$3.5x = 5.5 \times 7$$

$$\frac{3.5x}{3.5} = \frac{38.5}{3.5}$$
$$x = 11$$

The length of $\overline{FG}$ is 11 centimeters.

EXAMPLE

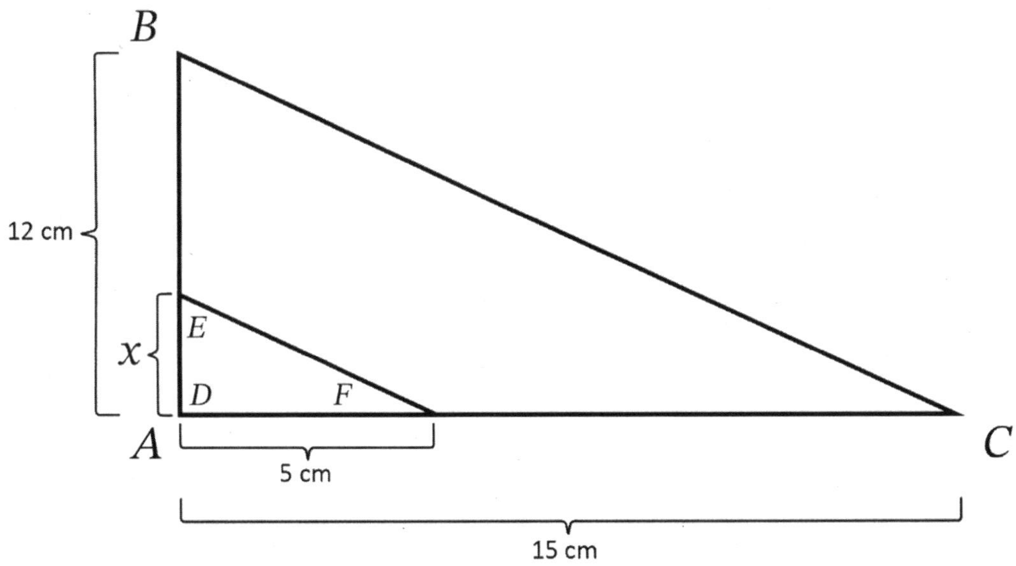

Triangle ABC and DEF are similar. What is the value of x in centimeters?

This problem focuses on solving problems involving similar shapes. We know that ABC and DEF are similar triangles. This means that their side lengths are proportional, so we can set up a proportion to solve this problem.

The first step to setting up a proportion is to identify the missing side length and its corresponding side. We want to find the value of x, which is the length of $\overline{DE}$, and the corresponding side is $\overline{AB}$. So, we will use the ratio $\frac{DE}{AB}$, $\frac{x}{AB}$, or $\frac{x}{12}$ to solve for x.

To set the other side of the proportion we will compare two other corresponding side lengths. $\overline{DF}$ corresponds with $\overline{AC}$, so we can also use the proportion $\frac{DF}{AC}$, or $\frac{5}{15}$.

Now we can set up a proportion and solve.

$$\frac{DE}{AB} = \frac{DF}{AC}$$
$$\frac{x}{12} = \frac{5}{15}$$
$$15x = 60$$
$$x = 4$$

The value of x is 4 centimeters.

EXAMPLE

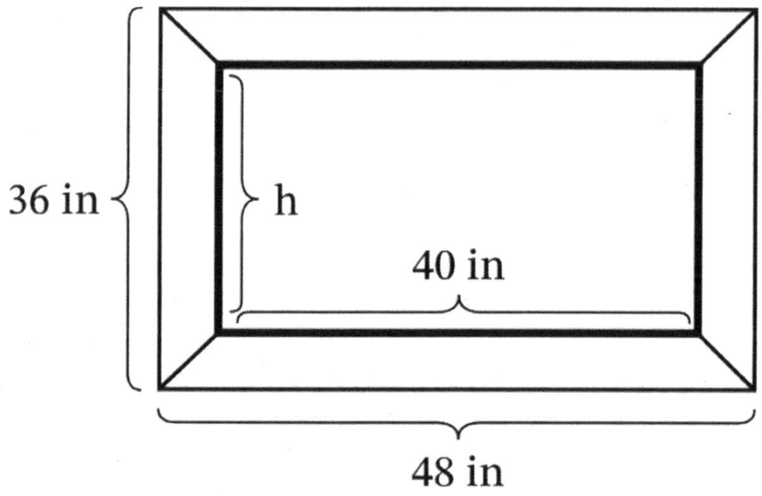

The diagram shows a painting in a frame. The two rectangles are similar. What is the height, *h*, of the painting in inches?

We know that the two rectangles are similar, so we can use a proportion to solve for the height of the painting.

$$\frac{h}{36} = \frac{40}{48}$$
$$48h = 1{,}440$$
$$\frac{48h}{48} = \frac{1{,}440}{48}$$
$$h = 30$$

The height of the painting is 30 inches.

SCALE FACTOR

Similar figures are the same shapes but different sizes. The change between similar figures can be described as a scale factor. The **scale factor** is the ratio between corresponding side lengths.

Let's say that we start with the smaller figure and increase the size to create the larger figure.

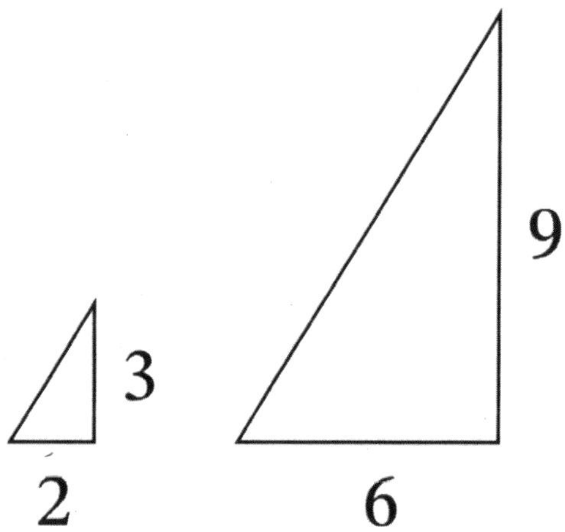

We can see that the ratio between side lengths is proportional and can identify the scale factor by identifying the value of the ratio of the new figure (the larger figure) to the original figure (the smaller figure).

$$\frac{\text{new figure}}{\text{original figure}} = \frac{6}{2} = 3$$
$$\frac{\text{new figure}}{\text{original figure}} = \frac{9}{3} = 3$$

When we compare the new figure side length to the original figure side length, we can see that the side lengths are proportional because the ratios are equivalent. We can also see that the change from figure 1 to figure 2 is an increase by a scale factor of 3.

Review Video: Proportional Change of Dimensions
Visit mometrix.com/academy and enter code: 186545

Scale Drawings

A **scale drawing** is a drawing used to represent similar figures. A map is an example of a scale drawing. Maps represent distances and measurements that are much too large to fit on a wall or sheet of paper, and the distance between locations on a map is proportional to the distance between those locations on earth. A scale drawing is a proportional representation, which means that the real measurements are proportional to the drawn measurements. A scale is used to define this proportional relationship.

The **scale** in a scale drawing is included in the key and shows the relationship between the original item and the scale drawing. The scale includes a measurement from the scale drawing and gives an equivalent measurement from the original item. An example of a scale is 1 inch = 100 miles. This means that in the scale drawing, 1 inch is equivalent to 100 miles in the original.

Example

Let's say you are building a bird house. You may encounter a scale drawing in the directions to represent the size of the real-life bird house you will make. A realistic sized drawing of a bird house cannot fit on a small sheet of paper, so scale drawings are used to represent the dimensions of the bird house.

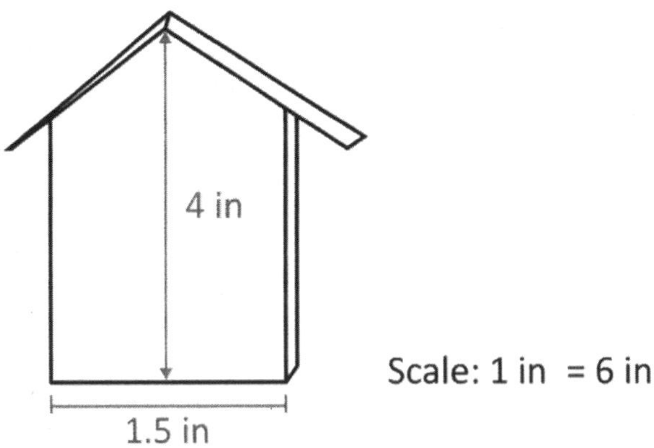

This scale drawing has the same proportions of the real-life bird house. There is a scale included with the scale drawing that says that 1 inch is equivalent to 6 inches. This means that in the scale drawing, 1 inch is equivalent to 6 inches in the real-life bird house.

In the drawing, the length of the bottom of the bird house measures 1.5 inches. This means that the length of the bottom of the real-life bird house will be $1.5 \times 6 = 9$ inches. The height of the bird house is 4 inches in the scale drawing. If the scale is 1 inch = 6 inches, the real-life bird house will be $4 \times 6 = 24$ inches tall.

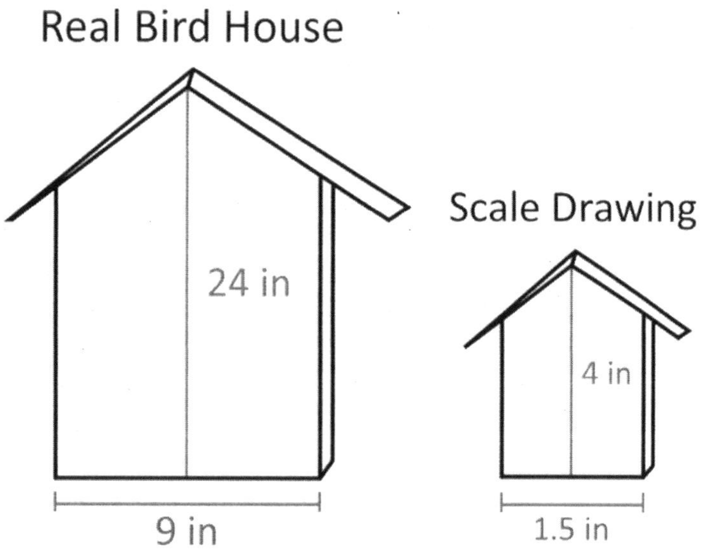

EXAMPLE

The relationship between scale drawings and the real items they represent is proportional.

Let's say that on the scale drawing, one side of the roof measures 2.5 inches. What is the measurement of the side of the roof in the real bird house?

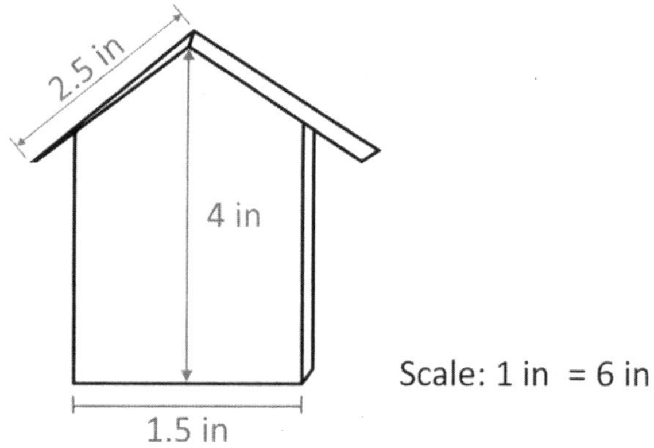

Since the side lengths of the two figures are proportional, we can find the missing side length by using the scale provided.

$$x = 2.5 \times 6$$
$$x = 15$$

The length of one side of the roof is 15 inches.

Example

A pool has a length of 30 meters and width of 25 meters. On a scale drawing of the pool, the length is 6 centimeters. What is the width of the pool in the scale drawing in centimeters?

This problem focuses on solving for a missing side length. Because scale drawings are similar figures, we can use a proportion to solve for the missing side length.

$$\frac{\text{length}}{\text{width}} = \frac{\text{length}}{\text{width}}$$
$$\frac{30}{6} = \frac{25}{x}$$
$$30x = 25 \cdot 6$$
$$30x = 150$$
$$\frac{30x}{30} = \frac{150}{30}$$
$$x = 5$$

The width of the pool in the scale drawing is 5 centimeters.

Angles

Angles and Vertices

An **angle** is formed when two lines or line segments meet at a common point. It may be a common starting point for a pair of segments or rays, or it may be the intersection of lines. Angles are represented by the symbol $\angle$.

The **vertex** is the point at which two segments or rays meet to form an angle. If the angle is formed by intersecting rays, lines, and/or line segments, the vertex is the point at which four angles are formed. The pairs of angles opposite one another are called vertical angles, and their measures are equal.

- An **acute** angle is an angle with a degree measure less than 90°.
- A **right** angle is an angle with a degree measure of exactly 90°.
- An **obtuse** angle is an angle with a degree measure greater than 90° but less than 180°.
- A **straight angle** is an angle with a degree measure of exactly 180°.
- A **reflex angle** is an angle with a degree measure greater than 180° but less than 360°.
- A **full angle** is an angle with a degree measure of exactly 360°.

Review Video: Angles
Visit mometrix.com/academy and enter code: 264624

Relationships Between Angles

Two angles whose sum is exactly 90° are said to be **complementary**. The two angles may or may not be adjacent. In a right triangle, the two acute angles are complementary.

Two angles whose sum is exactly 180° are said to be **supplementary**. The two angles may or may not be adjacent. Two intersecting lines always form two pairs of supplementary angles. Adjacent supplementary angles will always form a straight line.

Two angles that have the same vertex and share a side are said to be **adjacent**. **Vertical angles** are not adjacent because they share a vertex but no common side.

Review Video: Adjacent Angles
Visit mometrix.com/academy and enter code: 100375

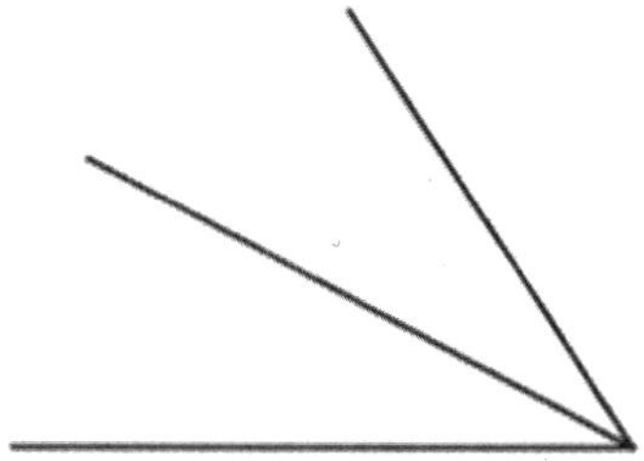

Adjacent
Share vertex and side

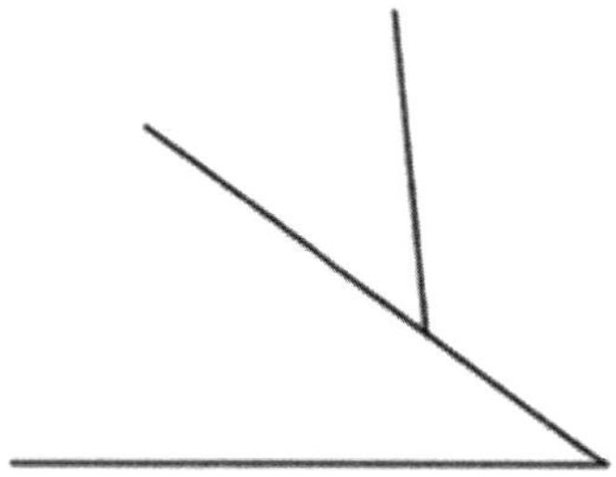

Not adjacent
Share part of a side, but not vertex

Constructing Triangles

According to the **Triangle Inequality Theorem,** the **sum** of any two sides of a triangle must be greater than the third side. In general, if a triangle has sides a, b, and c, this theorem can be represented using the following inequalities:

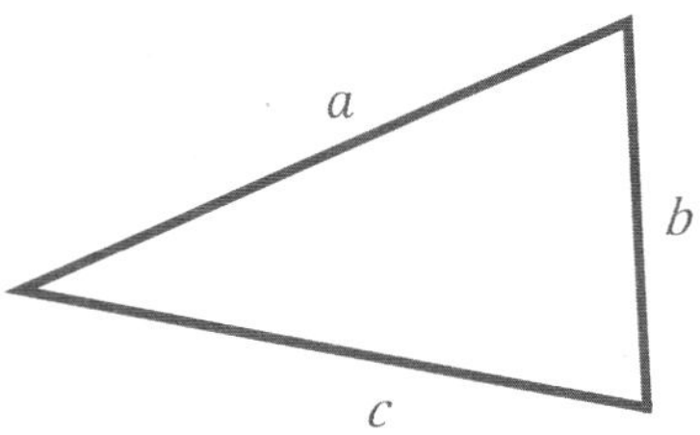

$$a + b > c$$
$$a + c > b$$
$$b + c > a$$

For example, if given the measurements of three different line segments with lengths of two units, three units, and six units, it is geometrically impossible for them to create a triangle, as shown below. The sum of the two shortest sides, $2 + 3 = 5$, is less than the third side, 6, so there is no way for all three of the sides to meet to form a triangle. To illustrate this, the arcs in the picture below show the side lengths of 2 and 3 would never meet. To create a triangle, the sum of any two line segments must be greater than the third line segment.

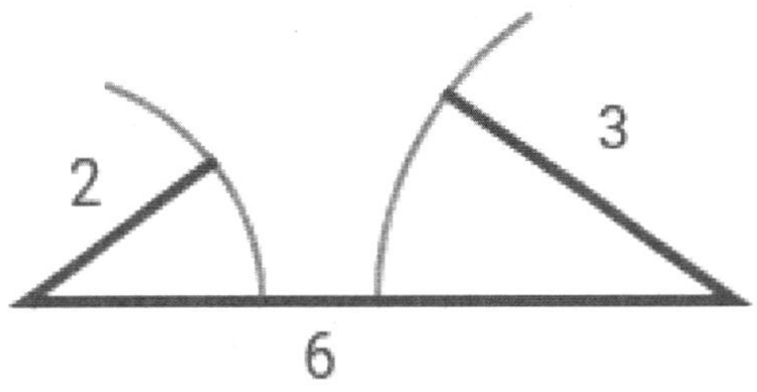

Understanding the Triangle Inequality Theorem leads to being able to determine if a set of given sides and angles makes a **unique triangle** (only one triangle), a **non-unique triangle** (more than one triangle), or **no possible triangle.**

A unique triangle is a triangle that can be drawn in only one way. Five cases result in a unique triangle.

Side-Side-Side (SSS)	Side-Angle-Side (SAS)	Angle-Side-Angle (ASA)	Angle-Angle-Side (AAS)	Hypotenuse-Leg (HL)
If three sides are given, AND the three sides satisfy the Triangle Inequality Theorem, the triangle is unique.	If two sides and their included angle (the angle between the given sides) are given, the triangle is unique.	If two angles and their included side (the side in between the given angles) are given, the triangle is unique.	If two angles and the non-included side (side *not* in between the given angles) are given, the triangle is unique.	In a right triangle (a triangle with a right angle), if the hypotenuse (longest side) and one leg (a side that is not the hypotenuse) are given, the triangle is unique.
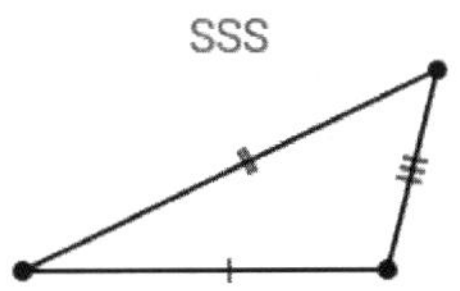	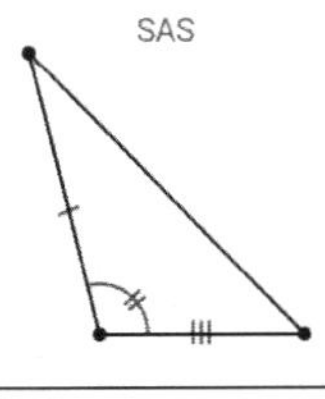	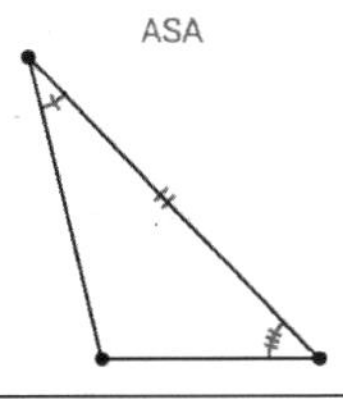	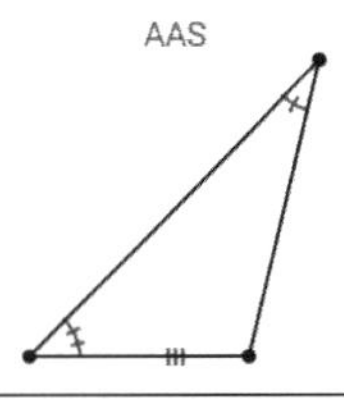	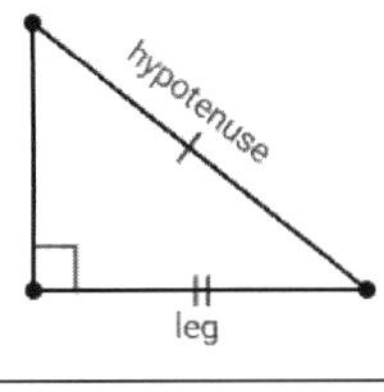

A non-unique triangle can be drawn in more than one way. Two cases result in a non-unique triangle.

Angle-Angle-Angle (AAA)	Side-Side-Angle (SSA)
If three angles are given and their sum is 180°, the triangle is non-unique. Many different triangles with different side lengths can be drawn given three angles.	If two sides and the non-included angle are given, the triangle is non-unique. In this case, two possible triangles can be formed, as the side not attached to the given angle can be in two different positions.
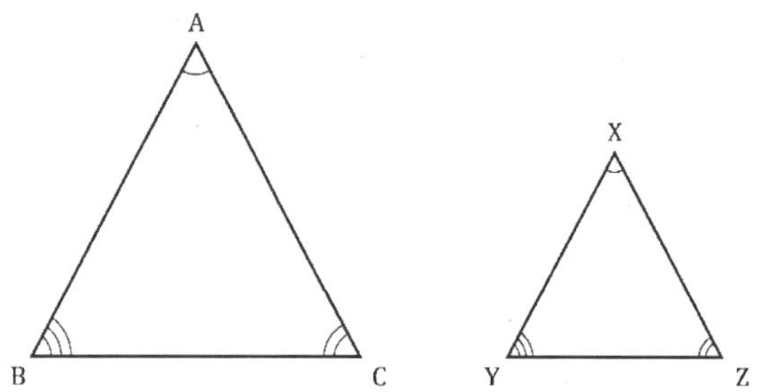 Triangles ABC and XYZ have all the same angle measures but are two different triangles.	Fig. 1 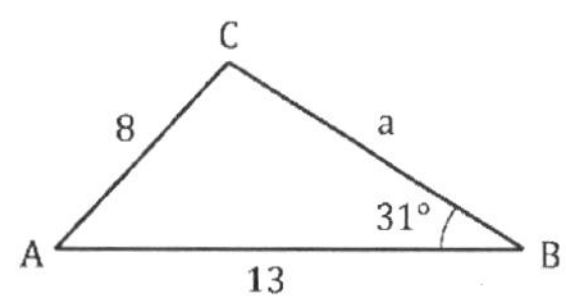 Fig. 2 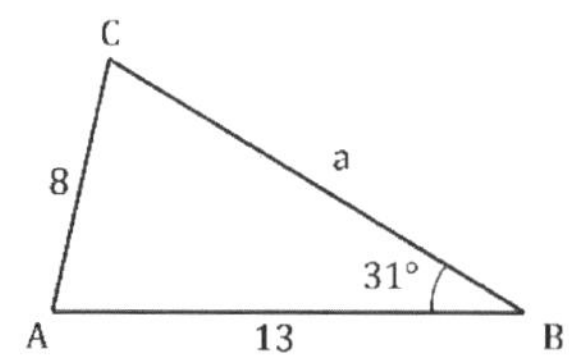 Side AC can swing to form two distinct triangles. Figure 1 shows one possible position of AC, and Figure 2 shows the other possible position of AC.

Two cases result in no possible triangle.

Sum of Angles ≠ 180°	Triangle Inequality Theorem Failure
By definition of a triangle, the sum of the interior angles of a triangle must equal 180°. If this is not true, there are no possible triangles that can be drawn.	If three sides are given and they fail to satisfy the Triangle Inequality Theorem, no possible triangles can be drawn. 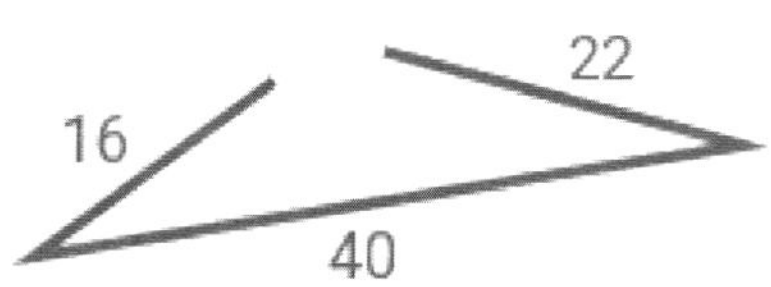 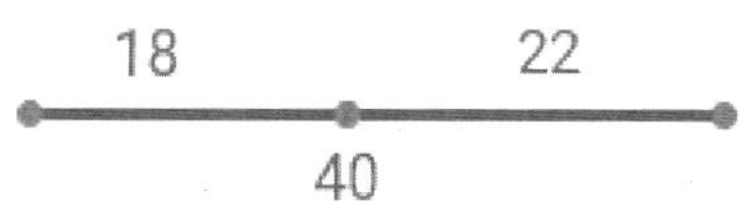 In the Figure A, $16 + 22 < 40$, so the two shorter sides cannot meet to form a triangle. In Figure B, $18 + 22 = 40$, so the two shorter sides are exactly as long as the third, and a triangle cannot be formed.

Writing and Solving Equations About Geometry

Equations with variables can be used to find missing measurements in geometric figures. By using what we know about geometry, we can create and solve equations to find these measurements.

Triangles have three interior angles. The sum of the three interior angles of a triangle is always 180°.

Let's use this information to solve a missing angle problem. Below, we are given a triangle whose angle measures are 35°, $(3x + 15)°$, and 85° and are directed to solve for the value of x.

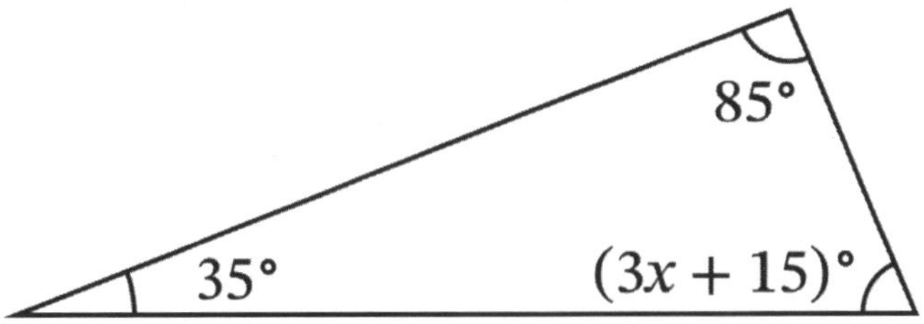

We can use an equation to solve for x and find the missing angle value.

First, we know that the sum of all angles in a triangle is 180°, so we can find the measurement of the angle that is equal to $3x + 15$ by isolating x.

$$35 + 85 + (3x + 15) = 180$$

$$135 + 3x = 180$$

$$135 - 135 + 3x = 180 - 135$$

$$3x = 45$$

$$\frac{3x}{3} = \frac{45}{3}$$

$$x = 15$$

Now we can solve for the missing angle measurement. Since we now know that $x = 15$, and the missing angle measurement is equal to $3x + 15$, we can plug x into the expression to find the angle measurement.

$$3(15) + 15$$

$$45 + 15$$

$$60$$

The missing angle measurement is 60°.

EXAMPLE

The angle measures of a triangle are shown in the diagram.

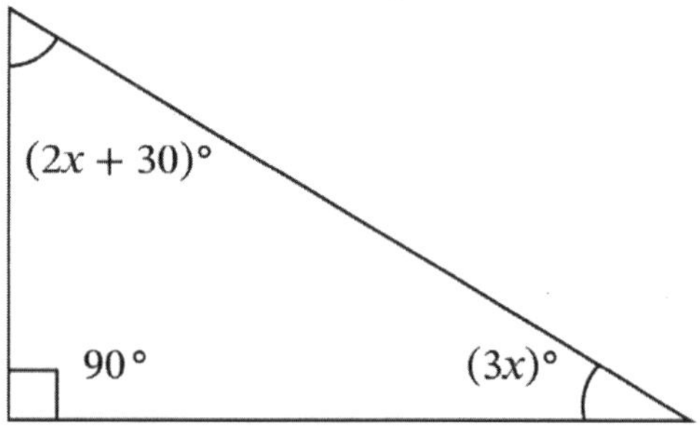

What is the value of x?

This triangle shows two angles with missing angle measures and one angle with a measure of 90°.

If we know that the sum of all angles of a triangle is 180°, then we can use subtraction to find the sum of the two missing angles.

$$180° - 90° = 90°$$

The sum of the two missing angles is 90°. This means that the sum of $3x$ and $2x + 30$ is 90°. Write and solve an equation that shows this.

$$3x + (2x + 30) = 90$$

Because the expressions on the left side of the equation are being added together, there is no need for parentheses.

$$3x + 2x + 30 = 90$$

Combine like terms.

$$5x + 30 = 90$$

Now, solve for x.

$$5x + 30 - 30 = 90 - 30$$
$$5x = 60$$
$$\frac{5x}{5} = \frac{60}{5}$$
$$x = 12$$

The value of x is 12.

We can check to see if this makes sense with the given triangle by using $x = 12$ to find the measurements of each angle.

$$3x = 3(12) = 36°$$

$$2x + 30 = 2(12) + 30 = 24 + 30 = 54°$$

The missing angle measures are 36° and 54°. If that were true, the sum of all angle measures would be 180°.

$$36 + 54 + 90 = 180$$
$$90 + 90 = 180$$
$$180 = 180$$

This is true, so we have confirmed the value of x is 12.

EXAMPLE

The angle measures of triangle *WXY* are listed below.

The measure of angle W is 65°.
The measure of angle X is $(4x + 5)$
The measure of angle Y is $(7x)$

What is the value of x?

In this problem, we are given the angle measures of a triangle and we need to find the value of x. We need to find the missing angle measurements and then use that information to find the value of x.

We know that the sum of the angles of a triangle is 180°, so we can find the sum of the missing angle measurements.

$$180 - 65 = 115$$

The missing angles have a sum of 115°. This means that the sum of $4x + 5$ and $7x$ is 115.

$$4x + 5 + 7x = 115$$
$$11x + 5 = 115$$
$$11x + 5 - 5 = 115 - 5$$
$$11x = 110$$
$$\frac{11x}{11} = \frac{110}{11}$$
$$x = 10$$

The value of x is 10.

Use $x = 10$ to find the measure of angle X and angle Y.

$$m\angle X = 4x + 5 = 4(10) + 5 = 40 + 5 = 45$$

$$m\angle Y = 7x = 7(10) = 70$$

The sum of all angles of a triangle is 180°.

$$45 + 70 + 65 = 180$$

We can confirm that the value of x is 10.

Statistics and Probability

Probability

Simple and Compound Events

Lists and tree diagrams can be used to represent sample spaces for simple and compound events. A **simple event** is an event where there is one trial. For example, a coin flip is a simple event, since it has one trial that has one outcome. A **compound event** is an event with multiple, separate trials. For example, flipping two coins would have two trials: one for the first coin and another for the second coin. Flipping one coin twice would also be a compound event, since a different trial occurs each time the coin is flipped.

> **Review Video: Intro to Probability**
> Visit mometrix.com/academy and enter code: 212374

Sample Spaces

A **sample space** is a representation of all possibilities in an event. In simple and compound events, lists and tree diagrams can be used to map all possible outcomes of an experiment.

Let's say that you are playing a game where you predict which number a die will land on before you roll it. There are six possible outcomes: 1, 2, 3, 4, 5, and 6. You will only roll the die once, meaning the event will have one trial. This means this is a simple event.

A sample space can be formed by identifying the possible outcomes of the roll. The outcome can be 1, 2, 3, 4, 5, or 6, so we can represent these possibilities on our tree diagram.

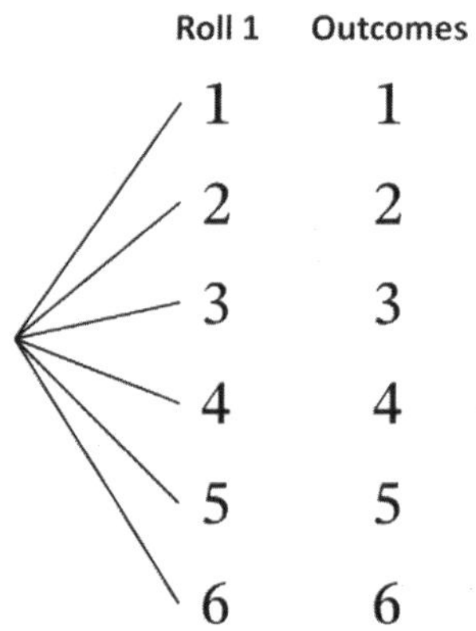

This tree diagram represents all possible outcomes for the simple event.

A tree diagram for a simple event only has one set of branches that come from one starting point. A tree diagram for a compound event has more branches, since more than one trial is represented.

Let's say that instead of only rolling once and making one prediction, you predict the outcome of two rolls of the die. You predict what number the die will land on with the first roll, and you predict whether the die will land on an even number or an odd number with the second roll. The game demonstrates a compound event, since two separate trials will occur.

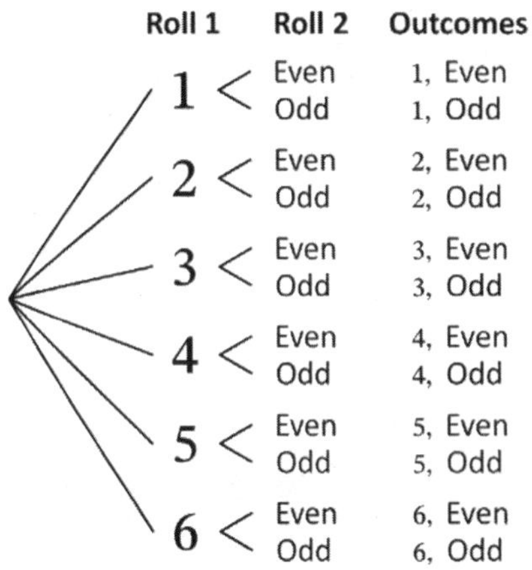

This tree diagram represents all possible outcomes for the compound event.

Since there are two different trials, the tree diagram has more than one set of branches. It has one set of branches for the possible outcomes of the first roll, and each of those branches is followed by another pair of branches. These pairs represent the possible results of the second roll. This shows that the result of the compound event has two parts, since there were two trials.

The sample space for a simple or compound event can also be represented by a list. Tree diagrams can be used to show what all the possible outcomes are for an event so they can be easily listed.

Consider the simple event of rolling the die once and guessing what number it will land on. There are only six possible results, and these are shown on the tree diagram. The list would be $\{1, 2, 3, 4, 5, 6\}$. This list shows the sample space for the simple event described.

Consider the compound event of predicting what number the die will land on for the first roll and then predicting whether it will land on an even or odd number for the second roll. These are shown on the tree diagram for this event. The list would be

$$\{(1, \text{Even}), (1, \text{Odd}), (2, \text{Even}), (2, \text{Odd}), (3, \text{Even}), (3, \text{Odd}), (4, \text{Even}), (4, \text{Odd}), (5, \text{Even}), (5, \text{Odd}), (6, \text{Even}), (6, \text{Odd})\}$$

. This list shows the sample space for the compound event described.

Review Video: Tree Diagrams
Visit mometrix.com/academy and enter code: 829158

EXAMPLE

You are picking buttons out of a bag. There are 4 red and 4 blue buttons in the bag. Which tree diagram shows all possible outcomes if you pick 4 buttons from the bag?

a.

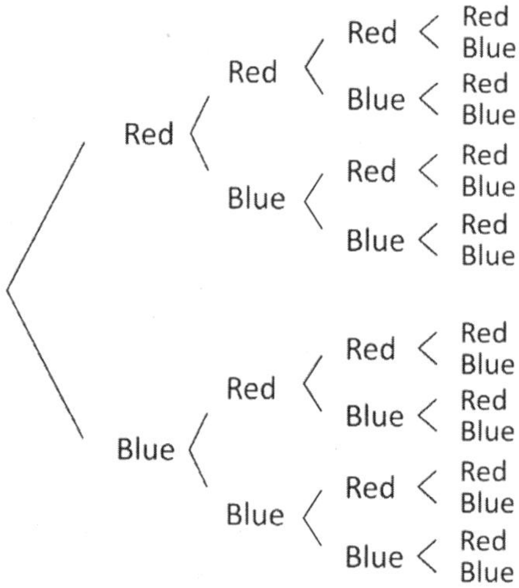

c.

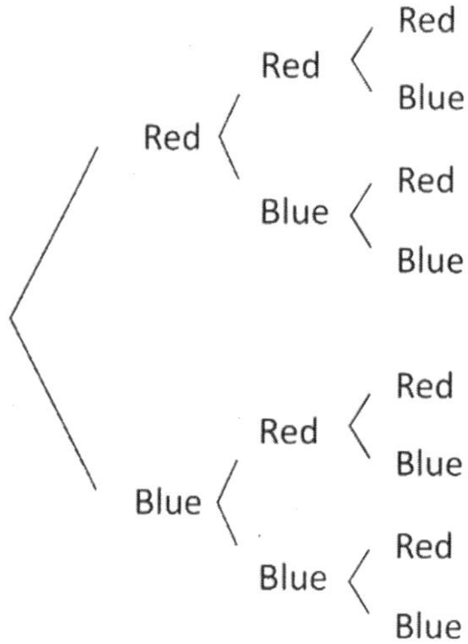

b.

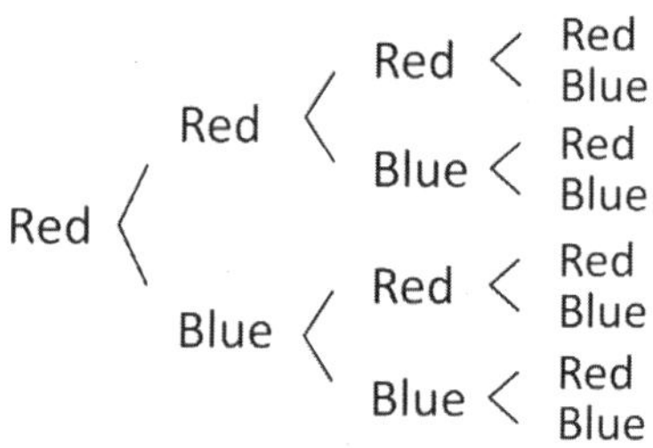

d.

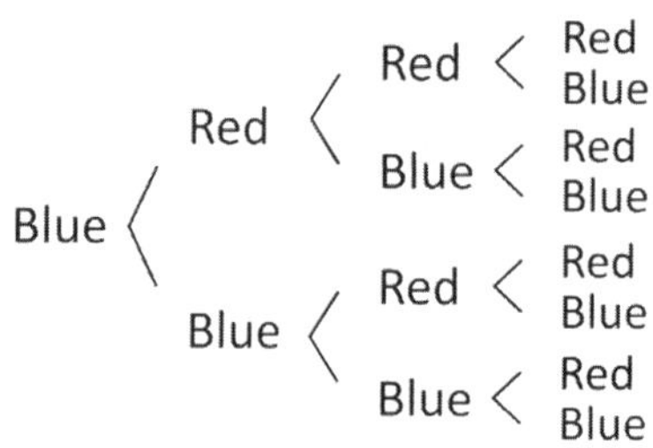

We can draw a tree diagram to represent this sample set.

First, we will identify the possible outcome for the first draw.

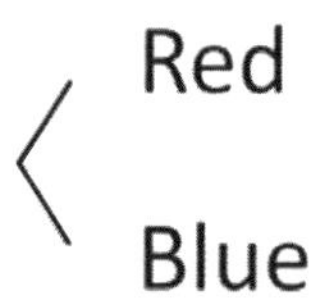

Next, we can add the possible outcomes for the second draw.

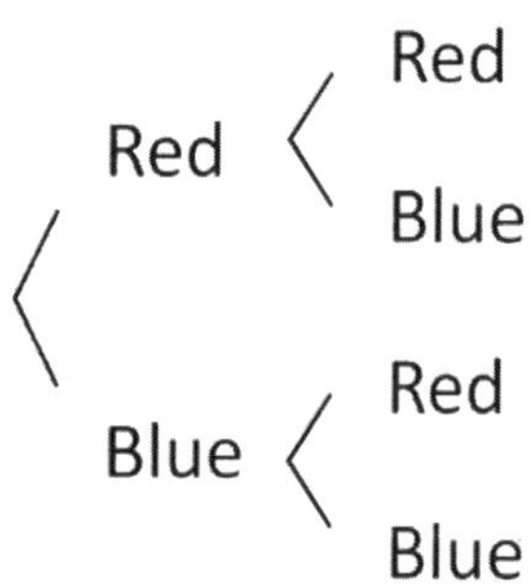

The third draw.

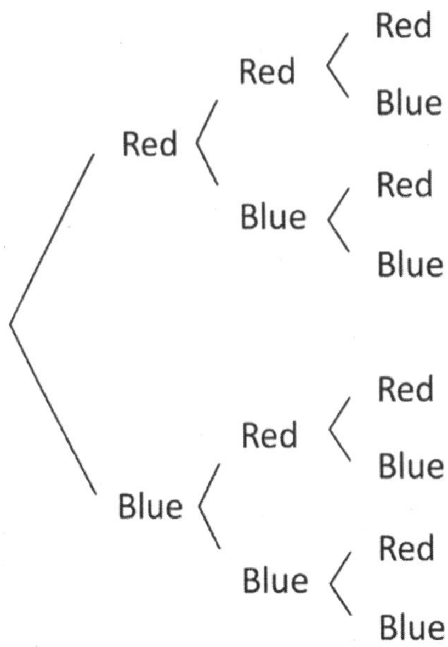

And the fourth draw.

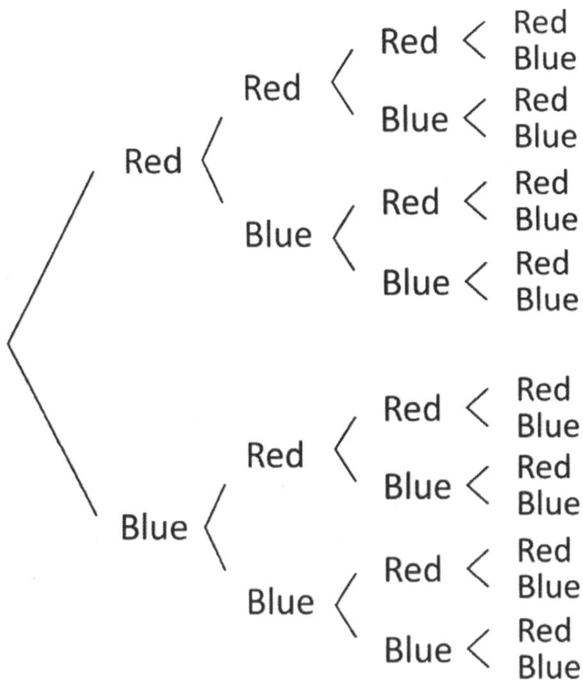

This tree diagram shows all possible outcomes. This tree diagram matches the tree diagram for option A.

The correct answer is A.

EXAMPLE

A student flips a coin in an experiment. The tree diagram shows all possible outcomes of the experiment.

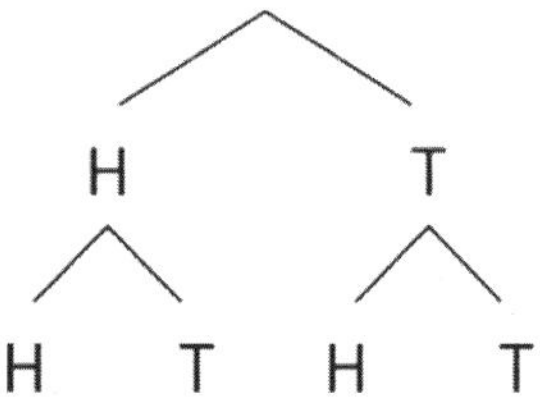

Which sample space is described by the tree diagram?

a. {HH, HT, TH, TT, H, T}
b. {HH, HT, TH, TT}
c. {HHH, HHT, HTH, HTT, TTT, TTH, THT, THH}
d. {H, T, H, T, H, T}

This problem focuses on identifying a sample space in list form. The given tree diagram shows all possible outcomes to the event. There are two tree diagrams that represent the two possible outcomes from the first coin flip. Each tree diagram has one level of branches which represent a second coin flip. It appears there were two-coin flips in this experiment.

Each "branch" of the tree diagram represents a possible outcome after two-coin flips.

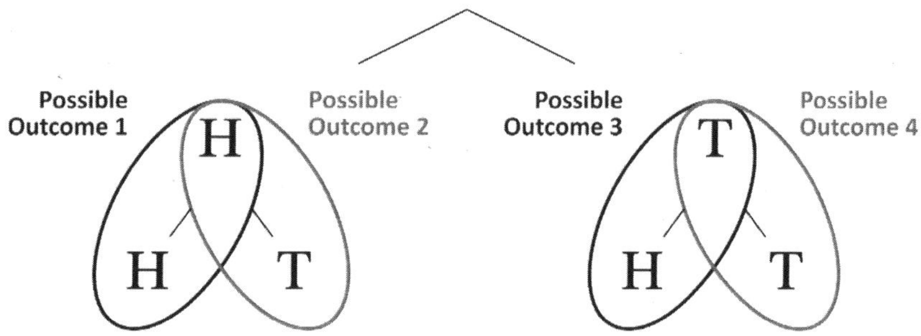

One outcome is heads then heads, HH, another is heads then tails, HT, the next is tails then heads, TH, and the last is tails then tails, TT.

The sample space for this experiment can be described by the list {HH, HT, TH, TT}.

The correct answer is B.

EXAMPLE

A sandwich shop has three different types of cheese and four different types of meats a customer can order on their sandwich. The choices are listed on the table below.

Cheese	Meat
Provolone (P)	Ham (H)
Swiss (S)	Turkey (T)
American (A)	Chicken (C)
	Beef (B)

Which list represents all possible sandwich combinations that a customer could order if they order one type of cheese and one type of meat on the sandwich?

a. {(P, S, A), (H, T, C, B)}

b. $\{(P, H), (P, T), (P, C), (P, B), (S, H), (S, T), (S, C), (S, B), (A, H), (A, T), (A, C), (A, B)\}$

c. $\{(P, S), (P, A), (P, H), (P, T), (P, C), (P, B), (S, P), (S, A), (S, H), (S, T), (S, C), (S, B), (A, P), (A, S), (A, H), (A, T), (A, C), (A, B)\}$

d. $\{(P, H, T, C, B), (S, H, T, C, B), (A, H, T, C, B)\}$

To identify the list that represents all possible outcomes to the experiment, we can start by identifying all possible outcomes for the first layer. The first set of possible options is three types of cheeses: Provolone, Swiss, or American.

Provolone Swiss American

The next set of possible options is four types of meats: Ham, Turkey, Chicken, or Beef.

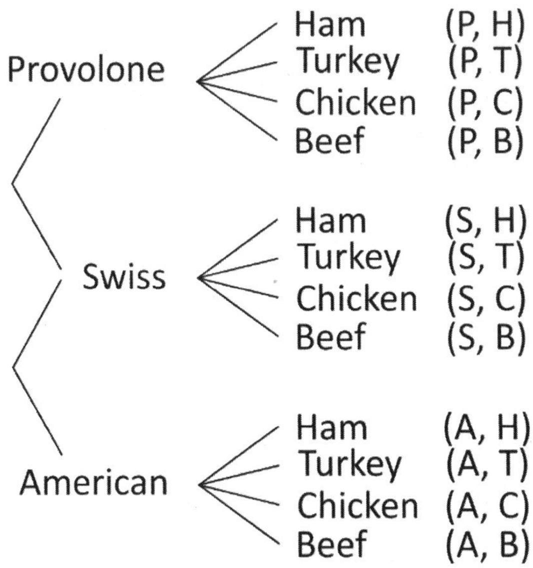

Now that we have made a diagram, we can see all possible outcomes.

The correct answer is B.

Experimental Probability

Predictions can be made about the outcomes of simple and compound events based on experimental data. A prediction based on experimental data is called **experimental probability**. Experimental data is the data that is collected by observing an experiment. The experimental probability can be found by reviewing experimental data then setting up and solving a proportion.

Let's say that an experiment is performed where a spinner is spun 100 times. One spin has three possible outcomes. The spinner could land on A, B, or C.

This table shows the experimental data.

Spin Outcome	Frequency
A	42
B	22
C	36

The table includes the three possible outcomes from a spin and the frequency that the spinner landed in each section. With this information, we can determine the experimental probability that the spinner could land on each section. Let's find the experimental probability that the spinner will land on section A.

The experimental probability is a comparison between the frequency of an outcome and the total number of outcomes; usually written as a fraction. In this example, the spinner landed on section A 42 times, so the frequency of the outcome is 42. The total number of outcomes is the total number of spins, which in this case is 100.

In this example, the experimental probability the spinner will land on A is $\frac{42}{100}$.

$$\frac{\text{frequency}}{\text{total}} = \frac{\text{number of times the spinner landed on A}}{\text{number of times the spinner was spun}} = \frac{42}{100}$$

Review Video: Empirical Probability
Visit mometrix.com/academy and enter code: 513468

EXAMPLE

We can make predictions using experimental data.

The table shows the experimental data of a spinner landing in section A, B, or C.

Spin Outcome	Frequency
A	42
B	22
C	36

Using this data, we can make reasonable predictions about future spins. We can predict the number of times the spinner will land on a certain section when it is spun in the future based on the experimental probability.

Let's explore how many times the spinner will land on section B in the next 50 spins.

The spinner landed on B 22 times out of 100 spins, which means that the experimental probability the spinner will land on B is $\frac{22}{100}$.

To predict the number of times the spinner will land on B in the next 50 spins, we can use a proportion.

$$\frac{22}{100} = \frac{x}{50}$$
$$22 \cdot 50 = 100x$$

$$1{,}100 = 100x$$
$$\frac{1{,}100}{100} = \frac{100x}{100}$$
$$11 = x$$

This means that the experimental probability that the spinner will land on B in 50 spins is $\frac{11}{50}$. Based on the experimental data, we can expect the spinner to land on B 11 times in the next 50 spins.

EXAMPLE

Other predictions can be made about experimental data.

The table shows the experimental data when a spinner is spun 100 times.

Spin Outcome	Frequency
A	42
B	22
C	36

Based on this experimental data, we can predict the number of times the spinner will not land on C in the next 250 spins.

The experimental data shows that the spinner was spin 100 times and the spinner did NOT land on C $42 + 22 = 62$ times. This is the number of times the spinner landed on A or B.

This means that the experimental probability that the spinner will not land on C is $\frac{62}{100}$.

To find the number of times the spinner will not land on C in the next 250 spins, we can set up a proportion and solve.

$$\frac{62}{100} = \frac{x}{250}$$
$$62 \cdot 250 = 100x$$

$$15{,}500 = 100x$$
$$\frac{15{,}500}{100} = \frac{100x}{100}$$
$$155 = x$$

EXAMPLE

A bag contains four different colored buttons. A student pulls buttons out of the bag at random, records the color, then places the button back in the bag. The outcome of the first 15 pulls is recorded in the table below.

Color of the button	Frequency
Red	2
Green	4
Blue	5
Yellow	4

Based on the data, how many buttons will be red or yellow in the next 20 pulls?

To solve this problem, we will use the experimental probability and set up a proportion.

The number of buttons pulled from the bag that were red or yellow is $2 + 4 = 6$. The total number of buttons pulled is 15. The experimental probability that the button will be red or yellow is $\frac{6}{15}$.

Based on this, we can predict the number of buttons that will be red or yellow over the next 20 pulls by setting up a proportion.

$$\frac{6}{15} = \frac{x}{20}$$
$$20 \cdot 6 = 15x$$

$$120 = 15x$$

$$\frac{120}{15} = \frac{15x}{15}$$
$$8 = x$$

Based on the data, it is expected that the number of buttons that will be red or yellow in the next 20 pulls is 8.

THEORETICAL PROBABILITY

The theoretical probability of an outcome differs from the experimental probability. An experimental probability represents the probability of an outcome after reviewing experimental data. This means that an experiment has been completed, there is experimental data, and you can make predictions about future events based on what happened already. **Theoretical probability** represents the probability of an outcome before an experiment, based on formulas. This means the experiment hasn't happened yet, but we can make predications based on calculated likelihood. The theoretical probability of an outcome can be described as the comparison between the number of desired outcomes and the number of possible outcomes.

Let's say a coin will be flipped. This is a simple event with two outcomes: heads or tails. Because there are only two options, the theoretical probability that the coin will land on heads in one flip is $\frac{1}{2}$.

$$\frac{\text{outcome of heads}}{\text{total possible outcomes}} = \frac{1}{2}$$

Now let's say we are rolling a six-sided dice. This is a simple event with six possible outcomes: 1, 2, 3, 4, 5, or 6. The theoretical probability that the dice will land on 5 in one roll is $\frac{1}{6}$.

$$\frac{\text{outcome of 5}}{\text{total possible outcomes}} = \frac{1}{6}$$

Or we can find the theoretical probability that the dice will land on an even number. Out of the total possible outcomes, there are three even numbers: 2, 4, and 6. And there are six possible outcomes.

$$\frac{\text{outcome of an even number}}{\text{total possible outcomes}} = \frac{3}{6}$$

This fraction can be reduced.

$$\frac{3}{6} = \frac{1}{2}$$

The theoretical probability that the dice will land on an even number is $\frac{1}{2}$.

By identifying the theoretical probability within experiments, we can make predictions about the frequency of outcomes using proportions.

EXAMPLE

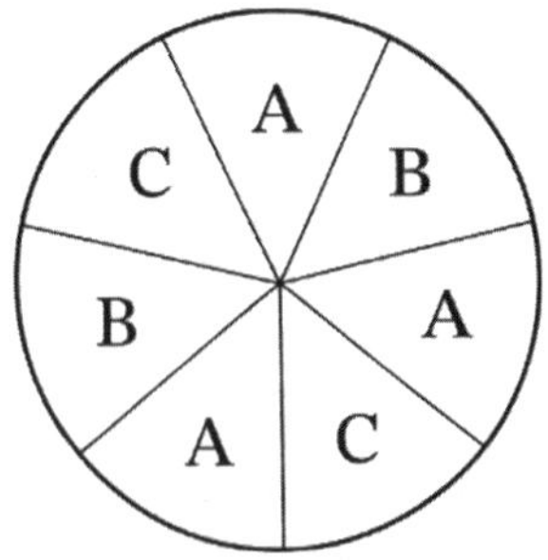

The spinner has seven congruent sections and is spun 35 times. What is a reasonable prediction for the number of times the spinner will land on B?

To solve this problem, we will find the theoretical probability and use a proportion.

The spinner shows seven congruent sections. Out of the seven sections, two are labeled with a B. There are seven possible outcomes for each spin, and two of them are B, so the theoretical probability that the spinner will land on B is $\frac{2}{7}$.

$$\frac{\text{outcome}}{\text{total possible outcomes}} = \frac{\text{sections labeled B}}{\text{total sections}} = \frac{2}{7}$$

Now, we need to calculate a reasonable prediction for the number of times the spinner will land on B when the spinner is spun 35 times. We can set up a proportion to solve this problem.

$$\frac{2}{7} = \frac{x}{35}$$
$$2 \cdot 35 = 7x$$
$$70 = 7x$$
$$\frac{70}{7} = \frac{7x}{7}$$
$$10 = x$$

A reasonable prediction for the number of times the spinner will land on B when the spinner is spun 35 times is 10 times.

PROBABILITIES AND COMPLEMENTS OF A SIMPLE EVENT

The **probability** of an outcome describes the comparison between a proposed outcome and the total possible outcomes of an event. The **complement** of a probability is the probability that a proposed outcome will not happen.

If the probability that something will happen is 100%, then there is a 0% probability that it will not happen. This shows that a probability and its complement, when expressed as percentages, must add up to 100%.

When performing calculations involving probability, these percentages are usually expressed as decimals or fractions. In this form, the probability and its complement should add up to 1. This means that the formula $1 - P = C$, where P is the original probability and C is its complement, can be used to find the complement of a probability.

For instance, a six-sided dice is rolled. The probability that the dice will land on the number 1 is $\frac{1}{6}$ because there is one side that reads 1 and there are six total sides.

The complement of this probability is the probability that the dice will not land on the number 1. There are five sides on the dice that are not the number 1, out of a total of six sides, so the probability that the dice will not land on the number 1 is $\frac{5}{6}$. This means that the complement of the probability that the dice will land on the number 1 is $\frac{5}{6}$.

EXAMPLE

A student selects a bead out of the bag at random. There are 16 red beads, 14 green beads, 24 blue beads, and 18 yellow beads. Which statement is true?

a. The probability of selecting a blue bead is $\frac{1}{4}$, and the probability of selecting a bead that is not blue is $\frac{3}{4}$.

b. The probability of selecting a blue bead is $\frac{3}{4}$, and the probability of selecting a bead that is not blue is $\frac{1}{4}$.

c. The probability of selecting a blue bead is $\frac{1}{3}$, and the probability of selecting a bead that is not blue is $\frac{2}{3}$.

d. The probability of selecting a blue bead is $\frac{2}{3}$, and the probability of selecting a bead that is not blue is $\frac{1}{3}$.

This problem focuses on identifying the probability of an outcome and its complement. To identify the true statement, we will identify the probability of selecting a blue bead and probability of NOT selecting a blue bead.

There are 24 blue beads in the bag and a total of $16 + 14 + 24 + 18 = 72$ beads in the bag. The probability of selecting a blue bead is $\frac{24}{72}$. This can be simplified by dividing the numerator and denominator by the greatest common factor, 24.

$$\frac{24 \div 24}{72 \div 24} = \frac{1}{3}$$

The probability that a blue bead will be selected is $\frac{1}{3}$.

The probability of selecting a bead that is not blue can be determined by finding the complement of this probability. The formula $1 - P = C$ can be used to find the complement.

$$1 - \frac{1}{3} = C$$

$$\frac{3}{3} - \frac{1}{3} = C$$

$$\frac{2}{3} = C$$

$$\frac{48 \div 24}{72 \div 24} = \frac{2}{3}$$

The probability of selecting a bead that is not blue is $\frac{2}{3}$.

The correct answer is C.

Interpreting Data

Bar Graphs

A **bar graph** organizes data by showing the frequency of data in certain categories. A bar graph contains a vertical and horizontal axis. Typically, the frequency is listed vertically. Bar graphs can illustrate many types of data sets.

The bar graph below shows the birthdays of students in a middle school.

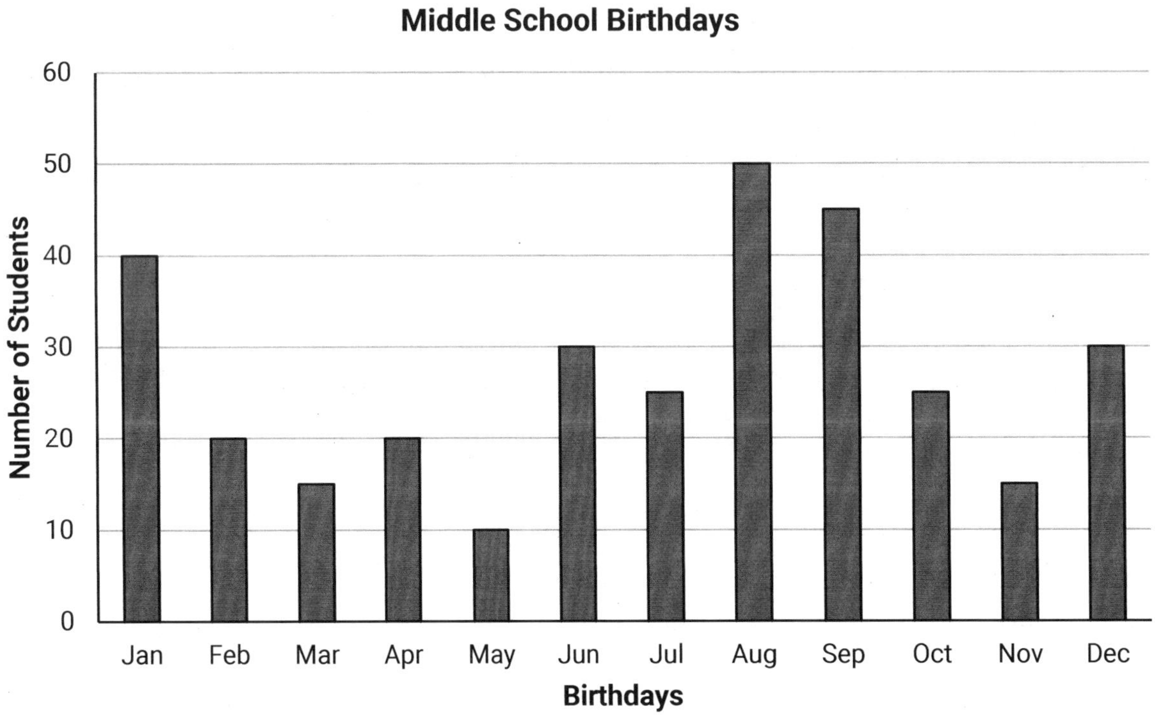

In this bar graph, you can see that the birthday months are listed along the bottom, horizontally, and the categories are divided by months. Then the frequency, or number of students, is listed along the left of the graph, vertically.

In the graph, you can see that there are 40 students that were born in January. We can see this because the bar that is above January goes up to the line that reads 40.

There are 25 students that were born in July. We can see this because the July bar goes up halfway between the lines for 20 and 30.

Bar graphs can also illustrate data horizontally. This bar graph displays the same values, just represented with horizontal bars.

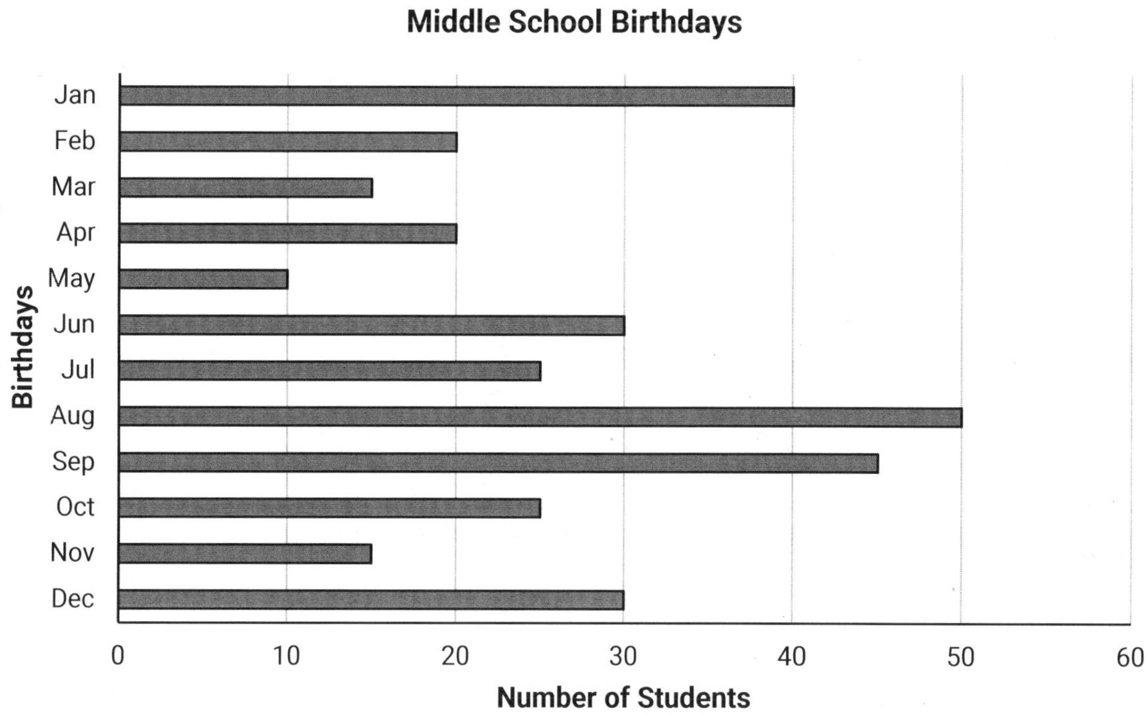

EXAMPLE

Eliza is planning a picnic for her family and asked each person which side dish he or she prefers. The bar graph below shows the number of people who chose each side dish as their preferred dish.

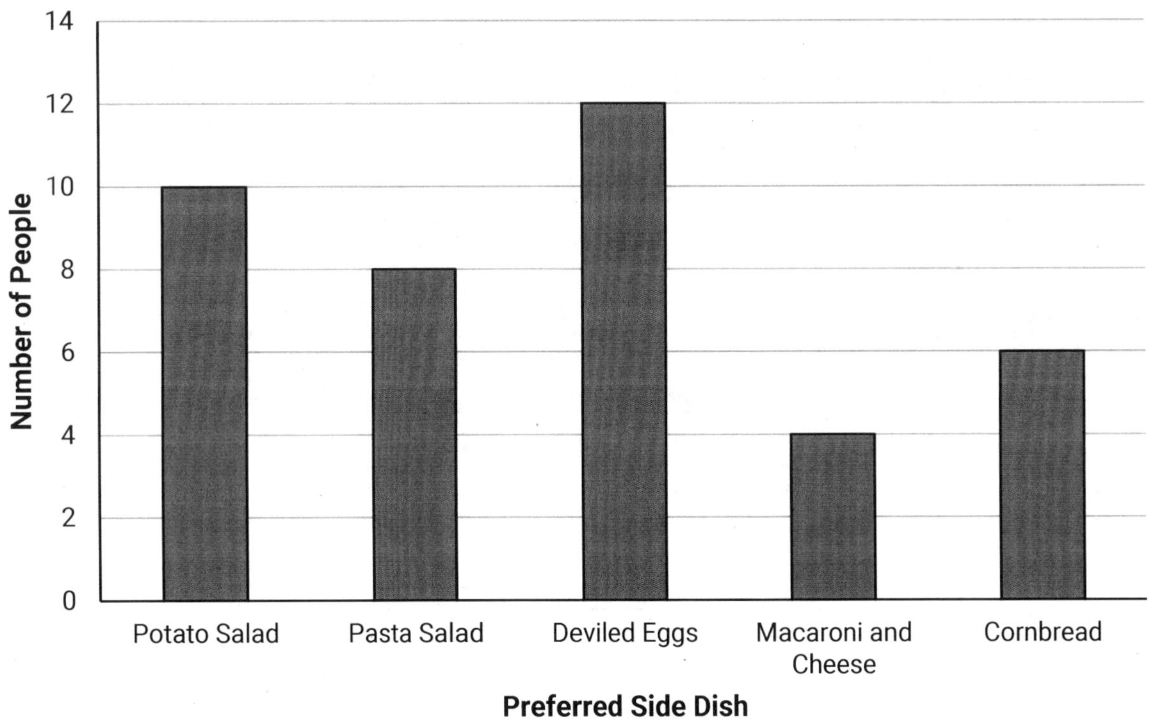

Which statement does NOT describe the data displayed on the graph?

a. Half as many people prefer cornbread than prefer deviled eggs.
b. One fourth of the people chose deviled eggs as their preferred side dish.
c. One tenth of the people chose macaroni and cheese as their preferred side dish.
d. Twice as many people prefer potato salad or cornbread than prefer pasta salad.

The first step when approaching this problem is to examine the data represented by the bar graph. Based on the bar graph, we can see that there are 5 categories of side dishes: potato salad, pasta salad, deviled eggs, macaroni and cheese, and cornbread. We can also see the number of people who chose each side dish as their favorite.

Option A states that half as many people prefer cornbread than prefer deviled eggs. To determine whether this statement is true or not, we need to compare the values for cornbread and deviled eggs. In the graph, we can see that 6 people prefer cornbread and 12 people prefer deviled eggs. $12 \div 2 = 6$, so 6 is half of 12. The statement that half as many people prefer cornbread than prefer deviled eggs is true.

Option B states that one fourth of the people chose deviled eggs as their preferred side dish. To determine if this statement is true of not, we need to compare the number of people who chose deviled eggs to the total number of people who were surveyed. We know 12 people chose deviled eggs. By adding the responses from each category, we see that 40 people were surveyed in total. Now, we can use division to find the fraction.

$$\frac{12}{40} = \frac{3}{10}$$

We can see that $\frac{3}{10}$ of people chose deviled eggs, which is not equal to $\frac{1}{4}$, so option B is not true.

Option C states that one tenth of the people chose macaroni and cheese as their preferred side dish. To determine if that statement is true, we will compare the number of people who chose macaroni and cheese, 4, and the total number of responses, 40. So, we can use division to find the fraction.

$$\frac{4}{40} = \frac{1}{10}$$

Option C is true. One tenth of the people chose macaroni and cheese as their preferred side dish.

Option D states that twice as many people prefer potato salad or cornbread than prefer pasta salad. To determine if this statement is true or not, we need to compare the number of responses for cornbread and potato salad to pasta salad. On the graph, we can see that 6 people prefer cornbread, 10 people prefer potato salad, and 8 people prefer pasta salad. The number of people who prefer potato salad or cornbread is 16 because $6 + 10 = 16$. The number of people who prefer pasta salad is 8. 16 is twice as much as 8 because $16 \div 2 = 8$, so option D is true. Twice as many people prefer potato salad and cornbread than prefer pasta salad.

All statements are true except the statement in option B, so the correct answer is B.

Dot Plots

A **dot plot** is a type of graph where values are lined up vertically, like a number line, and dots or x's are used to show the frequency of each value, or how many times that value appears in the data. Dot plots are used to show how often something happens. Dot plots are mostly used when gathering data from multiple trials or surveys. It is a way to represent these types of results in an organized way.

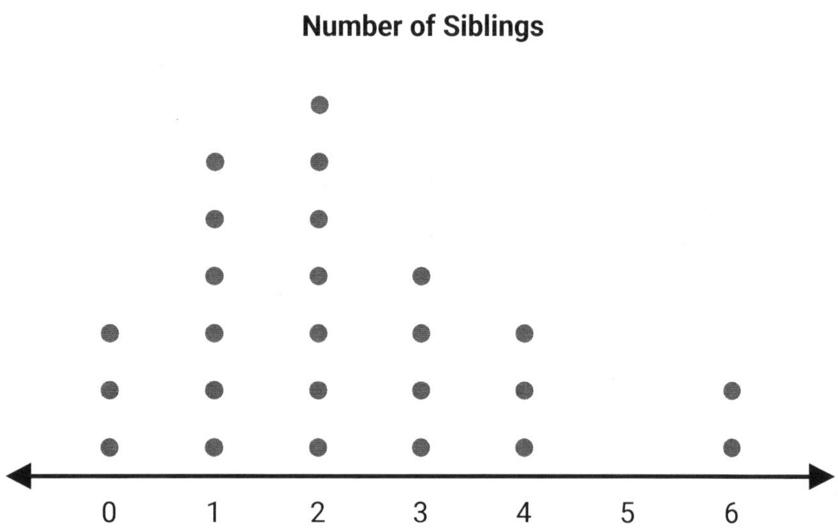

This dot plot shows the data from a survey of the 6th graders in a classroom. The survey gathered data about the number of siblings each 6th grader has in their family. The numbers along the bottom represent the number of siblings and the dots represent the number of students. Each dot is equal to one student. Based on this dot plot, you can determine that 7 people said they have 2 siblings because there are 7 dots above 2.

Review Video: Line Plot
Visit mometrix.com/academy and enter code: 754610

EXAMPLE

The dot plot shows the scores of a middle school basketball season.

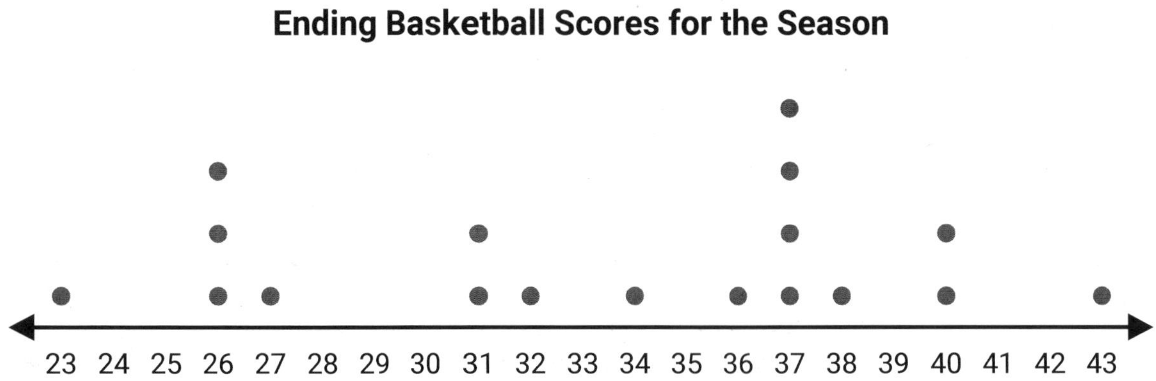

Which statement is true about the data represented by the dot plot?

a. Less than half of the scores were between 30 and 39 points.
b. The range of the scores is 18.
c. There were more games that ended with a score of 31 than there were that ended with a score of 40.
d. Half of the games ended with fewer than 35 points.

Read each answer choice and compare the statements to the data provided in the graph.

Option A states that less than half of the scores were between 30 and 39 points. To decide if that statement is true or not, we need to compare the number of values between 30 and 39, to the total number of values.

Based on the graph, we can see that 10 scores are between 30 and 39, and there are 18 total scores. 10 is more than half of 18, since 9 is half of 18, so this statement is not true. The answer is not A.

Option B states that the range of the scores is 18. We know that the range of a data set is the distance between the lowest value and the highest values. The lowest value on this graph is 23 and the highest value is 43. To calculate the distance between 23 and 43, we can use subtraction. $43 - 23 = 20$, so, the range of the data set is 20. The range is NOT 18, so this statement is not true. The answer is not B.

Option C states that there were more games that ended with a score of 31 than there were that ended with a score of 40. Based on the graph, we can see that 2 games had a score of 31 and 2 games had a score of 40. There were NOT more games that ended with a score of 31 than with a score of 40, there were an equal number of games that ended in these scores. This is not a true statement, so the answer is not C.

Option D states that half of the games ended with less than 35 points. To decide if this statement is true or not, we need to identify how many games ended with fewer than 35 points and compare that value to the total number of values.

Based on the graph, we can see that 9 games ended with less than 35 points, and the total number of games was 18. We know that 9 is half of 18 because $18 \div 2 = 9$, so this statement is true.

The correct answer is D.

CIRCLE GRAPHS

A **circle graph**, also known as a pie graph, is a type of graph used to represent the distribution of data. A circle graph uses a circle to represent the total data and each portion of the circle is divided based on the way the data is distributed. Circle graphs are commonly used with percentages and to illustrate how something is distributed across groups.

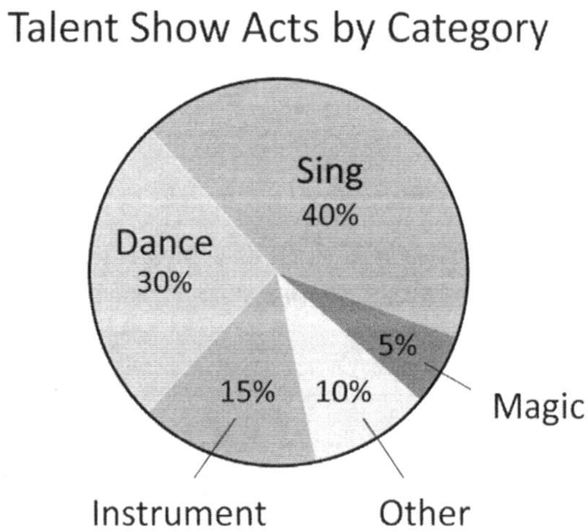

This circle graph shows the data collected from a middle school talent show. At the talent show, there were 80 students participating. 40% of the students performed a singing act, 30% of the students performed a dancing act, 15% of students played a musical instrument, 5% of students performed a magic act, and the remainder of the students, 10%, performed some other type of act.

A complete circle of the circle graph represents all students who participated in the talent show, or 100%. The size of each "slice" of the circle is proportional to the number of students who participated in a specific type of act.

EXAMPLE

A 7th grader spent 60 hours on their phone last week. The circle graph shows their phone's screen time report from last week.

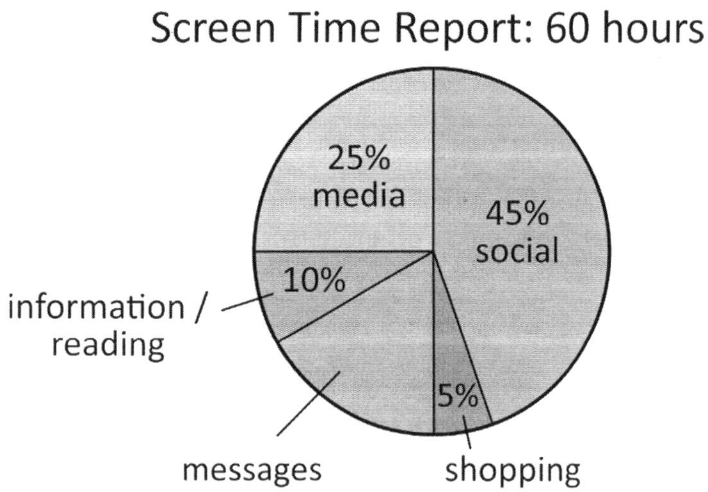

Based on the circle graph, how many hours were spent in messages?

A circle graph shows the percentage distribution of data from a data set. To solve this problem, we will need to identify the percentage of the hours spent in messages and identify the number of hours this percentage represents.

Based on the circle graph, we can see that this person spent 45% of the time on social, 25% on media, 10% on information/reading, 5% on shopping, and the rest in messages. We can use subtraction to find the percentage of hours spent in messages.

$$45\% + 25\% + 10\% + 5\% = 85\%$$
$$100\% - 85\% = 15\%$$

This person spent 15% of 60 hours in messages.

Now that we know the percentage of time spent in messages, we can set up a proportion and use cross multiplication to solve for the number of hours 15% represents.

$$\frac{15}{100} = \frac{x}{60}$$
$$15 \cdot 60 = 100x$$
$$\frac{900}{100} = \frac{100x}{100}$$
$$9 = x$$

This person spent 9 hours in messages last week.

Qualitative Predictions and Comparisons

Qualitative predictions are predictions based on observation and words rather than using numbers. Typical qualitative predictions include likelihood comparisons and uses words to describe the probability of an outcome. Qualitative predictions use the words more likely, less likely, very likely, or not likely to describe the probability of an outcome.

A group of 7th graders were asked, "If you could have any superpower, what would it be?" The results are shown in the table.

Superpower	Number of People
Super strength	5
Time travel	15
Fly	20

Based on the results of the survey, there are some predictions we can make about future surveys, and we can use qualitative statements to express these observations.

We can see that there were 40 students surveyed, $5 + 15 + 20 = 40$.

We can see that the superpower with the most votes was flight. Strength was chosen the least. Time travel was chosen three times as often as strength, and flight was chosen four times as often as strength.

We can make predictions about future surveys with this information.

It is more likely that time travel will be voted for than strength.

It is much more likely that flight will be voted for than strength.

It is less likely strength will be voted for than flight or time travel.

EXAMPLE

The table shows the number of different types of merchandise sold last week.

Type of Merch	Number Sold
Keychains	35
Stickers	70
T-shirts	5
Beanie	14

Based on the results of the table, which statement is NOT true about the type of merchandise sold monthly?

a. It is twice as likely for a sticker to be sold than a keychain.
b. It is equally likely for a sticker to be sold than a t-shirt, beanie, or keychain.
c. It is more likely for a beanie or sticker to be sold than a keychain.
d. It is five times more likely for a sticker to be sold than a beanie.

To solve this problem, we need to analyze the data in the table and compare the statements provided.

Statement A says that it is twice as likely for a sticker to be sold than a keychain. There were 70 stickers sold and 35 key chains sold. 35 is half of 70, $35 \times 2 = 70$. This statement is true. It is twice as likely for a sticker to be sold than a keychain.

Statement B says that it is equally likely for a sticker to be sold than a t-shirt, beanie, or keychain. There were 70 stickers sold and $5 + 14 + 35 = 54$ t-shirts, beanies, and keychains sold. These numbers are not equal, so this statement is not true.

Statement C stays that it is more likely for a beanie or sticker to be sold than a keychain. There were $70 + 14 = 84$ beanies or stickers sold, and 70 keychains sold. There were more beanies or stickers sold than keychains. This statement is true.

Statement D says that it is five times more likely for a sticker to be sold than a beanie. There were 70 stickers sold and 15 beanies sold. $70 \div 14 = 5$, which means that 70 is five times as much as 14. It is five times more likely for a sticker to be sold than a beanie. This statement is true.

The correct answer is B.

QUANTITATIVE PREDICTIONS AND COMPARISONS

Quantitative predictions are predictions based on calculations. Experimental probability and theoretical probability are examples of quantitative predictions. These predictions are described using numbers whether it be a fraction or a percentage.

We can use quantitative predictions to express the probability of the outcome of future surveys.

We can see that there are 5 votes for strength, 15 votes for time travel, 20 votes for flight, and 40 total students surveyed. Based on this information, and what we know about probability, we can make predictions about future surveys.

> It is three times more likely for a student to vote for time travel than super strength.
>
> It is four times more likely for a student to vote for flight than super strength.

We can also make predictions about future surveys with numerical data.

> The probability of a student voting for strength is $\frac{1}{8}$.

The probability of a student voting for flight or time travel is $\frac{7}{8}$.

There is a 50% chance a student will vote for flight.

We cannot confirm what will happen in the future, but we can make educated predictions based on data from past events.

If there are 496 7th graders, what can be said about the outcomes of a survey of the whole 7th grade?

There will be about $\frac{1}{8} \times 496 = 62$ votes for strength.

There will be about $\frac{1}{2} \times 492 = 246$ votes for flight.

There will be about $246 - 62 = 184$ more votes for flight than strength.

We make predictions about future outcomes using quantitative and qualitative predictions. Both of these predictions can be made by analyzing the data and comparing the probability of each outcome.

EXAMPLE

Many kindergarteners were surveyed about their favorite Halloween candy. The table shows the result of that survey.

Favorite Candy	Number of Votes
Chocolate	12
Lollipops	4
Sour Candy	9
Gummy Candy	8
Other	2

Based on this information, which prediction about the preferred candy for a group of 70 kindergarteners is most reasonable?

a. The number of kindergarteners who prefer chocolate will be 3 more than the number who prefer sour candy.
b. The number of kindergarteners who prefer lollipops is twice the number who prefer gummy candy.
c. The number of kindergarteners who prefer gummy candy will be 4 more than the number who prefer "other".
d. The number of kindergarteners who prefer chocolate will be 3 times more than the number who prefer lollipops.

To solve this problem, we will analyze the data and compare each statement.

The data shows the results of a survey of kindergartener's favorite Halloween candy. There was a total of $12 + 4 + 9 + 8 + 2 = 35$ votes counted.

Statement A says that the number of kindergarteners who prefer chocolate will be 3 more than the number who prefer sour candy. There were 12 votes for chocolate and 9 votes for sour candy in a group of 35. In this sample, there are 3 more children who prefer chocolate to sour candy. Since 70 is twice as many as 35, it would be reasonable to predict that the difference between the number of children who chose chocolate versus sour candy will also be doubled. We can predict that there will be about 6 more children who prefer chocolate than sour candy. This statement is not true.

Statement B says that the number of kindergarteners who prefer lollipops is twice the number who prefer gummy candy. There 8 votes for gummy candy, and twice as many as 8 is 16. There were only 4 votes for lollipops. There are half the number of students who prefer lollipops to gummy candy. This statement is not true.

Statement C says that the number of kindergarteners who prefer gummy candy will be 4 more than the number who prefer "other". Gummy candy received 8 votes and there were 2 votes for "other" in a survey of 35 kids. If there were 70 kids surveyed, it would be reasonable to predict that gummy candy would receive 8 more votes than "other". This statement is not true.

Statement D says that the number of kindergarteners who prefer chocolate will be 3 times more than the number who prefer lollipops. There were 12 votes for chocolate and 4 votes for lollipops. $12 = 3 \times 4$, so this statement is true.

The correct answer is D.

DATA AND EXPERIMENTAL PROBABILITY

Experimental probability is the probability of an outcome based on the results of an experiment. Experimental probability is described using fractions, decimals, or percentages. The experimental probability is the comparison of the frequency of an outcome, or how many times an outcome occurred during an experiment, and the total number of outcomes, or the total number of trials in an experiment.

$$\frac{\text{frequency of an outcome}}{\text{total \# of outcomes}}$$

Let's say there is bag of 50 buttons in different sizes. You pulled a button out of the bag at random and put the button bag in the bag before pulling a new button. The results of 10 pulls are recorded.

Size	Frequency
Large	1
Medium	6
Small	3

This is experimental data, so we can determine the experimental probability from the data. The frequency that a small button was pulled is 3 and the total number of pulls is 10. The experimental probability that a button pulled at random will be a small button is $\frac{3}{10}$, 0.3, or 30%.

$$\frac{\text{frequency of an outcome}}{\text{total \# of outcomes}} = \frac{3}{10} = 0.3 = 30\%$$

EXAMPLE

You flip two coins at the same time. The results of the experiment are represented in the table where H represents heads and T represents tails.

H, T	T, T	T, T	T, H	H, H
H, H	T, H	T, H	H, H	H, T
T, T	T, T	H, H	H, T	H, H

Based on the results, what is the experimental probability that the next time the coins are flipped, they will land with one coin on heads and one coin on tails?

To solve this problem, we will need to identify the frequency of the outcome and compare this to the total number of outcomes.

The trial shows 15 outcomes because there are 15 boxes with outcomes to the coin tosses. There are 6 outcomes where one coin landed on heads and one coin landed on tails. This means that based on the experimental data, the experimental probability that the coins will land with one coin on heads and one coin on tails the next time they are flipped is $\frac{6}{15}$. This can be written as a fraction, decimal, or percentage.

$$\frac{6}{15} = 0.4 = 40\%$$

Data and Theoretical Probability

Theoretical probability is the probability of an outcome based on calculations. The theoretical probability is the comparison of the possible frequency, the number of possible times a selected outcome could occur in the future, to the total number of outcomes.

$$\frac{\text{possible frequency of an outcome}}{\text{total \# of outcomes}}$$

Let's say there is a bag of 50 buttons in different colors. The contents of the bag are as follows:

- 5 green buttons
- 35 orange buttons
- 10 purple buttons

This data explains the frequency of button colors that appear in the bag. We can determine theoretical probability based on this information. There is no experiment performed, but we know the contents of the bag, which is enough information to allow us to calculate the probability of selecting a purple button.

The frequency that a purple button appears in the bag is 10 and there are a total of 50 buttons in the bag. The theoretical probability that a purple button will be selected at random is $\frac{1}{5}$, 0.2, or 20%.

$$\frac{\text{possible frequency of an outcome}}{\text{total \# of outcomes}} = \frac{10}{50} = \frac{1}{5} = 0.2 = 20\%$$

Example

A variety snack pack contains 6 bags of potato chips, 4 bags of popcorn, 8 bags of fruit snacks, and 7 bags of trail mix, all of equal size. Your teacher selects a stack at random. What is the theoretical probability that your teacher will select a bag of popcorn from the snack pack?

To solve this problem we will identify the possible frequency of an outcome and compare this to the total outcomes.

In this story, there are 4 bags of popcorn in the snack pack. There are a total of 25 snack items in the snack pack. This means that the theoretical probability that your teacher will select a bag of popcorn is $\frac{4}{25}$. This can be written as a fraction, decimal, or percentage.

$$\frac{4}{25} = 0.16 = 16\%$$

Comparing Data

To compare data, we first need to understand measures of center, the spread of data distribution, the shape of data, and how to interpret data from dot plots and box plots.

Measures of Center

The **measures of center** are different methods for estimating or measuring the center of a data set. The center of a data set can be described by the most frequent value in a data set, the value appearing in the middle of a data set arranged from least to greatest, or the value that is the average of that data set. The terms used to describe the center of a data set are mode, median, and mean.

Mode

The **mode** of a data set is the number that shows up most frequently.

Let's say we are given this data set.

$$\{0, 0, 1, 1, 1, 1, 1, 1, 1, 1, 1, 1, 2, 2, 2, 2, 3, 4, 5\}$$

The mode in a data set is the number that repeats the most, or shows up most frequently. If we look at this list of values, we can see that 1 shows up the most often, so the mode of this data set is 1.

Median

The **median** of a data set is the literal middle value in a set of values. If you have a list of values, the median is going to be the value directly in the middle of a list of these values.

Let's say we have a set of data in a list.

$$\{3, 2, 2, 3, 0, 1, 2, 1, 1, 6, 2, 4, 2, 3, 6, 0, 0, 1, 1, 2, 4, 2, 4, 3, 1\}$$

This is a list of values, and we can determine the center, or median value in the data set by lining the values up from least to greatest and finding the middle value.

$$\{0, 0, 0, 1, 1, 1, 1, 1, 1, 2, 2, 2, 2, 2, 2, 2, 3, 3, 3, 3, 4, 4, 4, 6, 6\}$$

Now that we have our data set listed from least to greatest, the median will be the middle number in the set.

$$\overbrace{0\ 0\ 0\ 1\ 1\ 1\ 1\ 1\ 1\ 2\ 2\ 2}^{12}\ \textcircled{2}\ \overbrace{2\ 2\ 2\ 3\ 3\ 3\ 3\ 4\ 4\ 4\ 6\ 6}^{12}$$

The center, or median value in this data set is 2, because when you list the values from least to greatest, 2 is the middle number. It is in the middle because it is the same distance from the smallest value to the greatest value and there are the same number of values, 12, on each side.

Finding the median of a data set that has even number of values requires a slightly different approach.

Let's say we are given this data set.

$$\{15, 16, 18, 20, 22, 12, 13, 14, 19, 21, 21, 11, 12, 14\}$$

First, we need to list the values from least to greatest to find the middle.

$$\{11, 12, 12, 13, 14, 14, 15, 16, 18, 19, 20, 21, 21, 22\}$$

Now, we can count to find the middle.

11 12 12 13 14 14 15|16 18 19 20 21 21 22

In this data set, there is not a middle number. Instead, the middle position lies between 15 and 16. So, to find the median value, we will have to find the mean of 15 and 16, the two middle numbers.

To find the mean of these middle values, we will add them together and divide by 2 because when we are calculating mean, we find the sum of the values and divide by the number of values.

$$15 + 16 = 31$$

$$31 \div 2 = 15.5$$

So, the median of this data set is 15.5.

Mean

The **mean** of a data set is often called the **average**. To find the mean of a data set, add the values in the data set together, and divide the total sum by the total number of values.

In school, we are familiar with the mean of data sets because this is the way average grades are calculated. To get a final grade, often teachers will add the grade on each assignment or test together and divide by the total number of assignments or tests.

Let's say you are in a math class and your scores are listed in a data set.

$$\{76, 82, 82, 84, 87, 90, 85, 100, 94, 90\}$$

To find the mean, or average, of your scores, add the values and divide by the number of values. In this data set, if we add all the given grades together, we will get a total of 870. Now, if we divide 870 by the total number of grades, 10, we will get 87. That means that the final grade, the average grade, or the mean of the data set is 87.

Review Video: Mean, Median, and Mode
Visit mometrix.com/academy and enter code: 286207

Spread of a Data Distribution

The **spread** of data distribution is a way to describe how far apart or close together the data is within the set. Data with a large spread means that there is a huge variety of values, or the values are far away from each other. Data with a small spread means that there is not very much variety of values, or the values are close to each other. There are two ways we describe the spread of data. One way to describe the spread is through **range**. The range of data describes the difference between the smallest value and the largest value.

Let's say you are given two sets of data.

Data Set 1					
953	1,634	1,348	450	2,349	879
1,334	2,145	587	994	1,045	950
2, 231	1,287	1,898	1,934	2,150	2,476

Data Set 2		
3	6	1
2	3	2
2	0	7

Data Set 2		
4	4	3
5	2	3

Let's compare the range of these data sets. To compare the ranges, we need to identify the difference between smallest and largest values in each data set.

In data set 1, the smallest value is 587 and the largest value is 2,476. The rage in this data set is the difference between these two values, so use subtraction to identify the range.

$$2{,}476 - 587 = 1{,}889$$

The range of data set 1 is 1,889.

In data set 2, the smallest value is 0 and the largest value is 7. So, the range is the difference between these values.

$$7 - 0 = 7$$

The range of data set 2 is 7.

Now, we can compare. Data set 1 has a large range compared to data set 2 because 1,889 is greater than 7.

Interquartile Range

A **quartile** is one quarter of the values in a data set when they are arranged from least to greatest. Another way to describe the spread is by identifying the **interquartile range**, or IQR. The interquartile range is a way to describe the middle 50% of a data set. The interquartile range is the distance between the first quartile and the third quartile.

To identify the interquartile range of a data set, you need to identify the first quartile and the third quartile. The difference between these two values is the interquartile range. The interquartile range is the "box" of a box plot.

Let's say you are given a list of values: $\{44, 41, 40, 43, 41, 45, 43, 42, 45\}$.

To find the interquartile range, we need to identify the first and third quartiles. To find the first and third quartiles, we will start with finding the median.

So, the first step to finding the interquartile range of a data set, is to identify the median. The median in this data set is 43.

40 41 41 42 (43) 43 44 45 45

The next step is identifying the first quartile. The first quartile is the median of the values to the left of the median. In this case, the first quartile lies between 41 and 41, or is the mean of 41 and 41, which is 41.

40 41 41 42 (43) 43 44 45 45

↑

First Quartile

The next step is identifying the third quartile. The third quartile is the median of the values to the right of the median. In this case, the third quartile lies between 44 and 45, or is the mean of 44 and 45, which is 44.5.

40 41 41 42 (43) 43 44 45 45

↑

Third Quartile

So, now that we have identified the first quartile value, 41, and the third quartile value, 44.5, we can identify the interquartile range. The interquartile range is the distance between the first and third quartiles, so subtract to find this difference.

$$44.5 - 41 = 3.5$$

The interquartile range, or IQR, of this data set is 3.5.

Review Video: Statistical Range
Visit mometrix.com/academy and enter code: 778541

Shape of a Data Distribution

The **shape** of data distribution describes the way that a set of data looks when it is represented visually. Graphs are visual illustrations of data, and we can observe the way data is displayed to make judgements. We can describe the shape of data based on symmetry, uniformity, peaks, gaps, clusters, and if it is skewed to one side or another.

Symmetry

A graph with **symmetry** is a graph that has a symmetrical shape, or it is the same shape on both sides. A symmetrical graph can be folded in half and look the same on both sides. Each side is a mirror image. The bar graph, dot plot, and box plot below show symmetrical sets of data.

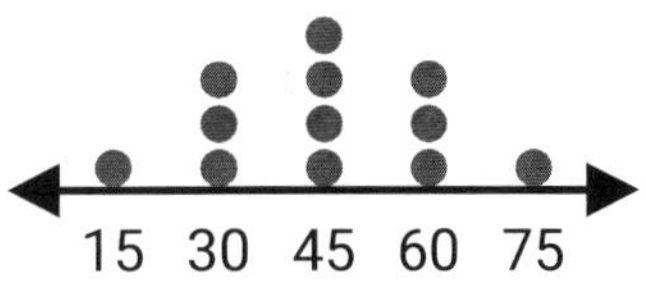

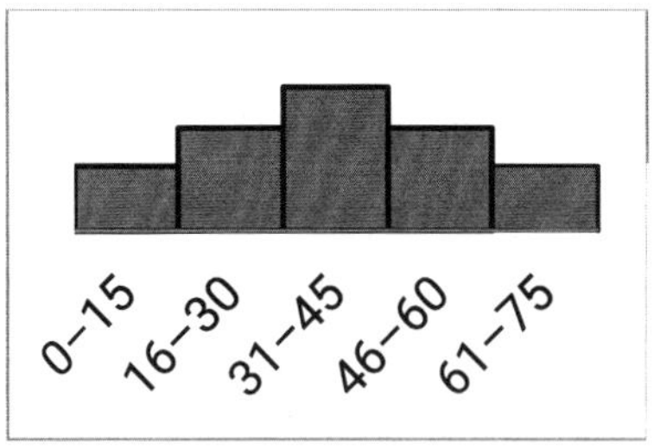

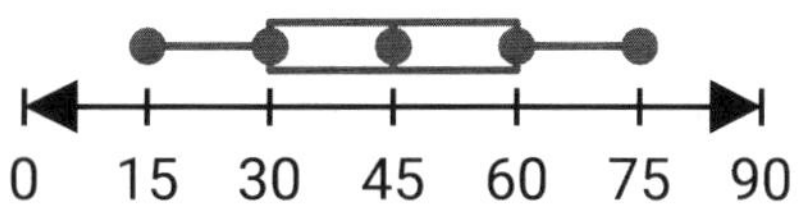

PEAKS

A **peak** on a graph is an area where there is an increase in data. A peak will be a tall part of a graph, where there is one area with the most data. The bar graph below shows a graph with two peaks. There is a peak at 16–30 and another peak at 46–60.

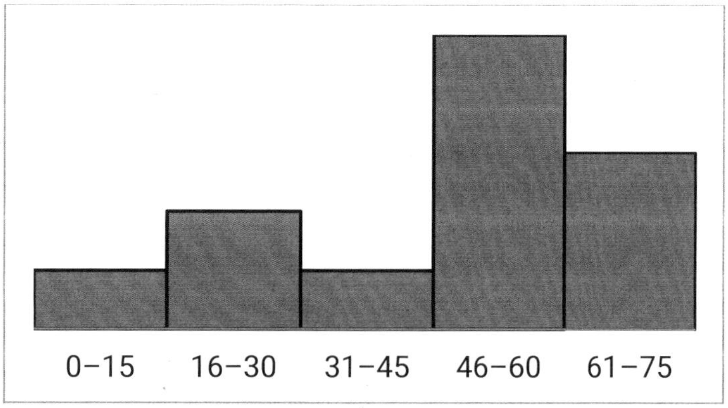

A uniform graph does not have any peaks.

GAPS

A **gap** on a graph is an area on the graph where there is no data and there is a blank area, or gap, in the graph. The dot plot below shows a graph with a gap at 60 because there is no data at 60, but there is data surrounding 60.

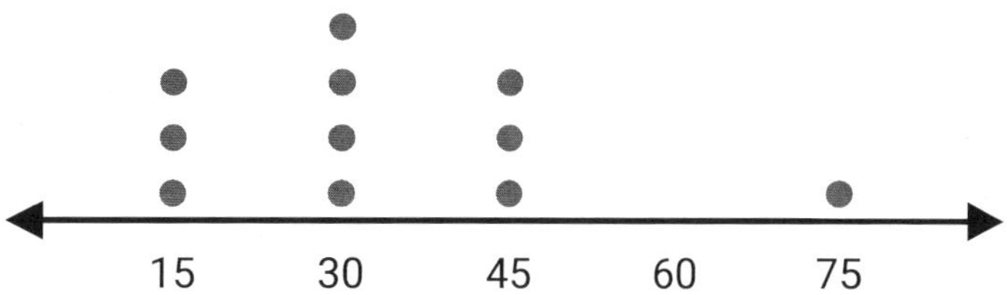

CLUSTERS

A **cluster** on a graph is an area where the majority of data lies. When data is mostly displayed in one area, this is described as a cluster. The bar graph below shows a graph with a cluster from 0 to 45 because the majority of the data is at 0–15, 15–30, and 30–45.

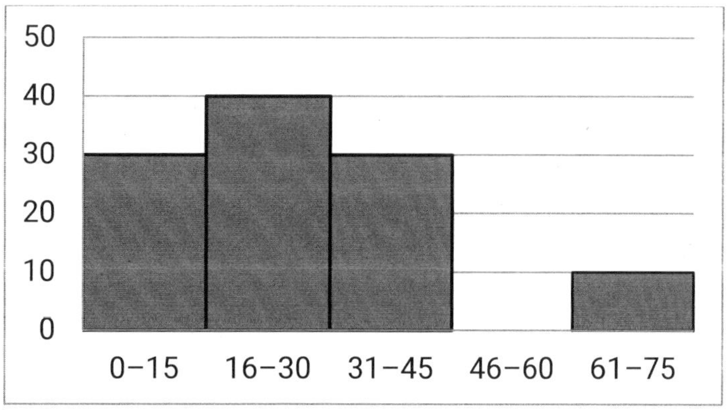

Skews

A **skewed** graph shows more data on one side of a graph than another. In a skewed graph, there is a peak and a tail. The peak in a graph is an area with the most data. The **tail** in a graph is an area with the least data. A graph with the tail to the right is described as "skewed to the right". A graph with the tail to the left is described as "skewed to the left".

Skewed to the right:

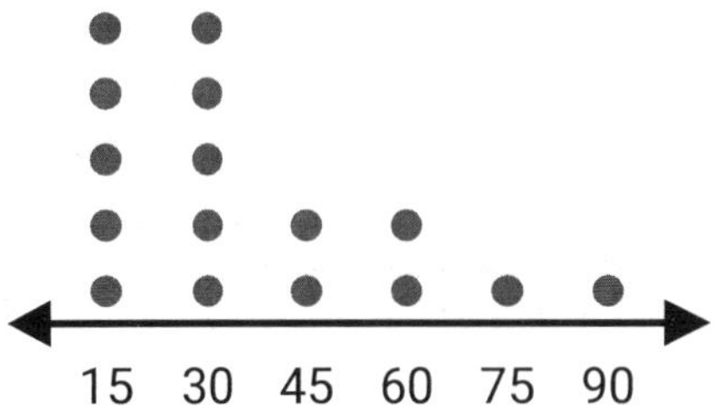

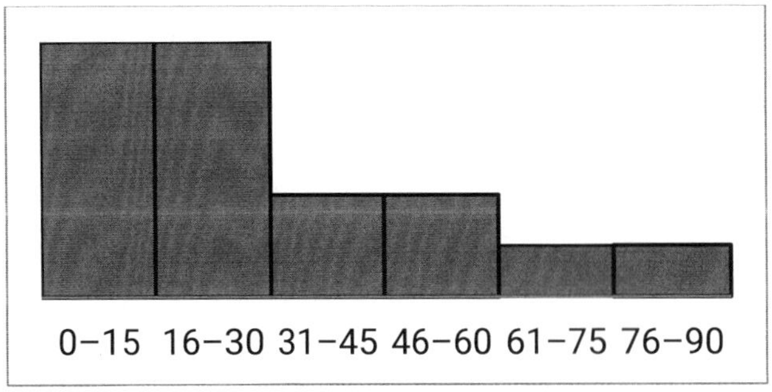

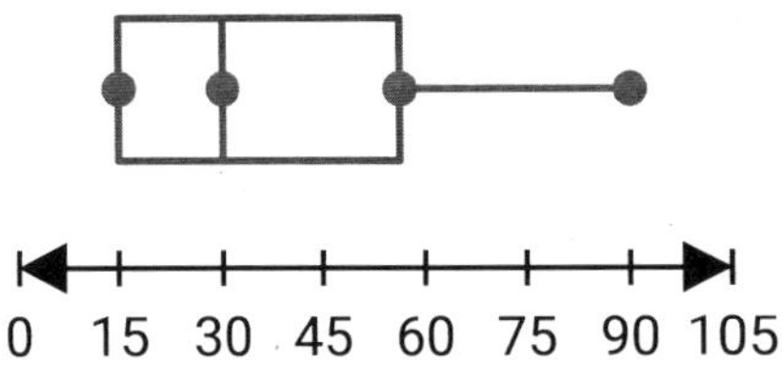

Skewed to the left:

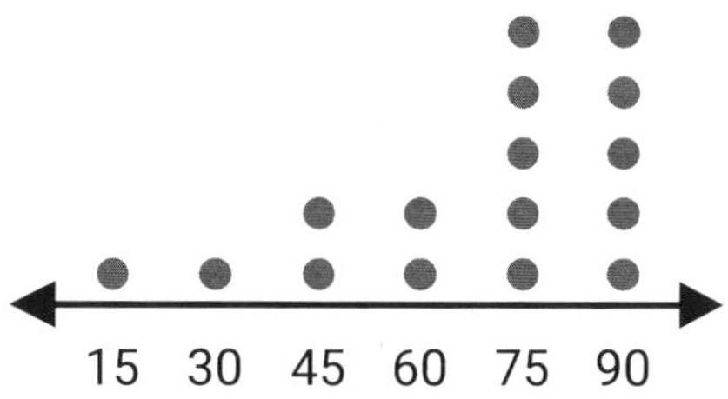

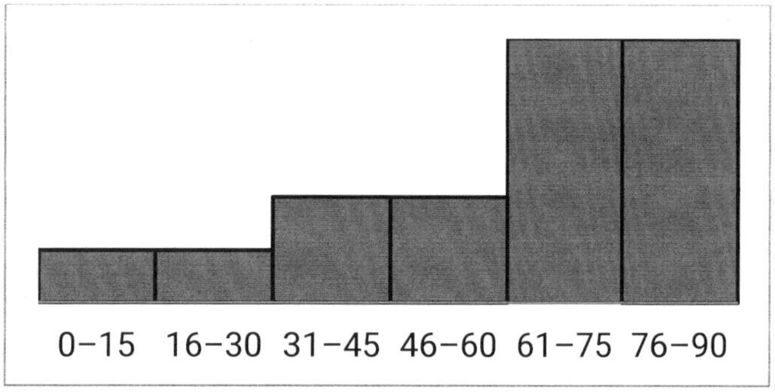

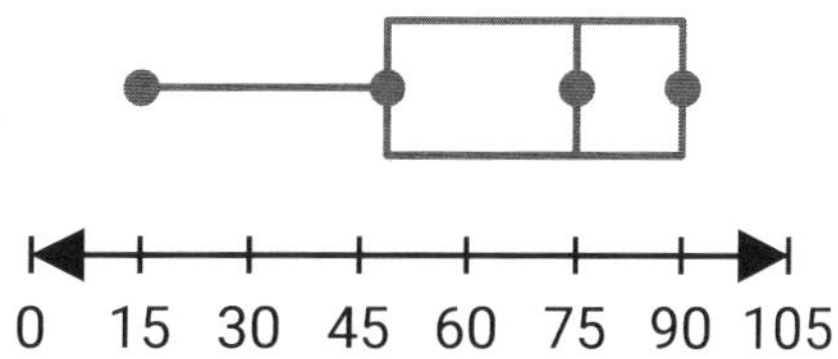

Review Video: Skew
Visit mometrix.com/academy and enter code: 661486

Dot Plots

A **dot plot** is a type of graph where values are lined up vertically, like a number line, and dots, or x's are used to show the frequency of each value. Dot plots are used to show how often something happens. Dot plots are mostly used when gathering data from multiple trials or surveys. It is a way to represent results in an organized way.

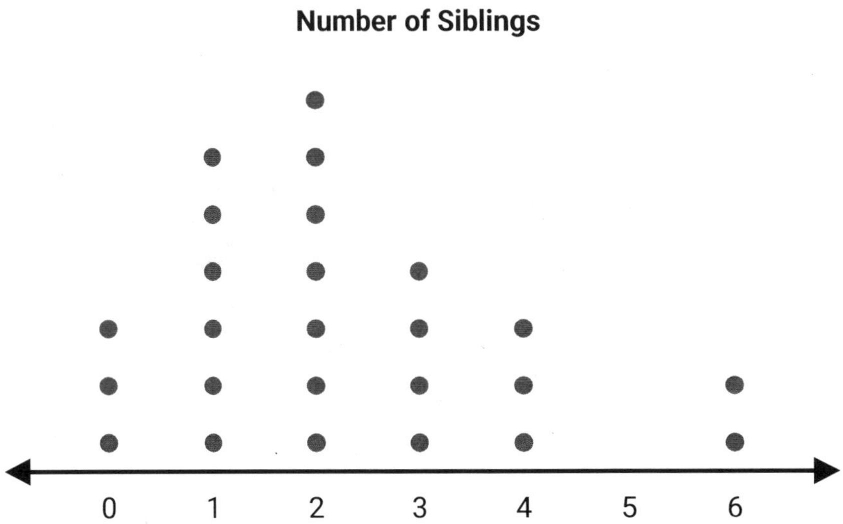

This dot plot shows the data from a survey of 6th graders in a classroom. The survey gathered data about the number of siblings each 6th grader has in their family. The numbers along the bottom represent the number of siblings and the dots represent the number of students. Each dot is equal to one student. Based on this dot plot, you can tell that 7 people said that they have 2 siblings because there are 7 dots above 2.

Example

The dot plots show the number of miles two runners ran each week.

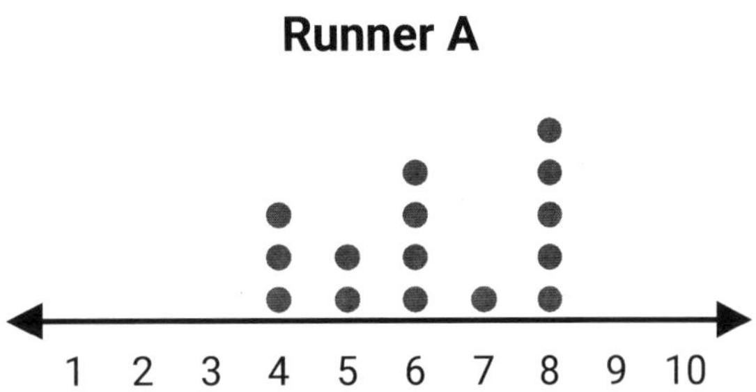

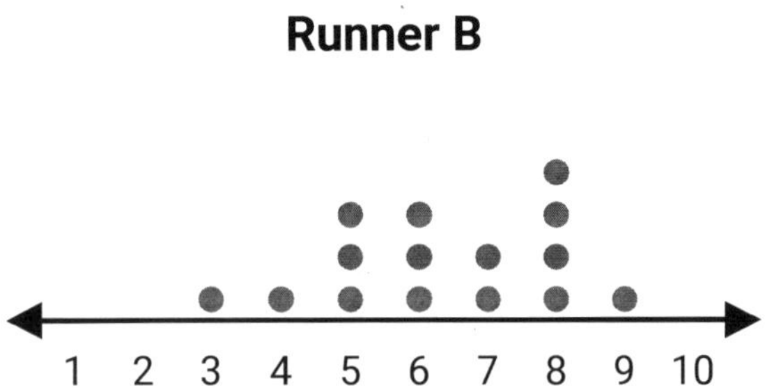

Which statement correctly compares these two data sets?

a. The range of the data for Runner A is greater than the range of the data for Runner B.
b. The mode of the data for Runner A is less than the range of the data for Runner B.
c. The mean of the data for Runner A is less than the mean of the data for Runner B.
d. The peak of the data for Runner A is greater than the peak of the data for Runner B.

To solve this problem, we will analyze the data from each dot plot and identify if each statement is true.

Choice A states that the range of the data for runner A is greater than the range of the data for Runner B. The range of the data is the difference, or distance, between the highest and lowest data point. For Runner A, the greatest data point is 8 and the lowest data point is 4, so the range of the data is $8 - 4 = 4$. For Runner B, the greatest data point is 9 and the lowest data point is 3, so the range of the data is $9 - 3 = 6$. The range of the data for Runner A is less than the range of the data for Runner B. Choice A is incorrect.

Choice B states that the mode of the data for Runner A is less than the range of the data for Runner B. The mode of the data is the data value that appears the most often. Runner 1 ran 8 miles more often than he or she ran the other distances. The range of the data for Runner B is 6. The mode of the data for Runner A is greater than the range of the data for Runner B. Option B is incorrect.

Choice C states that the mean of the data for Runner A is less than the mean of the data for Runner B. The mean of a data set is the sum of the data divided by the number of data points.

$$4 + 4 + 4 + 5 + 5 + 6 + 6 + 6 + 6 + 7 + 8 + 8 + 8 + 8 + 8 = 93$$

$$93 \div 15 = 6.2$$

The mean of the data for Runner B is also the sum of all miles run divided by the number of weeks recorded.

$$3 + 4 + 5 + 5 + 5 + 6 + 6 + 6 + 7 + 7 + 8 + 8 + 8 + 8 + 9 = 95$$

$$95 \div 15 = 6.\overline{3}$$

The mean of the data for Runner A is less than the mean of the data for Runner B. Choice C is supported by the data.

Choice D states that the peak of the data for Runner A is greater than the peak of the data for Runner B. On a dot plot, the peak is the data value with the highest column. The peak of the data for Runner A is 8. The peak of the data for Runner B is also 8. The peak of the data for Runner A is the same as the peak of the data for Runner B. Option D is incorrect.

The correct answer is C.

EXAMPLE

The dot plots show the number of students in each 6th and 7th grade homeroom class.

7th Grade Homeroom Populations

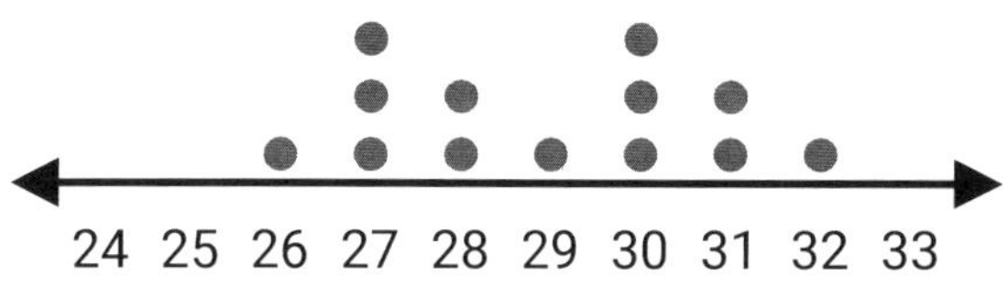

6th Grade Homeroom Populations

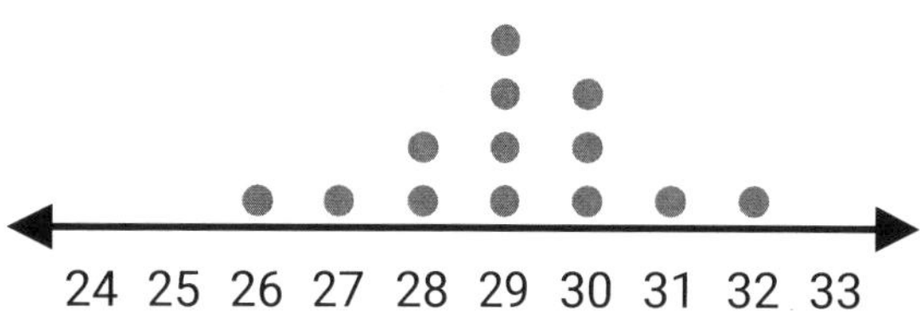

Which statement is NOT supported by the data?

a. The median of the data is the same for both sets.
b. The data set for 7th grade has more peaks than the data set for 6th grade.
c. The range of the data is the same for both sets.
d. The distribution of the data is the same for both sets.

To solve this problem, we will analyze the data sets and compare each statement and choose the statement that is NOT supported by the data.

Based on the dot plots, the 7th grade homeroom classrooms' populations can be listed in this data set $\{26, 27, 27, 27, 28, 28, 29, 30, 30, 30, 31, 31, 32\}$.

The $6th$ grade homeroom classrooms' populations can be listed in this data set $\{26, 27, 28, 28, 29, 29, 29, 29, 30, 30, 30, 31, 32\}$.

Choice A states that the median of the data is the same for both sets. The median of a data set is the physical center of the data. The median for 7th grade is 29. The median for 6th grade is also 29. The median of the data set is the same for both sets. This statement is true.

Choice B states that the data set for 7th grade has more peaks than the data set for 6th grade. A peak is an area with the most data. In a dot plot, peaks are the areas where there are the most dots in a column. 7th grade has two peaks, one at 27 and one at 30. 6th grade has one peak at 29. The data set for 7th grade has more peaks (2) than the data set for 6th grade (1). This statement is true.

Choice C states that the range of the data is the same for both sets. The range of data is the difference, or distance between the highest and lowest data point. The range for 7th grade is $32 - 26 = 6$. The range for 6th grade is also $32 - 26 = 6$. The range of the data is the same for both sets. This statement is true.

Choice D states that the distribution of the data is the same for both sets. The distribution of the data is the way the data is spread across the data points. In a dot plot, this would also refer to the shape of the data. The data for 7th grade shows two peaks and a dip in the middle. The data for 6th grade is symmetrical with a peak in the middle. The distribution of data is not the same for both data sets. This statement is false.

The correct answer is D.

Box Plots

A **box plot** is a type of graph that illustrates 5 parts of a data set: the minimum value, the maximum value, the median value, the first quartile, and the third quartile. The minimum value is the smallest value and the maximum value is the largest value. The median is the exact center of a data set.

The **first quartile** is the median of the lower half of the data set, or the median of the values to the left of the original median. The **third quartile** is the median of the upper half of the data set, or the median of the values to the right of the original median.

This list gives the heights in inches of students in a 6th grade math class.

$$\{52, 52, 53, 55, 56, 56, 57, 57, 57, 57, 58, 58, 59, 59, 59, 59, 60, 60, 62, 62, 64, 64, 65, 65\}$$

This box plot represents the data in this list.

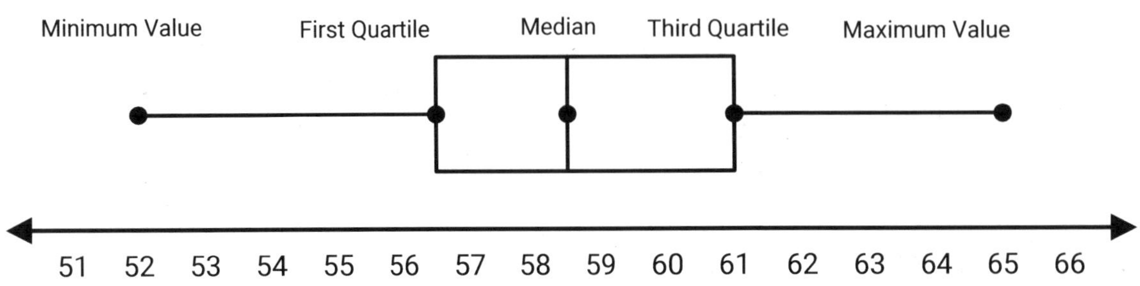

The point farthest to the left represents the minimum value in the data set, 52 inches.

The point farthest to the right represents the maximum value in the data set, 65 inches.

The point inside the box represents the median value in the data set, 58.5 inches, the mean of 58 and 59.

The first quartile is represented by the edge of the box to the left of the median. This value is the median of the values to the left of the median, 56.5 inches.

The third quartile is represented by the edge of the box to the right of the median. This value is the median of the values to the right of the median, 61 inches.

A box plot represents the four quarters of a data set.

The first 25% of a data set lies between the minimum and first quartile.

The next 25% of the data lies between the first quartile and the median.

The next 25% of the data lies between the median and the third quartile.

And the last 25% of a data set lies between the third quartile and the maximum.

Review Video: Box and Whisker Plots
Visit mometrix.com/academy and enter code: 810817

EXAMPLE

The box plots represent the data collected from measuring the daily temperatures during the months of July and December in degrees Fahrenheit.

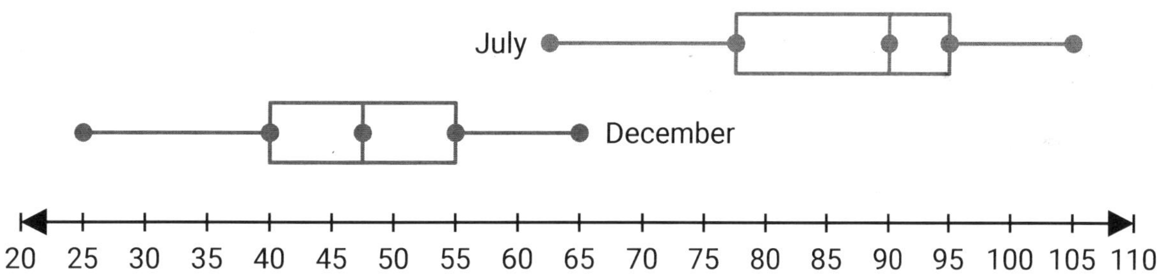

Which statement is NOT true about the data represented by the box plots?

a. The range in temperatures for December is 80.
b. Half of the temperatures in July were equal to or above 90 degrees.
c. The interquartile range for December is 15.
d. More than half of the temperatures in December were less than or equal to 55 degrees.

In this problem we are given two box plots that represent the temperature data collected during July and December. We need to select the statement that does NOT describe the data in the provided graph.

To approach this problem, we need to examine the options and compare the statements with the data represented by the box plots.

Choice A states that the range in temperatures for December is 80. We know that the range is the difference between the highest and the lowest values. The lowest temperature recorded for December is 25 and the highest is 65. To find the range, we can use subtraction. $65 - 25 = 40$. The range for December is not 80, so this statement is untrue. Choice A is the correct answer.

Choice B states that half of the temperatures in July were equal to or above 90 degrees. As we observe the July box plot, we can see that the median value is at 90, and we know that the median is the middle value, or the halfway point. This means that half of the temperatures in July are equal to or above 90 degrees, so this statement is true.

Choice C states that the interquartile range for December is 15. We know that the interquartile range is the range between the first quartile and the third quartile. This means it is the range of the lowest and highest values that make the "box" in the box plot. We can see that the first quartile, or lower "box" value, is 40 and the third quartile, or higher "box" value, is 55. The range is the distance, or difference, between these numbers. We can use subtraction to find that $55 - 40 = 15$. The interquartile range is 15, so this statement is true.

Choice D states that more than half of the temperatures in December were less than 55 degrees. Based on the graph, we can see that the median value in the December box plot is halfway between 45 and 50, and the third quartile is at 55. This means three-fourths of the data is less than or equal to 55 degrees, which is more than half of the temperatures recorded in December. This statement is true.

The only statement that is NOT true is that the range in temperatures recorded in December is 80.

The correct answer is A.

EXAMPLE

The box plots show the number of assignments completed by each student in two different classrooms this week.

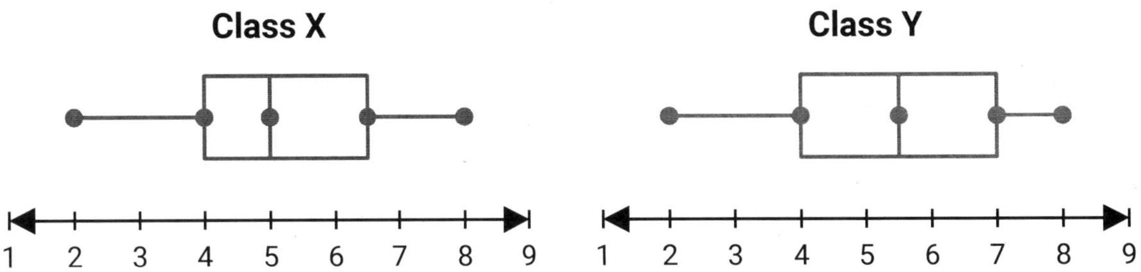

Which statement is best supported by the data?

a. The median of the data for Class X and Class Y is the same.
b. The first quartile of the data for Class Y is greater than the first quartile of the data for Class X.
c. The interquartile range of the data for Class X and Class Y is the same.
d. The third quartile of the data for Class Y is greater than for the data for Class X.

To solve this problem, we will analyze the data from both sets and review the statements.

Choice A states that the median of the data for Class X and Class Y is the same. The median of the data in a box plot is represented by the dot in the center of the box. The median of the data for Class X is 5 and the median of the data for Class Y is 5.5. The median of the data is not the same. This option is not supported by the data.

Choice B states that the first quartile of the data for Class Y is greater than the first quartile of the data for Class X. In a box plot, the first quartile is represented by the second dot, or the dot that aligns with the left of the box. The first quartile of the data for Class Y is 4 and for Class X is also 4. The first quartile is the same for both data sets, so this option is not supported by the data.

Choice C states that the interquartile range of the data for Class X and Class Y is the same. The interquartile range is the range of the middle 50% of the data, this is the range of the data represented by the box in the box plot. The interquartile range of the data for Class X is $6.5 - 4 = 2.5$. The interquartile range of the data for

Class Y is $7 - 4 = 3$. The interquartile range of the data for Class X is less than that of Class Y. This option is not supported by the data.

Choice D states that the third quartile of the data for Class Y is greater than for the data for Class X. The third quartile is represented by the dot that aligns with the right edge of the box. The third quartile of the data for Class Y is 7 and for Class X is 6.5. The third quartile of the data for Class Y is greater than the third quartile of the data for Class X. This option is supported by the data.

The correct answer is D.

Random Samples from Data

A **random sample** is a small group from a larger population that is selected randomly and without bias. A random sample can be used to make predictions and inferences about the larger population. Let's say that we would like to make predictions about all 7th graders in Texas. It would be very difficult to gather data from every single 7th grader in Texas, so we may select a random sample. To do this, we may select a few random students from every school in the state. Or perhaps a number of students from each school based on the number of students in the school. This would represent a random sample.

Let's say we selected all students from one 7th grade math class from which to gather data. Or perhaps we selected a few random male students from different schools. These would not be examples of random samples, since the students were not chosen at random. They all have something in common, which may influence the data from the sample. We could not use this data to make predictions or inferences about all 7th graders in Texas. This is because it would not represent all 7th grade students in Texas, and the group is not broad or inclusive enough to make predictions.

Comparisons and inferences can be made from the data collected from random samples about the larger populations they represent.

EXAMPLE

A high school conducted a survey among randomly selected 7th graders in Texas about their favorite extra-curricular activity. The results are represented in the table.

Activity	Number of 7th Graders
Team Sports	55
Individual Sports	40
Visual Arts	60
Music	45
Academics	35
Other	15

Which inference about all 7th graders in Texas is best supported by the data?

a. The number of 7th graders who prefer team sports is more than those that prefer visual arts.
b. The number of 7th graders who prefer academics is more than those that prefer individual sports.
c. The number of 7th graders who prefer music is less than those that prefer individual sports.
d. The number of 7th graders who prefer individual sports is less than those that prefer visual arts.

To solve this problem, we will review the options and compare the statements to the data.

Choice A states that the number of 7th graders who prefer team sports is more than those that prefer visual arts. The number who prefer team sports is 55 and the number that prefer visual arts is 60. 55 is not more than 60, so this statement is not supported by the data.

Choice B states that the number of 7th graders who prefer academics is more than those that prefer individual sports. The number who prefer academics is 35 and the number who prefer individual spots is 40. 35 is not more than 40, so this statement is not supported by the data.

Choice C states that the number of 7th graders who prefer music is less than those that prefer individual sports. The number who prefer music is 45 and the number who prefer individual sports is 40. 45 is not less than 40, so this statement is not supported by the data.

Choice D states that the number of 7th graders who prefer individual sports is less than those that prefer visual arts. The number who prefer individual sports is 40 and the number who prefer visual arts is 60. 40 is less than 60, so this statement is supported by the data.

The correct answer is D.

EXAMPLE

A pet store conducted a random survey at their store to determine the types of pets each customer had based on their age group. The results are shown in the bar graph.

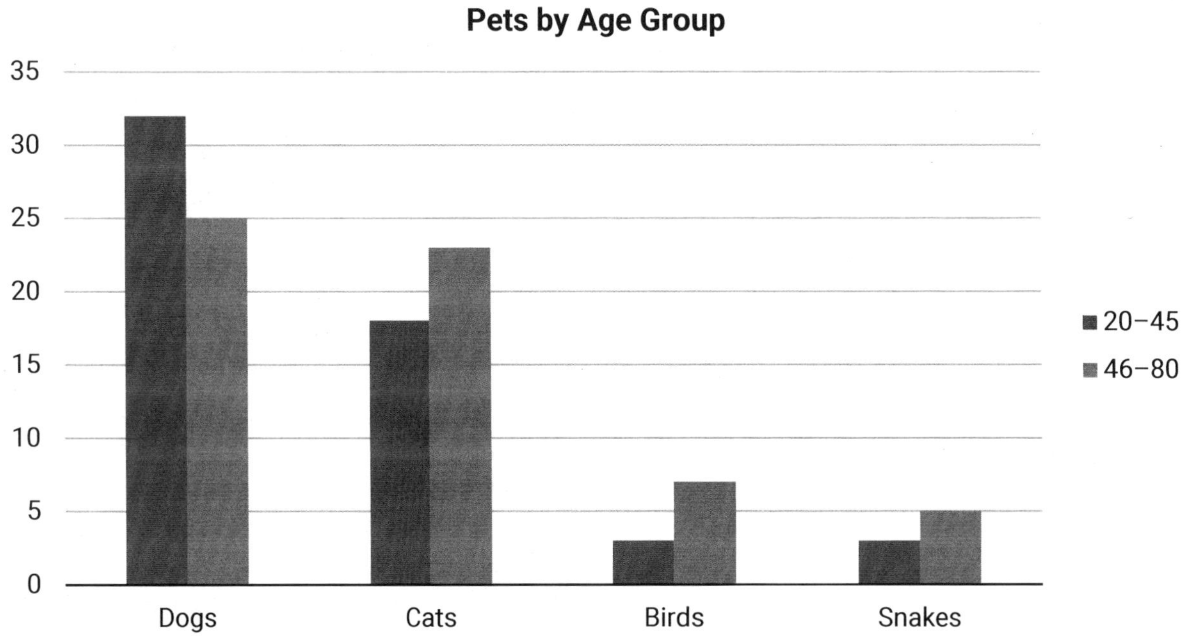

Based on the information in the graph, which inference about the general population of pet owners is NOT valid?

a. Pet owners aged 20–45 are more likely to own dogs than pet owners aged 46–80.
b. Pet owners aged 20–45 are more likely to own snakes than pet owners aged 46–80.
c. Pet owners aged 46–80 are more likely to own birds than pet owners aged 20–45.
d. Pet owners aged 46–80 are more likely to own cats than pet owners aged 20–45.

To solve this problem, we will review the statements and compare them to the data presented in the table.

Choice A states that pet owners aged 20–45 are more likely to own dogs than pet owners aged 46–80. Based on the data, more pet owners 20–45 owned dogs than pet owners aged 46–80. This statement is supported by the data.

Choice B states that pet owners aged 20–45 are more likely to own snakes than pet owners aged 46–80. Based on the data, more pet owners aged 46–80 owned snakes than those aged 20–45. This statement is not supported by the data.

Choice C states that pet owners aged 46–80 are more likely to own birds than pet owners aged 20–45. Based on the data, more pet owners aged 46–80 owned birds than pet owners aged 20–45. This statement is supported by the data.

Choice D states that pet owners aged 46–80 are more likely to own cats than pet owners aged 20–45. Based on the data, more pet owners aged 46–80 owned cats than pet owners aged 20–45. This statement is supported by the data.

The correct answer is B.

Practice Test #1

1. Rectangle $ABCD$ is similar to rectangle $EFGD$. Use the graphic below to determine the measure of side AB.

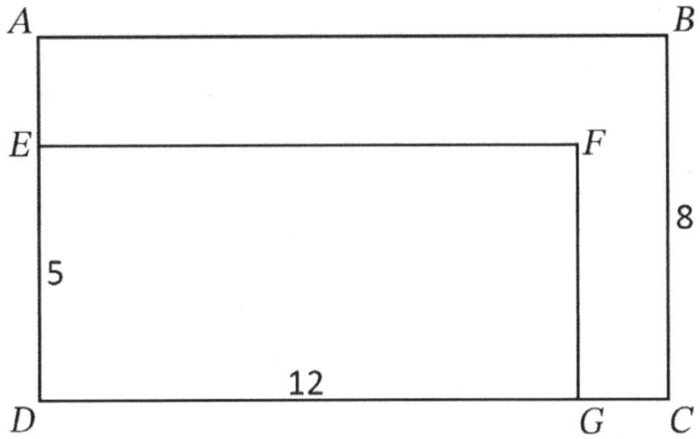

a. $7\frac{1}{2}$
b. $19\frac{1}{5}$
c. $3\frac{1}{3}$
d. $15\frac{1}{4}$

2. Dameon draws a circle with a circumference of 45 centimeters. Which equation represents an accurate way to solve for the diameter d?

a. Convert $45 = \pi d$ to $\frac{45}{\pi} = d$
b. Convert $45 = \frac{\pi}{d}$ to $\frac{45}{r} = d$
c. Convert $45 = \pi d$ to $\frac{45}{\pi} = C$
d. Convert $45 = \pi C$ to $\frac{45}{\pi} = d$

3. Elijah has prepared $2\frac{1}{2}$ gallons of lemonade to distribute to guests at a party. If there are 25 guests, how much lemonade is available to each guest, given that each guest receives an equal amount?

a. $\frac{1}{8}$ of a gallon
b. $\frac{1}{6}$ of a gallon
c. $\frac{1}{12}$ of a gallon
d. $\frac{1}{10}$ of a gallon

4. The points M, N, and O are plotted on the number line below. Plot point P based on the equation: $N - M + O = P$

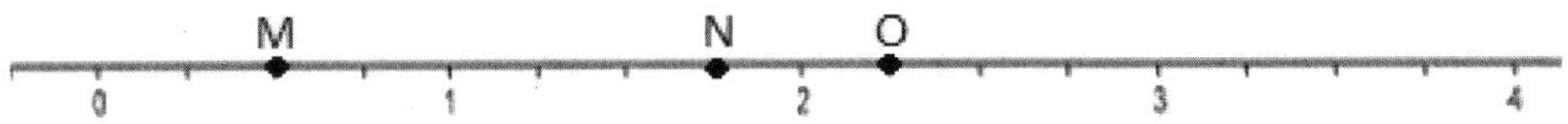

5. Part A: Edward spins the spinner below three times. He decides to spin it one more time. What is the probability that he will land on a number that he has already landed on?

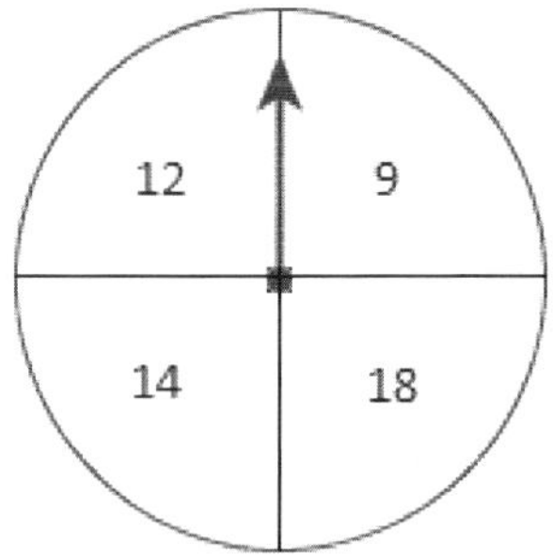

a. $\frac{1}{4}$
b. $\frac{2}{4}$
c. $\frac{3}{4}$
d. $\frac{4}{4}$

Part B: Based on the probability, what is the likelihood this will happen?

a. Not possible
b. Unlikely
c. Very likely
d. Definite

6. A bag of coffee costs \$9.85 and contains 16 ounces of coffee. Which of the following best represents the cost per ounce?

a. \$0.67
b. \$0.64
c. \$0.65
d. \$0.62

7. Angle x and angle y are complementary angles. Angle x is presented below.

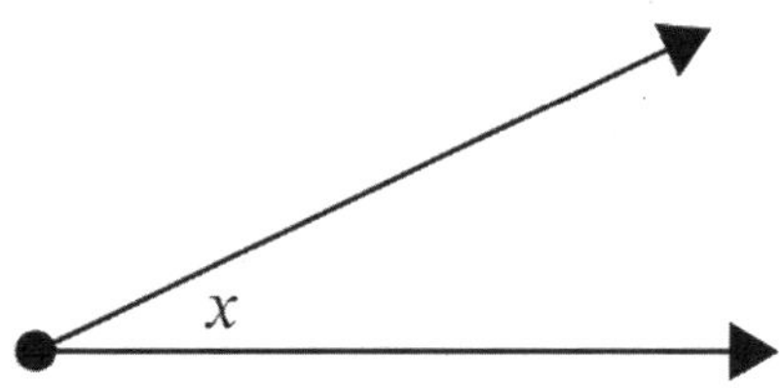

The measure of angle y is $(4t + 4)°$. Which equation can be used to determine the measure of angle x?

a. $x + 90 = 180$
b. $x + (4t + 4) = 180$
c. $x + (4t + 4) = 90$
d. $y + (4t + 4) = 90$

8. The ingredients needed for a cake are given below:

2 eggs
$1\frac{3}{4}$ cups of flour
2 teaspoons baking soda
½ cup butter
$1\frac{1}{4}$ teaspoons vanilla extract
$\frac{3}{4}$ cup of milk

What is the ratio of butter to flour?

a. 1 : 3
b. 2 : 5
c. 2 : 7
d. 3 : 2

9. Part A: The original price of a jacket is $36.95. The jacket is discounted by 25%. Before tax, which of the following best represents the cost of the jacket?

a. $27.34
b. $27.71
c. $28.82
d. $29.56

Part B: If tax is 8% how much does it cost in total?

a. $2.22
b. $25.49
c. $22.17
d. $29.93

10. Martin and his friends are taking a road trip from Houston, TX to Las Vegas, NV. The trip will take two days and they will spend the night in El Paso, TX. The first day they drove for 11 hours at a rate of 69 miles per hour. The next day they drove for 10 hours at a rate of 72 miles per hour. How far is it from Houston to Las Vegas?

a. 1479 miles
b. 1410 miles
c. 1482 miles
d. 1551 miles

11. A bottle of lotion contains 20 fluid ounces and costs $3.96. Which of the following best represents the cost per fluid ounce?

a. $0.18
b. $0.20
c. $0.22
d. $0.24

12. Lexi recorded the number of points she scored in her basketball games this month. What percentage of her total points this month were scored at home games?

Game Location	Points Scored
Home Game	30
Home Game	14
Away Game	18
Away Game	12
Home Game	26

a. 60%
b. 65%
c. 70%
d. 75%

13. Given the figure below what is the area of the shaded regions? Figure is not to scale.

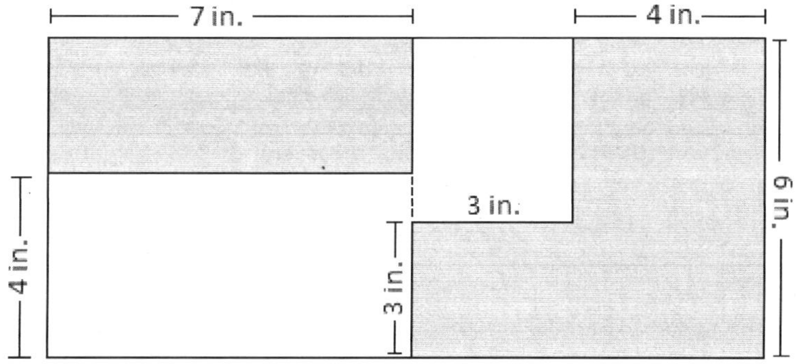

a. 47 in^2
b. 84 in^2
c. 66 in^2
d. 31 in^2

14. Choose the correct answer to go in each blank. Dot plot A shows the ages of visitors to a museum on Monday. Dot plot B shows the ages of visitors to the same museum on Tuesday.

Plot A

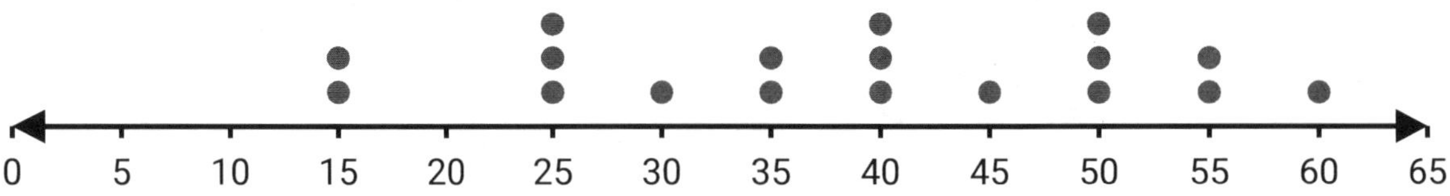

Plot B

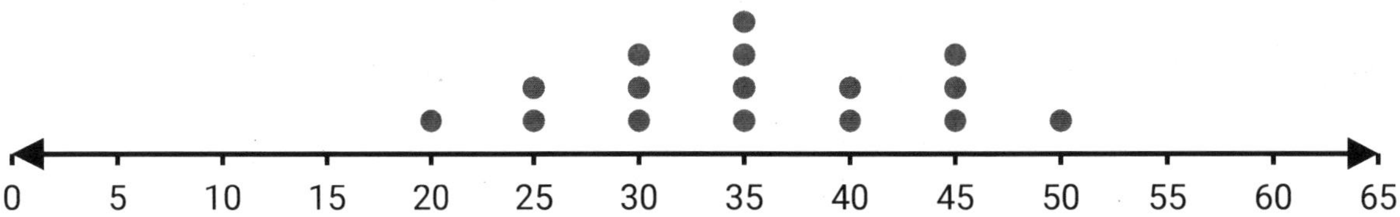

The range for plot A is ____ more than plot B. The median for plot A is ____ more than plot B.

First blank:
10
11
12
13
14
15

Second blank:
1
2
3
4
5
6

15. The trapezoids below are similar. What is the measure of side *NM*?

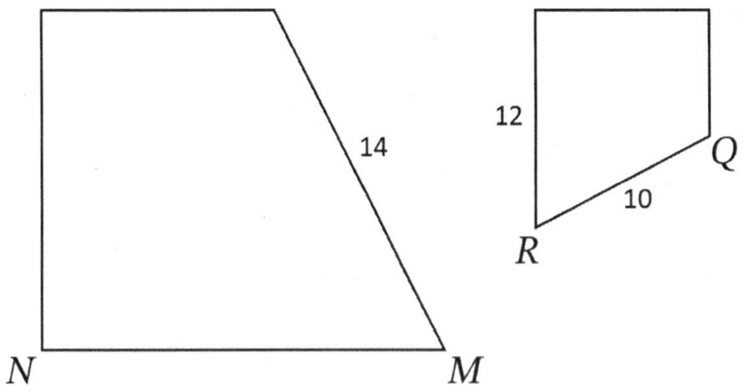

a. 11.7
b. 8.6
c. 21.7
d. 16.8

16. Kevin pays \$12.95 for a text messaging service plus \$0.07 for each text message he sends. Which of the following equations could be used to represent the total cost, *y*, when *x* represents the number of text messages sent?

a. $y = \$12.95x + \$0.07$
b. $y = \$13.02x$
c. $y = \frac{\$12.95}{\$0.07}x$
d. $y = \$0.07x + \$12.95$

17. Hannah draws two supplementary angles. One angle has a measure of 34°. What is the measure of the other angle?

a. 56°
b. 66°
c. 146°
d. 326°

18. Ray boards a train that travels at an average rate of 45 miles per hour. Which equation can be used to calculate the total number of miles, *y*, Ray travels in a *x* number of hours?

a. $y = x - 45$
b. $x = 45y$
c. $y = 45x$
d. $y = x + 45$

19. The number of tournaments a chess club member can compete in is directly proportional to the number of months they have been in the club. Charlie is in a chess club that competes in 15 tournaments every 6 months. What is the constant of proportionality relating the number of tournaments, *y*, to the number of months, *x*?

a. 2.5
b. 3
c. 3.5
d. 4

20. Part A: Jordan has a bag full of red and blue marbles. There are 16 red marbles and 24 blue marbles? What is the probability of him drawing a red marble?

a. $\frac{3}{5}$
b. $\frac{2}{5}$
c. $\frac{3}{10}$
d. $\frac{7}{10}$

Part B: Jordan has continued to draw marbles and has now taken out 4 red and 6 blue. What is the probability of him drawing a red marble now?

a. $\frac{3}{5}$

b. $\frac{3}{4}$

c. $\frac{2}{3}$

d. $\frac{2}{5}$

21. A group of 5 volunteers participate in a fitness challenge in order to increase their pushup ability. Participants documented the number of pushups they could complete in 5 minutes in June and then again in July.

Volunteer Identification	Number of Pushups (June)	Number of Pushups (July)
Volunteer A	50	80
Volunteer B	60	90
Volunteer C	45	100
Volunteer D	60	80
Volunteer E	80	120

Which two volunteers documented exactly a 50% increase in the number of pushups they were able to complete? Select all that apply.

a. Volunteer A
b. Volunteer B
c. Volunteer C
d. Volunteer D
e. Volunteer E

22. A travel agency conducts a survey of a random group of 250 citizens. The travel agency is offering a free trip to one of the four destinations. The survey is designed to gather feedback regarding the most desirable vacation destination from the list. Participants are asked to select one vacation destination from the list.

Destination Options	Number of People
Hawaii	68
Iceland	60
Fiji	77
Scotland	45

Which statement is most likely NOT accurate about all citizens based on the data collected in the survey?

a. The least popular vacation destination on the list will be Scotland.
b. The most popular destination will receive twice as many votes as the least popular destination.
c. More people will choose Fiji or Hawaii than will choose Iceland or Scotland.
d. The number of votes for Iceland will be lower than the number of votes for Hawaii.

23. Triangles *ABC* and *DEF* are similar.

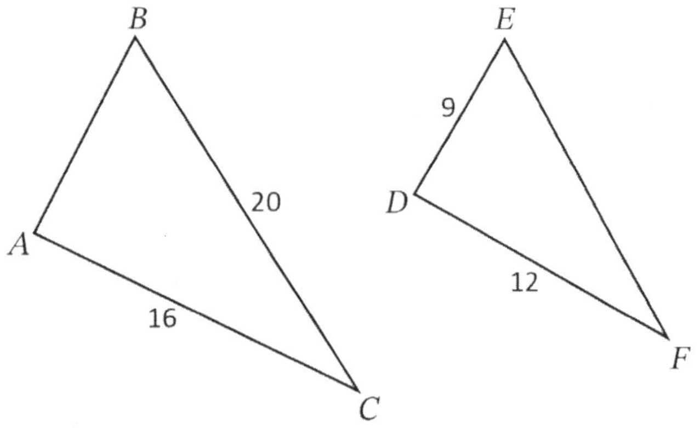

What is the value of *AB*?

a. 9
b. 10
c. 11
d. 12

24. A carpenter must fix a broken section of a kitchen cabinet. The intact portion of the cabinet forms a 76 degree angle with the wall. The width of the cabinet is supposed to form a 90 degree angle with the wall. What angle measure should the carpenter use when cutting the piece that will fit next to the 76 degree angle?

a. 12°
b. 14°
c. 104°
d. 136°

25. Joey sold 16 bouquets of flowers at the farmer's market for $8.50 each. Joey used the money from his bouquet sales to buy himself dinner. The total bill for Joey's dinner was $45.30. How much money does Joey have left after the dinner bill is paid?

a. $72.50
b. $93.45
c. $90.70
d. $91.70

26. A circle has a radius of 23 cm. Which of the following is the best estimate for the circumference of the circle?

a. 71.76 cm
b. 143.52 cm
c. 144.44 cm
d. 72.22 cm

27. Julia recently published her first book. Each book has a spine width of 2.5 centimeters. There is an open gap on Julia's bookshelf that is $28\frac{3}{5}$ centimeters wide. What is the greatest number of books Julia can place into the open gap on the shelf?

a. 11
b. 12
c. 13
d. 14

28. Mr. Thomas held a paper-airplane-throwing contest in each of his physics classes. He recorded the number of yards that the paper airplane flew after each student threw it and created the box plots below from the data.

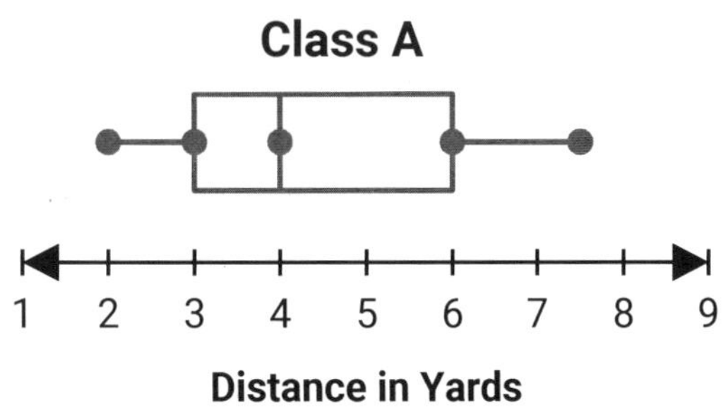

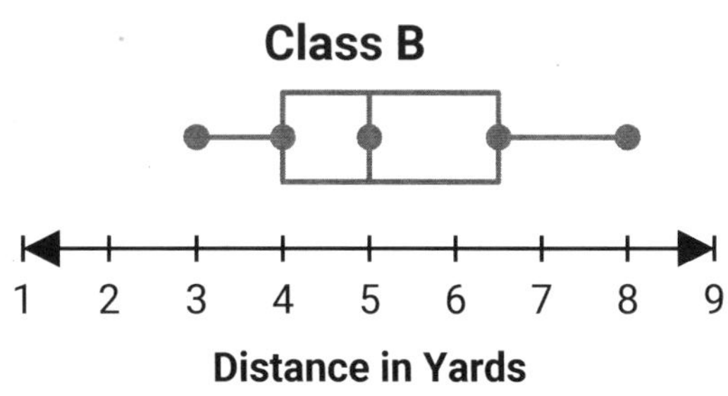

Based on the box plots above, which of the following statements are correct? Mark your answer for each statement below.

Statement	Correct	Not Correct
The longest flight length occurred in Class B.		
The range of the flight lengths in class B is higher than the range of flight lengths in class A.		
The median flight length was the same in both classes.		
The interquartile range of flight lengths in class A is greater than interquartile range of flight lengths in class B.		
The shortest flight length occurred in class B.		

29. Mr. Trey has a bag of pencils that vary in color. Mr. Trey lets each of his students randomly select a pencil from the bag.

Color	Number of Pencils Selected
Purple	11
Aqua	18
Green	3
Magenta	20

Which statement is supported by the data in the table?

a. It is equally likely to select a green pencil as it is a purple pencil.
b. Aqua pencils are least likely to be selected.
c. Purple pencils are approximately half as likely to be selected as magenta pencils.
d. Magenta pencils are approximately twice as likely to be selected than green pencils.

30. In the formula for the volume of the figure shown below, written as $V = B \cdot h$, h represents the height of the prism when it rests one of its bases. What does the B represent?

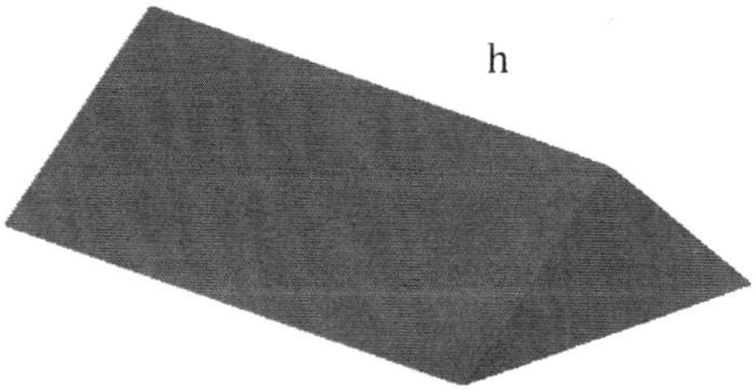

a. $\frac{1}{3}bh$, where b represents the length of the triangle's base and h represents the triangle's height
b. bh, where b represents the length of the triangle's base and h represents the triangle's height
c. $2bh$,where b represents the length of triangle's base and h represents the triangle's height
d. $\frac{1}{2}bh$, where b represents the length of triangle's base and h represents the triangle's height

31. A rectangular prism has a length of 14.3 cm, a width of 8.9 cm, and a height of 11.7 cm. Which of the following is the best estimate for the volume of the rectangular prism?

a. 1,512 cm^3
b. 1,287 cm^3
c. 1,386 cm^3
d. 1,620 cm^3

32. Mike goes to the fair with $25. He purchases an ice cream cone for $2.50 and a hamburger for $6.50. Mike wants to use the rest of his money on rides. Each ride cost $2. Which inequality describes the possible number of rides, x, Mike can afford?

a. $25 \leq 2x + 9$
b. $x = 25$
c. $2x < 25$
d. $2x + 9 \leq 25$

33. Fred designs a candy box in the shape of a triangular prism. The base of each triangular face measures 4 inches, while the height of the prism is 7 inches. Given that the length of the prism is 11 inches, what is the volume of the candy box?

a. 102 in^3
b. 128 in^3
c. 154 in^3
d. 308 in^3

34. Miranda rolls a standard die and spins a spinner with 4 equal sections. Which of the following represents the sample space?

a.

1, Section 1	1, Section 2	1, Section 3	1, Section 4	1, Section 5	1, Section 6
2, Section 1	2, Section 2	2, Section 3	2, Section 4	2, Section 5	2, Section 6
3, Section 1	3, Section 2	3, Section 3	3, Section 4	3, Section 5	3, Section 6
4, Section 1	4, Section 2	4, Section 3	4, Section 4	4, Section 5	4, Section 6

b.

1, Section 1	2, Section 1	3, Section 1	4, Section 1
1, Section 2	2, Section 2	3, Section 2	4, Section 2
1, Section 3	2, Section 3	3, Section 3	4, Section 3
1, Section 4	2, Section 4	3, Section 4	4, Section 4

c.

1, Section 1	2, Section 1	3, Section 1	4, Section 1	5, Section 1	6, Section 1
1, Section 2	2, Section 2	3, Section 2	4, Section 2	5, Section 2	6, Section 2
1, Section 3	2, Section 3	3, Section 3	4, Section 3	5, Section 3	6, Section 3
1, Section 4	2, Section 4	3, Section 4	4, Section 4	5, Section 4	6, Section 4
1, Section 5	2, Section 5	3, Section 5	4, Section 5	5, Section 5	6, Section 5
1, Section 6	2, Section 6	3, Section 6	4, Section 6	5, Section 6	6, Section 6

d.

1, Section 1	2, Section 1	3, Section 1	4, Section 1	5, Section 1	6, Section 1
1, Section 2	2, Section 2	3, Section 2	4, Section 2	5, Section 2	6, Section 2
1, Section 3	2, Section 3	3, Section 3	4, Section 3	5, Section 3	6, Section 3
1, Section 4	2, Section 4	3, Section 4	4, Section 4	5, Section 4	6, Section 4

35. A hat contains 6 red dice, 4 green dice, and 2 blue dice. What is the probability that Sarah pulls out a blue die, replaces it, and then pulls out a green die?

a. $\frac{1}{18}$
b. $\frac{1}{3}$
c. $\frac{1}{2}$
d. $\frac{1}{16}$

36. A landscape architect is creating a sand pathway. The project requires 24 bags of sand. All the sandbags weigh the same amount. The total weight of all the sandbags is 926.4 pounds. How many pounds does one bag of sand weigh?

a. 38.6 pounds
b. 38.2 pounds
c. 36 pounds
d. 36.8 pounds

37. Triangle ABC and triangle DEF are similar figures. What scale factor transforms triangle ABC to triangle DEF?

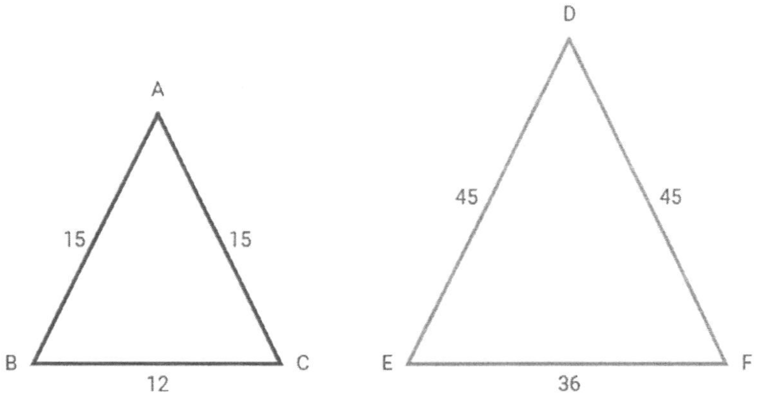

a. $\frac{1}{3}$
b. 2
c. 3
d. $\frac{1}{2}$

38. Describe the shape of the cross-section of a plane that slices the rectangular prism below parallel to its base.

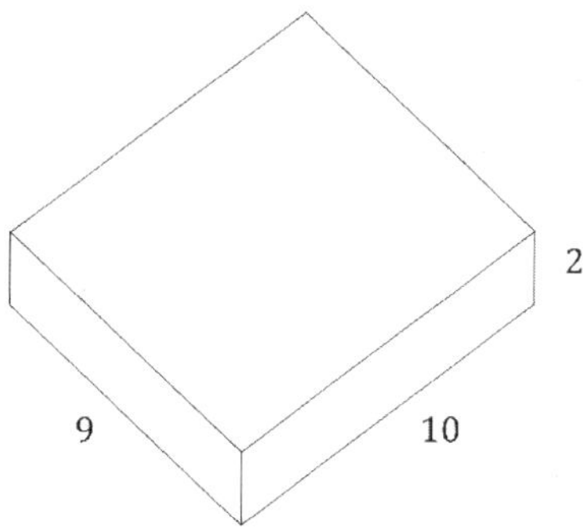

a. one 9 units by 10 units rectangle
b. one 9 units by 2 units rectangle
c. one 90 units by 2 units rectangle
d. one 2 units by 10 units rectangle

39. Gabriel went to a taco shop for lunch. He ordered 3 tacos and paid $4.14. The next day he decided to try a different taco shop and ordered 4 tacos and paid $4.80. How much more expensive was the first taco shop per taco?

a. $0.18
b. $0.66
c. $0.57
d. $0.28

40. Amy rolled a die and flipped a coin and spun a spinner with four equal sections numbered 1-4. What is the probability that she rolled an even number, got heads and then spun an even number?

a. $\frac{1}{4}$
b. $\frac{1}{2}$
c. $\frac{3}{4}$
d. $\frac{1}{8}$

41. A group of students are playing a game that requires a die to be rolled and then a spinner to be spun. The game die has 6 sides and the game spinner has 2 equal sections, one red and one green.

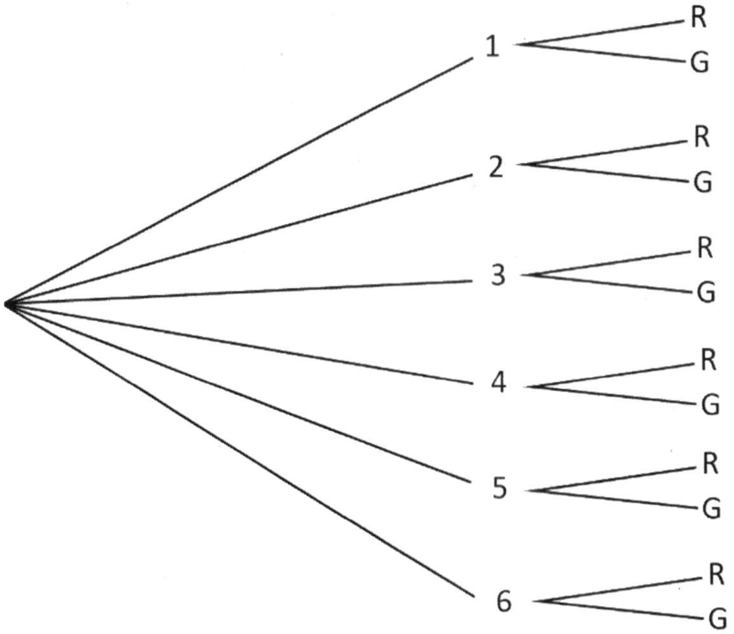

Which sample space is presented in the tree diagram?

a. $\{(1,R),(2,R),(3,R),(4,R),(5,R),(6,R)\}$
b. $\{(1,R),(1,G),(2,R),(2,G),(3,R),(3,G),(4,R),(4,G),(5,R),(5,G),(6,R),(6,G)\}$
c. $(1,RG),(2,RG),(3,RG),(4,RG),(5,RG),(6,RG)$
d. $\{(R),(G),(R),(G),(R),(G),(R),(G),(R),(G),(R),(G)\}$

42. Part A: Students at two schools recorded the number of steps they took daily as part of a health activity. The distribution of the number of steps taken at each school is shown in the boxplots below:

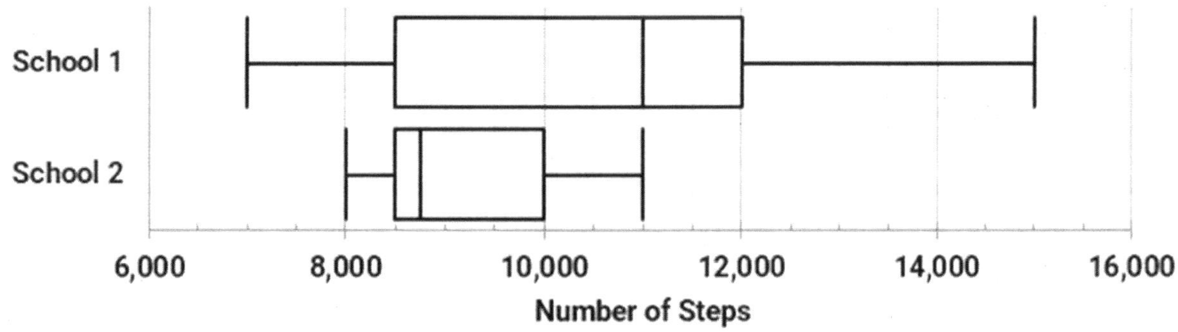

Determine the degree of visual overlap between the distribution of the number of steps at school 1 and school 2.

a. between the bottom 25% of school 1 and 100% of school 2
b. between the bottom 50% of school 1 and 100% of school 2
c. between the top 50% of school 1 and 100% of school 2
d. between the top 25% of school 1 and 100% of school 2

Part B: If school 1 has 1,000 students, how many students at school 1 took more steps than all the students at school 2?

a. 400
b. 300
c. 500
d. This cannot be determined.

43. Approximately 66% of US adults voted in the last presidential election. Tanya is selecting a random sample of four adults. She wants to find the probability that exactly three adults in her sample voted in the last presidential election. She has a random number generator that will generate a random number between 1 and 12. Describe how she could perform the simulation using this random number generator.

a. She could assign numbers 1-8 as "not voted" and numbers 9-12 as "voted." Then she should use the number generator to randomly select a number four times and record the results. This should be repeated.
b. She could assign numbers 1-8 as "voted" and numbers 9-12 as "not voted." Then she should use the number generator to randomly select a number three times and record the results. This should be repeated.
c. She could assign numbers 1-8 as "not voted" and numbers 9-12 as "voted." Then she should use the number generator to randomly select a number three times and record the results. This should be repeated.
d. She could assign numbers 1-8 as "voted" and numbers 9-12 as "not voted." Then she should use the number generator to randomly select a number four times and record the results. This should be repeated.

44. Patrick thinks that there is more than one way to draw a triangle with the angle measures of $71°, 47°$, and $62°$. Anna disagrees and says there is only one possible triangle with those angle measures. Who is correct?

a. Patrick is correct due to ASA.
b. Anna is correct due to AAA.
c. Anna is correct due to ASA.
d. Patrick is correct due to AAA.

45. Mike is ordering a new polo shirt for each of his 12 employees, spending at least $150. Which of the following inequalities represents the possible costs?

a. $150 < 12p$
b. $150 > 12p$
c. $150 \leq 12p$
d. $150 \geq 12p$

46. Gillian is deciding between two data plans for her cellphone. Plan A provides 2.5 GB of data for a flat rate of $20/month and charges $15 per GB for any extra use. Plan B provides unlimited data for $50/month. What amount of data would Gillian have to use in a month for both plans to cost the same amount?

a. 2 GB
b. 3.5 GB
c. 3.75 GB
d. 4.5 GB

47. Nurseries A, B, and C offer various plants for sale, as well as landscaping services to plant the trees and bushes. Prices are listed in the table below.

	A	B	C
Trees	$25	$30	$20
Bushes	$15	$20	$15
Landscaping (per hour)	$45	$55	$50

Isabella plans to hire one of the companies to plant 10 trees and 8 bushes. This project will take x hours. Which of the following inequalities represents x if Nursery A offers a better deal than Nursery C?

a. $x < 5$
b. $x < 10$
c. $x > 5$
d. $x > 10$

48. If a restaurant's salad dressing is made of a ratio of ¾ cup oil to ¼ cup vinegar, how many cups of vinegar are there in 6 cups of salad dressing?

a. $\frac{1}{2}$
b. $1\frac{1}{2}$
c. $1\frac{3}{4}$
d. $2\frac{1}{4}$

49. What is the value of the following:

$$12 - 14$$

a. 2
b. -26
c. -2
d. 26

50. Marcus is mowing yards and doing odd jobs to earn money for a new video game system that costs \$325. Marcus only charges \$6.50 per hour. Which of the following equations represents the number of hours Marcus needs to work to earn \$325?

a. $6.50x = 325$
b. $6.50 + x = 325$
c. $325x = 6.50$
d. $6.50x + 325 = x$

Answers and Explanations for Test #1

1. B: Rectangles $ABCD$ and $EFGD$ are similar, which means their side lengths are proportional. It is also true that opposite sides of a rectangle are congruent. This makes the ratio of DG to AB is the same as the ratio of ED to BC. The unknown value of side length AB can be determined by setting up a proportion.

$$\frac{12}{AB} = \frac{5}{8}$$

Solve for AB using cross multiplication.

$$5(AB) = 12(8)$$
$$5(AB) = 96$$
$$AB = \frac{96}{5}$$

$\frac{96}{5}$ is equivalent to the mixed number $19\frac{1}{5}$.

2. A: The formula $C = 2\pi r$ is used to determine the circumference of a circle. This formula can also be written as $C = \pi d$ because d is equivalent to $2r$. Substitute 45 in for C.

$$45 = \pi d$$

Now, solve for the variable d. Divide both sides of the equation by π to isolate the variable d.

$$\frac{45}{\pi} = d$$

3. D: In order to determine the amount available to each guest, the total amount of prepared lemonade should be divided by 25 guests. Thus, the expression $2\frac{1}{2} \div 25$ represents the amount that each guest has available for consumption. The mixed fraction can be rewritten as $\frac{5}{2}$. The expression can be simplified by writing $\frac{5}{2} \div 25 = \frac{5}{2} \times \frac{1}{25}$, which equals $\frac{5}{50}$, or $\frac{1}{10}$.

4. M=$\frac{1}{2}$, N=$1\frac{3}{4}$, and O=$2\frac{1}{4}$, so N-M+O= $1\frac{3}{4} - \frac{1}{2} + 2\frac{1}{4} = \frac{7}{4} - \frac{2}{4} + \frac{9}{4} = \frac{14}{4} = 3\frac{1}{2}$. The number line is shown below.

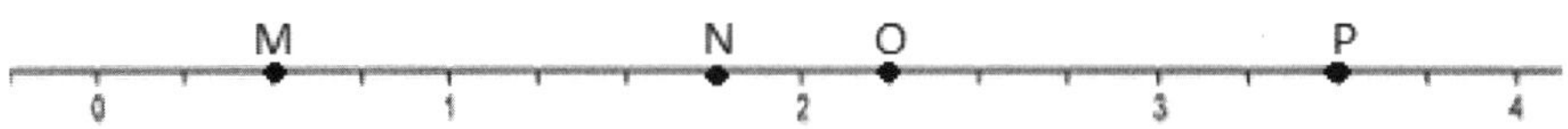

5. Part A: C: He has already landed on three of the four numbers so the probability is $\frac{3}{4}$.

Part B: C: A larger probability indicates that something is more likely to happen. A smaller probability indicates that something is less likely to happen.

6. D: The cost per ounce can be calculated by dividing the cost of the bag by the number of ounces the bag contains. Thus, the cost per ounce can be calculated by writing $9.85 ÷ 16, which equals approximately $0.62 per ounce.

7. C: Angle x and angle y are complementary angles, which means they have a sum of 90°. The sum of $x°$ and $(4t + 4)°$ is 90°. This can be expressed as the equation $x + (4t + 4) = 90$.

8. C: Both flour and butter are given in cups so they are easy to compare. First find a like denominator. $\frac{1}{2}$ is equal to $\frac{2}{4}$, and $1\frac{3}{4}$ is equal to $\frac{7}{4}$. So, the ratio is 2:7.

9. Part A: B: The discounted price is 25% less than the original price. Therefore, the discounted price can be written as $36.95 - ((0.25)(36.95))$, which equals approximately 27.71. Thus, the discounted price of the jacket is $27.71.

Part B: D: If sales tax is 8% then that can be written as ($27.71)(1.08), which is approximately $29.93.

10. A: The first day they went 69 miles per hour for 11 hours, so they went $11 \times 69 = 759$ miles. The second day they went 72 miles per hour for 10 hours, so they went $10 \times 72 = 720$ miles. When added together, they went a total of 1479 miles.

11. B: To find the unit rate, the cost of the bottle should be divided by the number of fluid ounces contained in the bottle: $\frac{\$3.96}{20} \approx 0.20$. Thus, the cost per fluid ounce is approximately $0.20.

12. C: Lexi scored a total of $30 + 14 + 18 + 12 + 26 = 100$ points this month. Out of those 100 points, $30 + 14 + 26 = 70$ points were scored at home games. 70 out of 100 is expressed as the decimal $\frac{70}{100} = 0.70$. Multiply the decimal 0.70 by 100 in order to convert it to decimal form: $0.70 \times 100 = 70\%$. 70% of Lexi's points were scored at home games.

13. A: The top left shaded region can be found by first finding the width. Since 6 in. is given as the width of the whole rectangle and 4 in. is given for the width of the non-shaded region then the width of the shaded region is the difference of 2 inches. So, the area of that region is 7 in.× 2in. = 14 square inches. The other shaded region can be broken into a 3 in. by 3 in. square and a 4 in. by 6 in. rectangle. So, 3 in.× 3 in. = 9 square inches and 4 in.× 6 in. = 24 square inches. Added together, $14 + 9 + 24 = 47$ square inches.

14. 15, 5: To determine the range for each dot plot subtract the lowest age from the highest age. The range for plot A is $60 - 15 = 45$. The range for plot B is $50 - 20 = 30$. This means that the range for plot A is 15 more than the range for plot B. Select 15 from the dropdown menu.

To determine the median age for each dot plot, start by arranging the values from least to greatest.

Plot A: 15, 15, 25, 25, 25, 30, 35, 35, 40, 40, 40, 45, 50, 50, 50, 55, 55, 60

Plot B: 20, 25, 25, 30, 30, 30, 35, 35, 35, 35, 40, 40, 45, 45, 45, 50

Now, locate the middle value for each set of numbers.

The middle, or median, age for plot A is 40 years old.

The middle, or median, age for plot B is 35 years old.

This means that the median for plot A is 5 more than the median for plot B.

Select 5 from the dropdown menu.

15. D: Solve for side length NM by setting up a proportion. The ratio $\frac{NM}{12}$ is proportional to the ratio $\frac{14}{10}$. Set both ratios equal to each other.

$$\frac{NM}{12} = \frac{14}{10}$$

Use cross multiplication to solve for NM.

$$NM(10) = 12(14)$$
$$NM(10) = 168$$

Divide both sides by 10 to isolate NM.

$$NM = 16.8$$

16. D: The constant amount Kevin pays is \$12.95; this amount represents the y-intercept. The variable amount is represented by the expression $\$0.07x$, where x represents the number of text messages sent and \$0.07 represents the constant rate of change or slope. Thus, his total cost can be represented by the equation $y = \$0.07x + \$12.95$.

17. C: Supplementary angles add to 180 degrees. Therefore, the other angle is equal to the difference between 180 degrees and 34 degrees: $180 - 34 = 146$. Thus, the other angle measures 146°.

18. C: A train traveling 45 miles per hour can be expressed as the equation $y = 45x$, where x is the number of hours, y is the number of miles traveled, and 45 is the number of miles traveled each hour. The number of miles Ray travels is dependent on the number of hours Ray in on the train. Any number of hours can be substituted in for x in the equation $y = 45x$ in order to solve for the total number of miles traveled.

19. A: The constant of proportionality is the value that relates two amounts. In the equation $y = kx$, k represents the constant of proportionality and y is directly proportional to x. In this scenario, the number of chess tournaments is directly proportional to the number of months where x represents the number of months, and y represents the number of tournaments. The constant of proportionality, k, is calculated as the number of tournaments divided by the number of months, $15 \div 6 = 2.5$. The constant of proportionality, k, is 2.5.

20. Part A: B: There are a total of 40 marbles in the bag. The probability of him drawing a red one is $\frac{16}{40}$ or $\frac{2}{5}$.

Part B: D: If 4 red and 6 blue are missing then there are only 12 red and 18 blue remaining. There are a total of 30 marbles left in the bag. The probability of drawing a red one then is $\frac{12}{30}$ or $\frac{2}{5}$.

21. B, E: Use the percent change formula to determine with volunteers increased their number of pushups by 50%.

Volunteer B:

$$\% \text{ change} = \frac{\text{final value} - \text{initial value}}{\text{initial value}} \times 100\%$$
$$\% \text{ change} = \frac{90 - 60}{60} \times 100\%$$
$$\% \text{ change} = 0.5 \times 100\%$$
$$\% \text{ change} = 50\%$$

The pushup ability for Volunteer B jumped from 60 to 90 which is an increase of 50%.

Volunteer E:

$$\% \text{ change} = \frac{\text{final value} - \text{initial value}}{\text{initial value}} \times 100\%$$
$$\% \text{ change} = \frac{120 - 80}{80} \times 100\%$$
$$\% \text{ change} = 0.5 \times 100\%$$
$$\% \text{ change} = 50\%$$

The pushup ability for Volunteer E jumped from 80 to 120 which is an increase of 50%.

Participants B and E were the only two volunteers that increased their number of pushups by 50%.

22. B: All statements are true except choice B. The most popular destination is Fiji, with 77 votes. The least popular destination is Scotland, with 45 votes. $45 \times 2 \neq 77$, which means the most popular destination received less than two times the number of votes that the least popular destination received.

23. D: Triangles ABC and DEF are similar, so their side lengths are proportional. The ratio of AB to AC is proportional to the ratio of DE to DF.

$$\frac{AB}{AC} = \frac{DE}{DF}$$

Substitute in the values for AC, DE, and DF.

$$\frac{AB}{16} = \frac{9}{12}$$

Cross multiply to solve for AB.

$$12(AB) = 9(16)$$
$$12(AB) = 144$$

Divide both sides by 12.

$$AB = 12$$

24. B: Since the intact portion of the cabinet and the missing piece form a 90 degree angle with the wall, the missing piece must have an angle equal to the difference between 90 degrees and 76 degrees. Thus, the newly cut cabinet piece should have an angle measure of 14 degrees.

25. C: Joey earned \$8.50 for every bouquet sold. The total amount of money earned can be calculated as $16 \times \$8.50 = \$136$. His dinner bill was \$45.30, so subtract this from \$136: $\$136 - \$45.30 = \$90.70$. Joey has \$90.70 remaining after the dinner bill is paid.

26. C: The circumference of a circle can be determined by using the formula $C = \pi d$. A radius of 23 cm indicates a diameter of 46 cm, or twice that length. Substitution of 46 cm for d and 3.14 for π gives the following: $C = 3.14 \cdot 46$, which equals 144.44. Thus, the circumference of the circle is approximately 144.44 cm.

27. Julia's shelf has a gap of $28\frac{3}{5}$ centimeters, and each book has a spine width of 2.5 centimeters. Start by expressing both values in decimal form. The mixed number $28\frac{3}{5}$ is equivalent to $28\frac{6}{10}$, which is 28.6 as a decimal.

Divide the shelf space by the width of one book to determine how many books will fit on the shelf. Use the long division algorithm to solve $28.6 \div 2.5$.

When dividing decimals, start by eliminating the decimal from the divisor (2.5). Multiply 2.5 by 10 in order to eliminate the decimal: $2.5 \times 10 = 25$. Now the dividend must also be multiplied by 10: $28.6 \times 10 = 286$. The division problem becomes $286 \div 25$.

```
       11.4 4
  25) 286.0 0
     -25
       36
      -25
       11 0
      -10 0
        1 0 0
       -1 0 0
            0
```

The result is 11.44. Julia will be able to place 11 books on the shelf.

28.

Statement	Correct	Not Correct
The longest flight length occurred in class B.	X	
The range of the flight lengths in class B is higher than the range of flight lengths in class A.		X
The median flight length was the same in both classes.		X
The interquartile range of flight lengths in class A is greater than interquartile range of flight lengths in class B.	X	
The shortest flight length occurred in class B.		X

The maximum of the data for class A is 7.5, while the maximum of the data for class B is 8, so the longest flight length occurred in class B. The minimum of the data for class A is 2, while the minimum of the data for class B is 3. This means that the range of the data for class A is 5.5, because $7.5 - 2 = 5.5$, and the range of the data for class B is 5, because $8 - 3 = 5$. So, the range of the flight lengths in class B is lower than the range of the flight lengths in class A. The median of the data for class A is 4, and the median of the data for class B is 5, so the two data sets do not have the same median. The interquartile range of the data for class A is 3, since $6 - 3 = 3$. The interquartile range of the data for class B is less than that, since $6.5 - 4 = 2.5$. The minimum of the data for class A is lower than the minimum of the data for class B, so the shortest flight length occurred in class A.

29. C: 11 purple pencils were selected from the bag. 20 magenta pencils were selected from the bag. 11 is approximately half as much as 20. Choice C is supported by the data in the table.

30. D: The B in the formula $V = Bh$ represents the area of the triangular base. The formula for the area of a triangle is $\frac{1}{2}bh$, where b represents the length of the triangle's base and h represents the triangle's height.

31. A: The dimensions of the rectangular prism can be rounded to 14 cm, 9 cm, and 12 cm. The volume of a rectangular prism can be determined by finding the product of the length, width, and height. Therefore, the volume is approximately equal to $14 \times 9 \times 12$, or 1,512 cm^3.

32. D: Mike spends \$2.50 on an ice cream cone and \$6.50 on a hamburger. Before Mike spends any money on rides, he has already spent \$9, as $\$2.50 + \$6.50 = \$9$.

Each ride costs \$2. The amount Mike spends on rides can be expressed as $2x$, where x represents the number of rides.

Mike has \$25 to spend at the fair, so the amount that he spends on snacks and rides needs to be less than or equal to \$25. The inequality $2x + 9 \leq 25$ represents the scenario and can be used to calculate the possible number of rides Mike can purchase.

33. C: The volume of a triangular prism can be determined using the formula $V = \frac{1}{2}bhl$, where b represents the length of the base of each triangular face, h represents the height of each triangular face, and l represents the length of the prism. Substitution of the given values into the formula gives $V = \frac{1}{2} \cdot 4 \cdot 7 \cdot 11$, which equals 154. Thus, the volume of the candy box is 154 cubic inches.

34. D: The sample space can be displayed using an organized list. Answer choice D is correct because it pairs each section (4 total sections) with each side of the standard die (6 sides).

35. A: The events are independent since Sarah replaces the first die. The probability of two independent events can be found using the formula $P(A \text{ and } B) = P(A) \cdot P(B)$. The probability of pulling out a blue die is $\frac{2}{12}$. The probability of pulling out a green die is $\frac{4}{12}$. The probability of pulling out a blue die and a green die is $\frac{2}{12} \cdot \frac{4}{12}$, which simplifies to $\frac{1}{18}$.

36. A: There are 926.4 total pounds of sand. The sand is contained in 24 bags that all weigh the same amount. The scenario represents a decimal division problem.

$$\begin{array}{r} 38.6 \\ 24\overline{)926.4} \\ -72 \\ \hline 206 \\ -192 \\ \hline 144 \\ -144 \\ \hline 0 \end{array}$$

Since $926.4 \div 24 = 38.6$, one bag of sand weighs 38.6 pounds.

37. C: The scale factor equals the ratio of the two corresponding sides of triangle ABC and triangle DEF. Set up a ratio of any two similar sides. In this case, side DE and side AB will be used, and then the values of the lengths of each of those sides will be substituted in the scale factor ratio. Finally, simplify the fraction:

$$scale\ factor = \frac{DE}{AB} = \frac{45}{15} = \frac{3}{1} = 3$$

38. A: The cross-section parallel to the base is congruent to the base. Since the base is a rectangle with the dimensions 9 units by 10 units, the cross sections will also be a rectangle with the dimensions 9 units by 10 units.

39. A: First find the cost of the first taco shop by dividing $4.14 by 3, which comes out to $1.38 per taco. Then find the price at the second shop by dividing $4.80 by 4 to get $1.20 per taco. The difference is $0.18.

40. D: The probability of getting an even number is $\frac{3}{6}$. The probability of getting heads is $\frac{1}{2}$. The probability of spinning an even number is $\frac{2}{4}$. The probability of all three occurring can be calculated by multiplying the probabilities of the individual events: $\frac{3}{6} \cdot \frac{1}{2} \cdot \frac{2}{4}$ equals $\frac{1}{8}$.

41. B: A sample space lists all possible outcomes in an experiment. In this experiment, which is the game, a player rolls a 6-sided die and then spins a spinner containing 2 equal sections. The sample space for this game has 12 possible outcomes. The tree diagram represents all of the possible outcomes. For example, a player can roll a 1 and spin red $(1, R)$, or roll a 1 and spin green $(1, G)$, or roll a 2 and spin red $(2, R)$, or roll a 2 and spin green $(2, G)$. The pattern continues until every number on the die is paired with red and green.

Choice B is the only sample space containing all the possible outcomes.

Choice A is missing all outcomes containing Green.

Choice C lists RG as an option for the spinner. However, the spinner can only land on one section, R or G.

Choice D only lists options for the spinner. The outcomes listed in the sample space need to contain one roll of the die and one spin of the spinner.

42. Part A: B: There is a large overlap between the bottom 50% of school 1 and 100% of school 2. The bottom 50% of School 1 took between 7,000 and 11,000 steps, while all the students at School 2 took between 8,000 and 11,000 steps.

Part B: C: The top 50% of students at school 1 took more steps than the maximum number of steps taken at school 2. Find 50% of 1,000: $0.50 \times 1{,}000 = 500$ students.

43. D: 66% is approximately $\frac{2}{3}$, so she should label $\frac{2}{3}$ of the twelve numbers as voted and the other $\frac{1}{3}$ as not voted. For example, she could assign numbers 1-8 as "voted" and numbers 9–12 as "not voted." Then, she should use the number generator to randomly select a number four times since she needs to randomly select four adults and record the results. Tanya should repeat this process many times until she has enough outcomes to calculate the probability.

44. D: Since this is AAA, there are many ways to draw a triangle with those three angles. This is a non-unique triangle. The sum of all angles in a triangle must equal 180°.When all the provided angles are added together, the result is equal to 180°.

$$71 + 47 + 62 = 180$$

No side lengths are given, so this is a non-unique triangle. As shown below, triangles with different side lengths can share the same angle measures.

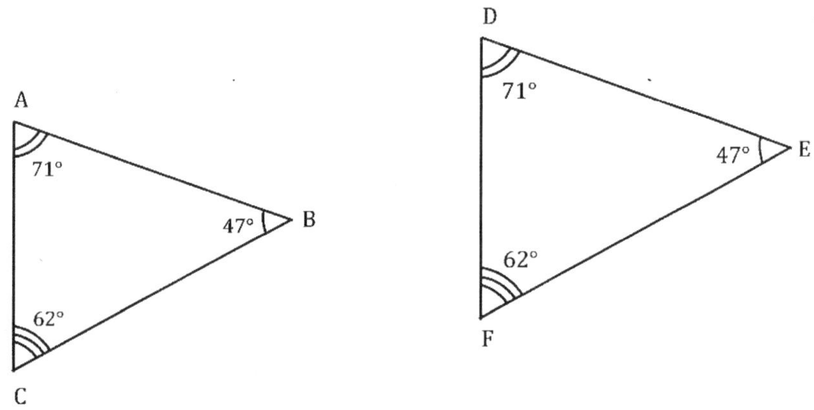

Therefore, Patrick is correct.

45. C: Since he spends at least \$150, the relation of the number of polo shirts to the minimum cost may be written as $12p \geq 150$. Alternatively, the inequality may be written as $150 \leq 12p$.

46. D: The expression representing the monthly charge for Plan A is $\$20 + \$15(d - 2.5)$, where d is the data used. This can be found by adding the flat rate to the price of any data used over the provided amount. Set this expression equal to the monthly charge for Plan B, which is \$50. Solve for d to find the number of GB for which the two plans charge the same amount.

$$\$20 + \$15(d - 2.5) = \$50$$
$$\$15(d - 2.5) = \$30$$
$$d - 2.5 = 2$$
$$d = 4.5$$

So, the plans have the same cost when Gillian uses 4.5 GB of data.

47. D: We can calculate the cost of each nursery's trees and bushes. Nursery A's cost is:

$$25(10) + 15(8) = 250 + 120 = \$370$$

Nursery C's cost is:

$$20(10) + 15(8) = 200 + 120 = \$320$$

So, we can set up an inequality, letting x be the number of hours to plant the bushes and trees. For Nursery A's services to be a better deal, they must cost less than Nursery C's.

$$370 + 45x < 320 + 50x$$

We solve for x by subtracting $45x$ and 320 from each side.

$$50 < 5x$$

We rewrite this as $5x > 50$ and divide each side by 5 to obtain $x > 10$. It is important to remember to reverse the inequality sign when we move the x to the left so we don't end up with $x < 10$ (answer choice B).

48. B: Determine what the ratio of vinegar to the salad dressing as a whole is. Vinegar is $\frac{1}{4}$ of a cup and the salad dressing as a whole is $\frac{1}{4}$ cup vinegar plus $\frac{3}{4}$ cup oil, or 1 cup. Thus, vinegar is $\frac{1}{4}$ of the salad dressing. Therefore, $\frac{1}{4}$ of 6 cups is $\frac{3}{2}$or $1\frac{1}{2}$ cups of vinegar.

49. C: Subtracting rational numbers is the same thing as adding the additive inverse. Therefore, $12 - 14 = 12 + (-14)$. To solve, find the difference between the two, $14 - 12 = 2$. Then the sign comes from the number that has the greatest absolute value or distance away from zero. 12 has an absolute value of 12, and -14 has an absolute value of 14. Therefore, the answer is -2 since 14 is greater than 12.

50. A: Marcus needs $325 for the new gaming system. If he earns $6.50 an hour, the number of hours he needs to work can be determined by dividing $325 by $6.50 which is written as $\frac{325}{6.50} = x$. Multiplying both sides of the equation by 6.50 yields $6.50x = 325$.

Practice Test #2

1. Sarah sells sweatshirts at a clothing store. Large sweatshirts cost $18.50, medium sweatshirts cost $16.00, and small sweatshirts cost $12.80.

- Sarah sold 45 sweatshirts by the end of her work shift.
- $\frac{1}{5}$ of the sweatshirts sold were a size medium.
- Twice as many large sweatshirts were sold than mediums.

How much money was earned from the sale of small sweatshirts?

a. $130.40
b. $235.40
c. $290.90
d. $230.40

2. A plane takes off from Dallas and lands in New York 3 hours and 20 minutes later. The distance from Dallas to New York is 1510 miles. Approximately how fast was the plane traveling?

a. 445 mph
b. 453 mph
c. 456 mph
d. 449 mph

3. The net below consists of 5 shapes. Which three items contribute to the total area of the net? Select all that apply.

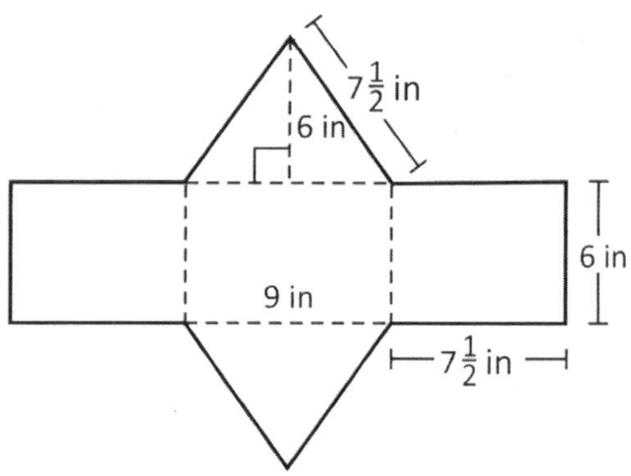

a. 2 triangles with an area of 27 square inches
b. 1 rectangle with an area of 54 square inches
c. 3 rectangles with an area of 45 square inches
d. 2 rectangles with an area of 45 square inches
e. 2 triangles with an area of 36 square inches

4. A parcel of land has 35 mature trees for every 3 acres. How many mature trees can be found on 18 of the acres?

a. 206
b. 212
c. 210
d. 214

5. The box plots below compare the ages of people at a public library. The upper box plot shows data from Monday. The lower box plot shows data from Friday. Which statement is true based on the data displays?

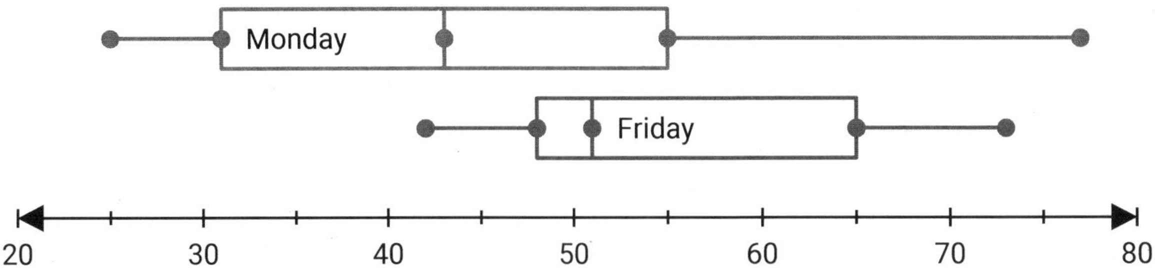

a. The median age of library visitors on Monday is 6 years greater than the median age of visitors on Friday.
b. The ages of Monday's visitors have a smaller range than the visitors on Friday.
c. The interquartile range of the ages of Friday's visitors is twice as much as the interquartile range of the ages of Monday's visitors.
d. The oldest visitor on Monday is older than the oldest visitor on Friday.

6. Nancy is shopping for cereal at the grocery store. If Nancy's goal is to purchase the cereal that is least expensive per serving, which option should she select?

Cereal Size Options	Number of Servings per Container	Cost per Container
Medium Box	10	$4.60
Bargain Bag	30	$3.30
Family Size Box	20	$3.80
Jumbo Bag	20	$8.60

a. Medium Box
b. Bargain Bag
c. Family Size Box
d. Jumbo Bag

7. Part A: What is the area of the shaded region below?

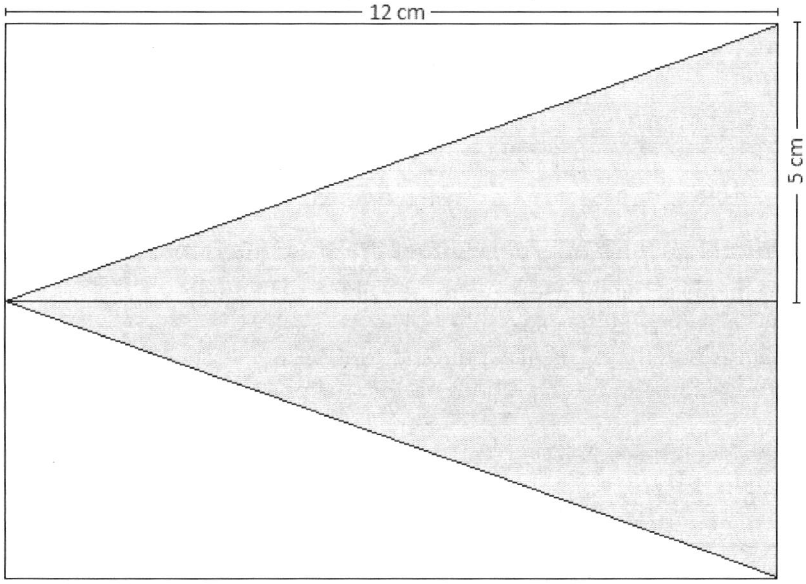

a. 60 cm^2
b. 120 cm^2
c. 68 cm^2
d. 34 cm^2

Part B: How does the shaded region compare to the non-shaded region?

a. The shaded region is bigger than the non-shaded region.
b. Both the shaded and non-shaded region are the same size.
c. The non-shaded region is bigger than the shaded region.
d. The area of the non-shaded region cannot be determined.

8. Calculate the product. Express your answer as a fraction in simplest form.

$$3.5 \times \frac{1}{4}$$

a. 14
b. $8\frac{5}{7}$
c. $\frac{7}{8}$
d. $\frac{5}{8}$

9. A sample of 7th and 8th graders are asked to vote on their preference for new school lunch menu items. The results are displayed in the table below. Students are asked to select one menu item from the list.

Menu Item	7th Graders	8th Graders
Corn Dogs	26	28
Vegetable Chili	11	14
Calzones	31	30
Shrimp Tacos	24	29

Based on the data in the table, which inference about the students is most valid?

a. Students will be equally satisfied with any of the following menu items.
b. Corn dogs are twice as popular as vegetable chili.
c. Calzones are twice as popular as the least popular option.
d. 7th graders prefer calzones, but 8th graders prefer shrimp tacos.

10. A landscaping company charges \$25 per $\frac{1}{2}$-acre to mow a yard. The company is offering a 20% discount for the month of May. If Douglas has a two-acre yard, how much will the company charge?

a. \$65
b. \$80
c. \$70
d. \$75

11. A house is priced at \$278,000. The price of the house has been reduced by \$12,600. Which of the following best represents the percentage of the reduction?

a. 3%
b. 4%
c. 5%
d. 6%

12. Amy buys 4 apples and 3 bananas at the grocery store. She spent a total of \$5.17. Each apple cost \$0.94. If each banana cost the same amount how much did one banana cost?

a. \$1.41
b. \$3.76
c. \$0.59
d. \$0.47

13. Melanie makes \$12 an hour and is taxed at 15% on her income. Lynn makes \$14 an hour and is taxed at 18% on her income. If they both work a 40-hour week, how much more does Lynn make than Melanie?

a. \$28.80
b. \$488.00
c. \$51.20
d. \$379.20

14. Four ordered pairs from a linear function are presented in the table.

x	y
1	9
2	11
3	13
4	15

Which linear equation can be used to represent the data in the table?

a. $y = -2x + 7$
b. $x = 2y + 7$
c. $y = 2x - 7$
d. $y = 2x + 7$

15. The measure of angle *b* can be described using an equation. Which equation is NOT an accurate way to calculate the value of angle *b*?

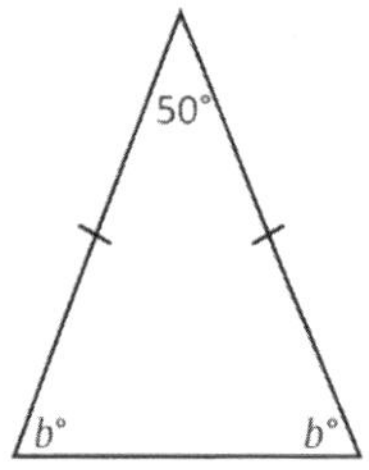

a. $180° = 50° + b° + b°$
b. $50° + 2b° = 180°$
c. $180° - 50° = 2b°$
d. $50° + b° + b° = 360°$

16. Eliza is planting flowers in a garden. The relationship between the number of flowers that are planted and the amount of time that expires is listed in the table below.

What is the value of *k*, the constant of proportionality?

Number of Minutes	1	2	3	4
Number of Flowers Planted	12	24	36	48

a. 10
b. 11
c. 12
d. 13

17. Point S and Point T are shown on the number line below. Which of the following equations produces a point, *R*, not on the number line?

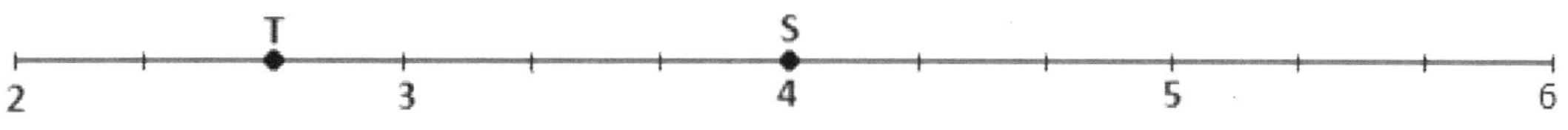

a. 2S-T=R
b. 2T-S=R
c. 3T-S=R
d. 3S-2T=R

18. Part A: The spinner below is spun once. What is the probability of landing on a 12 or greater?

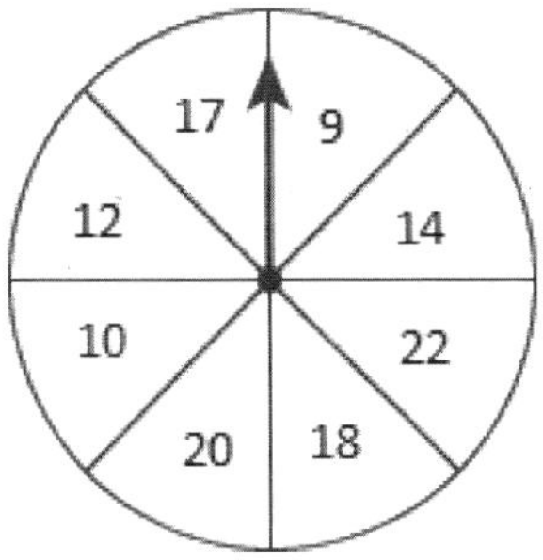

a. $\frac{5}{8}$
b. $\frac{1}{2}$
c. $\frac{3}{4}$
d. $\frac{2}{8}$

Part B: What is the probability of spinning it a second time and getting a 12 or greater both times?

a. $\frac{9}{16}$
b. $\frac{3}{4}$
c. $\frac{5}{8}$
d. $\frac{25}{64}$

19. A toy store owner sells action figures. He buys each one from the manufacture for $4.10. He has labor and other costs of $1.35 per action figure. He wants to make a 30% profit on each one. How much does he need to sell them for?

a. $1.62
b. $7.02
c. $5.33
d. $3.58

20. Angle A and Angle B are complementary. Angle B measures 28°. What is the measure of Angle A?

a. 62°
b. 92°
c. 72°
d. 152°

21. Which of the following describes *all* requirements of similar polygons?

a. Similar polygons have congruent corresponding angles and proportional corresponding sides
b. Similar polygons have congruent corresponding angles and congruent corresponding sides
c. Similar polygons have proportional corresponding sides
d. Similar polygons have congruent corresponding angles

22. **The dot plots below compare the heights of students in two classes. Class A is displayed above, and Class B is displayed below. All heights are measured and displayed in centimeters. Each dot represents one student.**

Class A

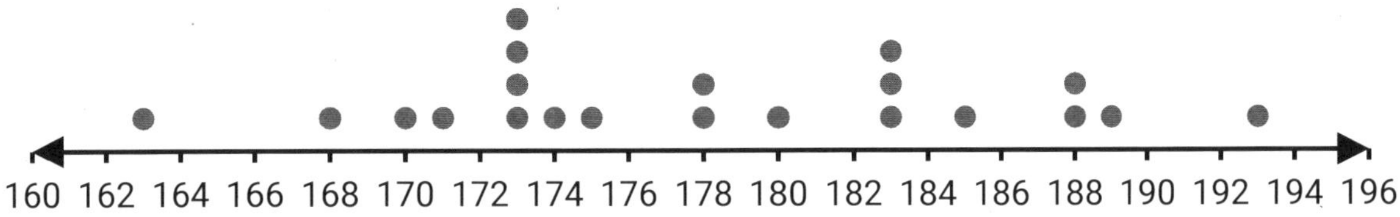

Class B

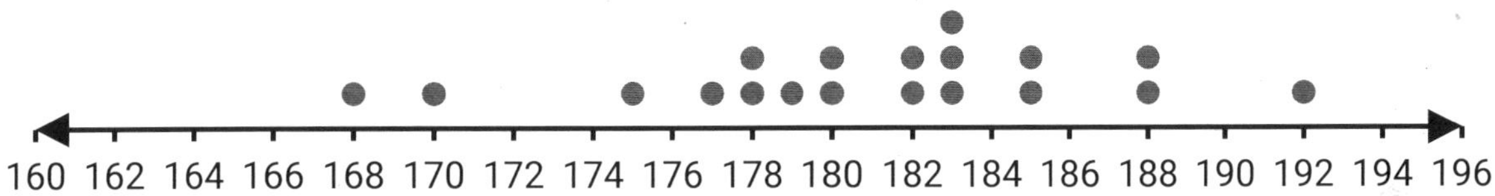

Which statement is true?

a. The mode in class A is 4, because 4 is the greatest number of dots over any height.
b. The mode in class B is 2 because there are 5 heights with 2 dots.
c. Class A has 2 modes because there are two heights with 4 dots.
d. The mode in Class B is 10 more than the mode in Class A.

23. **Eric can dribble the soccer ball down $\frac{2}{3}$ of the field in $\frac{2}{5}$ of a minute. How long will it take him to dribble the whole field?**

a. 36 seconds
b. 24 seconds
c. 30 seconds
d. 32 seconds

24. **Kaleb has a bike rim that is 18 inches in diameter. He puts a tire on it that is 2 inches thick. What is the circumference of the tire?**

a. 20π
b. 22π
c. 24π
d. 18π

25. Quadrilateral $ABCD$ is displayed below.

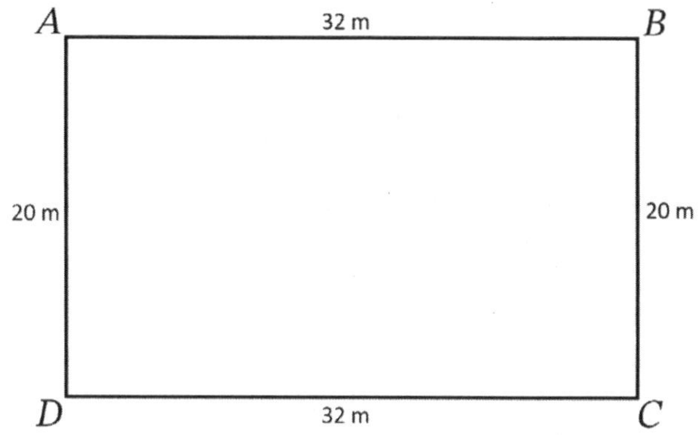

Which set of side lengths represent a quadrilateral that is similar to quadrilateral $ABCD$?

a. 60 m, 65 m, 96 m, 90 m
b. 60 m, 60 m, 96 m, 96 m
c. 16 m, 16 m, 40 m, 40 m
d. 32 m, 32 m, 40 m, 40 m

26. Harry is shopping around for a new cell phone provider. Company 1 charges \$45 each month plus a \$30 startup fee. Company 2 charges \$50 each month with a \$20 startup fee. Company 3 charges \$60 each month and has no startup fee. Company 4 charges \$30 each month and a \$30 startup fee. The cell phone pricing structure for one of the companies is graphed below.

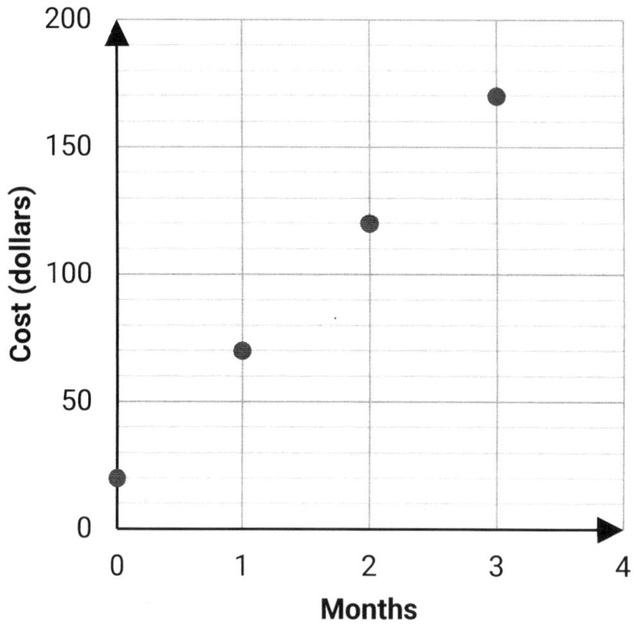

Which company does the graph represent?

a. Company 1: $y = 45x + 30$
b. Company 2: $y = 50x + 20$
c. Company 3: $y = 60x$
d. Company 4: $y = 30x + 30$

27. A parallelogram has two bases, each equal to 18 cm, and a height of 8 cm. What is the area of the parallelogram?

a. 288 cm^2
b. 72 cm^2
c. 144 cm^2
d. 96 cm^2

28. Select the correct answer for each blank below. Craig purchased a bundle of 4 baseball game tickets. The ticket price is the same for all games. The total price of the bundle was $287.16.

The price of one baseball game is ________.

$73.79
$72.79
$71.79
$70.79

29. Judith purchased a box from the U.S. Postal Service with dimensions of 12 inches by 8 inches by 6 inches. How many cubic inches of space inside the box does she have available for use?

a. 576 in^3
b. 26 in^3
c. 288 in^3
d. 1296 in^3

30. A pothole has a radius of 9 inches. Which of the following best represents the distance around the pothole?

a. 14.13 inches
b. 28.26 inches
c. 42.39 inches
d. 56.52 inches

31. What is the area of a trapezoid with base lengths of 7 cm and 10 cm and a height of 5 cm?

a. 85 cm^2
b. 42.5 cm^2
c. 28 cm^2
d. 8.5 cm^2

32. What is the sample space when rolling two standard dice?

a. 18
b. 6
c. 12
d. 36

33. What is the sample space when flipping a coin 3 times?

a. TTT, HHH, THT, HTH, TTH, HHT, THH, HTT
b. TTT, HHH, THT, HTH, TTH, HHT, THH, HTT, THT
c. TTT, HHH, THT, HTH, HHT, THH, HTT
d. TTT, HHH, THT, HTH, TTH, HHT, THH, HTT, THT, HTH, HHT, THH

34. **Kevin spins a spinner with 8 sections labeled 1 through 8. He also flips a coin. What is the probability he will land on a number less than 5 and get tails?**

a. $\frac{7}{8}$
b. $\frac{1}{4}$
c. $\frac{5}{16}$
d. $\frac{1}{2}$

35. **A box contains 8 yellow marbles, 9 orange marbles, and 1 green marble. What is the probability that Ann pulls out a yellow marble, replaces it, and then pulls a green marble?**

a. $\frac{4}{153}$
b. $\frac{1}{2}$
c. $\frac{4}{9}$
d. $\frac{2}{81}$

36. **An architect is creating a blueprint of an apartment for a client. The blueprint is a scale drawing of the actual apartment being built. In the architect's first draft of the blueprint shown below, 1 inch = 4 feet; however, she wants to use a different scale to make her next draft slightly bigger. Use her new scale of 1 inch = 2 feet to find the dimensions of the study in the new blueprint.**

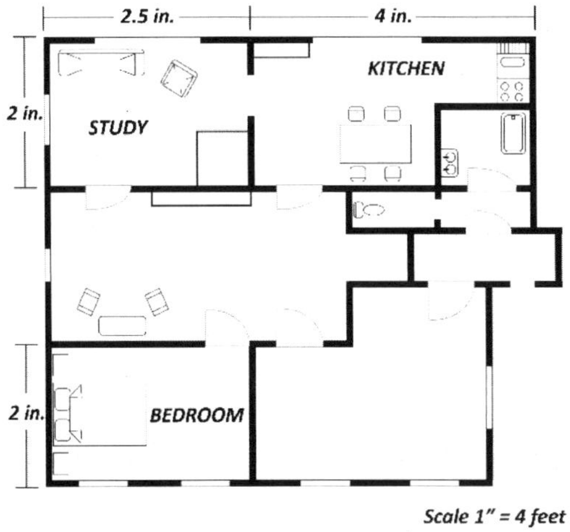

a. Length = 8 inches, Width = 4 inches
b. Length = 5 inches, Width = 8 inches
c. Length = 5 inches, Width = 4 inches
d. Length = 4 inches, Width = 4 inches

37. In the given rectangular prism, describe a possible cross section perpendicular to the base. Select all that apply.

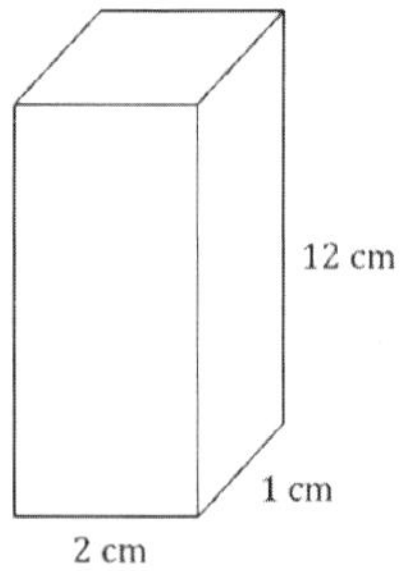

a. one 2 cm by 1 cm rectangle
b. one 12 cm by 2 cm rectangle
c. one 3 cm by 12 cm rectangle
d. one 13 cm by 2cm rectangle
e. one 12 cm by 1 cm rectangle

38. A local fruit stand records the number of apples and oranges sold each day in June. The data is shown in the dot plots below. Describe the degree of visual overlap between the distribution of apples and oranges sold.

a. moderate overlap between fruit amounts of 20 and 30
b. slight overlap between fruit amounts of 20 and 30
c. no overlap between fruit amounts of 20 and 30
d. large overlap between fruit amounts of 20 and 30

39. Part A: According to the latest estimates, approximately 35% of adults in the United States have 20/20 vision, which means they do not need glasses or corrective lenses of any kind. Jeremy is taking a random sample of five adults. He wants to know the probability of selecting three adults who have 20/20 vision and two adults who do not have 20/20 vision. He will run a simulation with a spinner that has twenty blank equal sections. How should Jeremy label the spinner to run a proper simulation?

a. 7 spaces with 20/20 and 7 spaces without 20/20
b. 13 spaces with 20/20 and 13 spaces without 20/20
c. 7 spaces with 20/20 and 13 spaces without 20/20
d. 13 spaces with 20/20 and 7 spaces without 20/20

Part B: After labeling the spinner, describe how Jeremy should run the simulation to estimate the probability of selecting five US adults at random, where three adults have 20/20 vision and two adults do not have 20/20 vision.

a. spin the spinner 5 times, record the results, and repeat the process
b. close his eyes, randomly point to a section 5 times, record the results, and repeat the process
c. spin the spinner 10 times, record the results, and repeat the process
d. close his eyes, randomly point to a section 10 times, record the results, and repeat the process

40. A sandwich shop allows customers to choose the size of their bread and the type of meat. The options for bread sizes are 6 inches and 12 inches. The options for the type of meat are turkey, ham, roast beef, tuna, and chicken. Suppose a customer orders a type of bread and meat at random. Which of the following tree diagrams properly represents the outcomes of the sample space?

a.
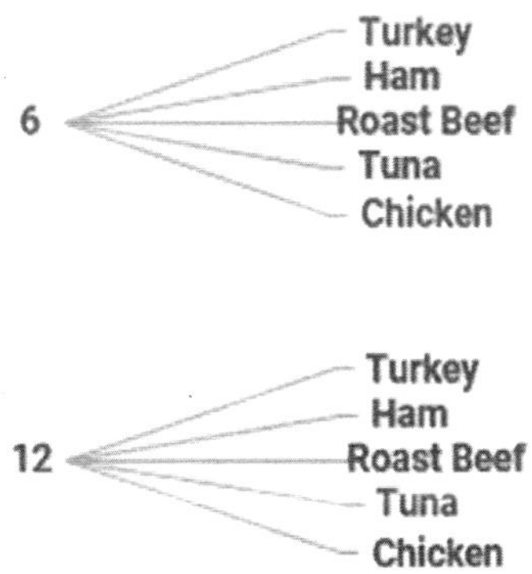

c.
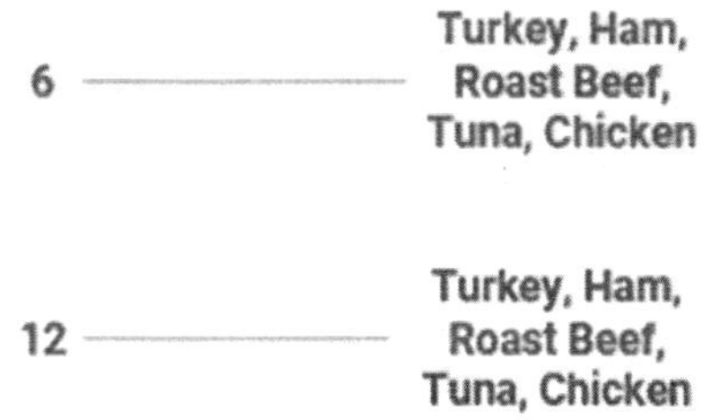

b.
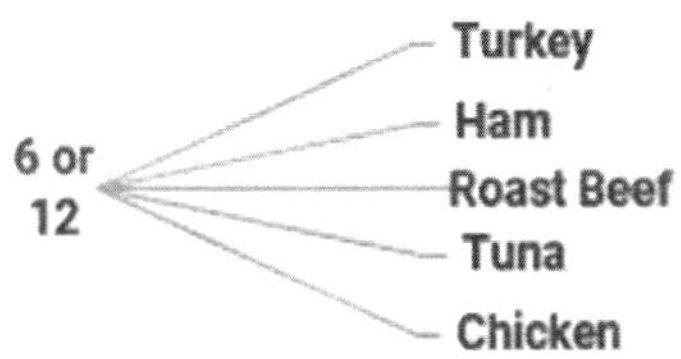

d.
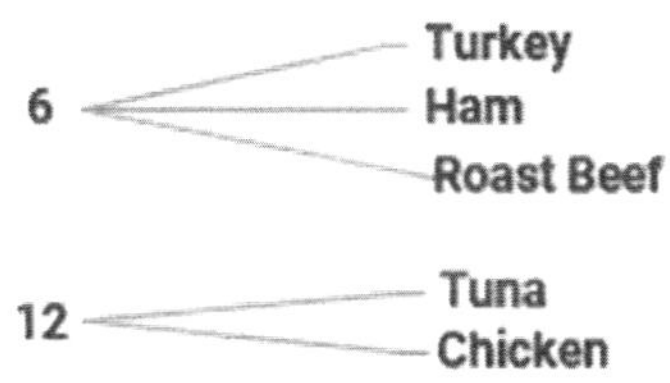

41. Given side lengths of 4 cm and 4 cm and the included angle of 45°, determine whether a unique triangle is possible.

a. A unique triangle is possible due to SSA.
b. A unique triangle is not possible due to SAS.
c. A unique triangle is not possible due to SSA.
d. A unique triangle is possible due to SAS.

42. Use the image below to find the measure of $\angle CAD$.

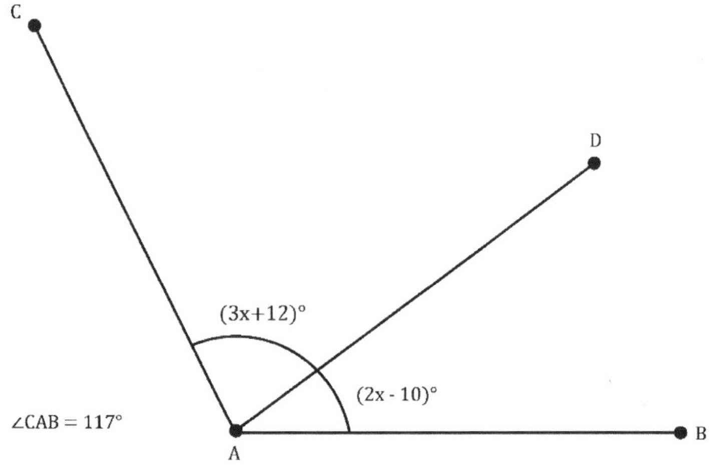

a. $m\angle CAD = 23°$
b. $m\angle CAD = 36°$
c. $m\angle CAD = 69°$
d. $m\angle CAD = 81°$

43. Trevor collects trading cards. The store where he typically buys his packs of trading cards is running a special promotion, claiming that 20% of the packs have a special, limited-edition card inside. Interested in getting one of these special cards, Trevor goes to the store and purchases five packs of cards. To his dismay, none of the packs contain the special card. He is interested in running a simulation to approximate the probability of having 0 out of 5 packs of cards containing the special card, assuming the true probability of selecting a special card is 20%. Which of the following simulations should Trevor use to approximate his probability?

a. Using a 10-sided spinner, label 2 of the sides "winners" and 8 of the sides "losers." Randomly spin the spinner five times, then record the number of times he gets a "winner." Do not repeat the process.
b. Using a 10-sided spinner, label 2 of the sides "winners" and 8 of the sides "losers." Randomly spin the spinner five times, then record the number of times he gets a "winner." Repeat this process 100 times and calculate the percentage of the 100 spins where 0 "winners" were recorded.
c. Using a 10-sided spinner, label 8 of the sides "winners" and 2 of the sides "losers." Randomly spin the spinner five times, then record the number of times he gets a "winner." Do not repeat the process.
d. Using a 10-sided spinner, label 8 of the sides "winners" and 2 of the sides "losers." Randomly spin the spinner five times, then record the number of times he gets a "winner." Repeat this process 100 times and calculate the percentage of the 100 spins where 0 "winners" were recorded.

44. Lucy has \$25 and needs to buy pens, highlighters, and notebooks. Each pack of pens costs \$4. Each pack of highlighters costs \$5. Each notebook costs \$1.50. Which of the following inequalities may be used to find the combinations of pens, highlighters, and notebooks that she may purchase?

a. $4p + 5h + 1.5n > 25$
b. $4p + 5h + 1.5n < 25$
c. $4p + 5h + 1.5n \leq 25$
d. $4p + 5h + 1.5n \geq 25$

45. Henry is three times as old as Truman. Two years ago, Henry was five times as old as Truman. How old is Henry now?

a. 4
b. 8
c. 12
d. 16

46. Elise, Max, and Rylie are each offering lawn care services. Their prices for each service are listed in the table below. Prices are per square foot.

	Elise	Max	Rylie
Mowing	\$0.0025	\$0.002	\$0.003
Edging	\$0.0015	\$0.0015	\$0.002
Weeding	\$0.055	\$0.065	\$0.05

Ms. Lin wants to have her 7,500 square foot lawn mowed and edged. She also has a flower bed of x square feet to be weeded. Which of the following inequalities represents x if Elise's services are a better deal than Max's?

a. $x < 250$
b. $x < 375$
c. $x > 250$
d. $x > 375$

47. Thirty-five boys went out for the soccer team. Of these, $\frac{5}{7}$ made the team. Of the boys who made the team, $\frac{4}{5}$ showed up for practice on Wednesday. How many boys were at the Wednesday practice?

a. 18
b. 20
c. 22
d. 25

48. What is the value of the following:

$$-6 + |-6|$$

a. 0
b. 12
c. -12
d. -6

49. Raquel pays \$12 per ticket to the fair, plus an \$8 parking fee. Let x represent the number of tickets she buys. Which of the following equations represents her total cost y?

a. $y = 8x + 12$
b. $y = 20x$
c. $y = 12x + 8$
d. $y = 12x + 20$

50. A local animal shelter recorded the monthly number of cats and dogs adopted. The data is shown in the histograms below. Describe the degree of visual overlap between the number of cats and dogs adopted monthly.

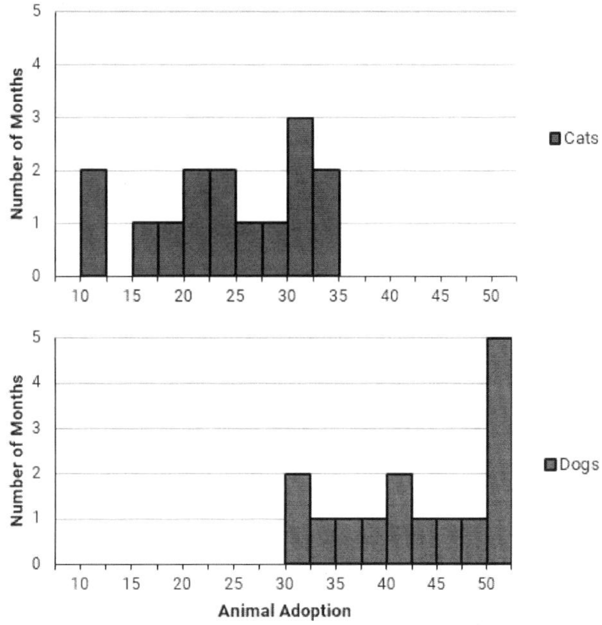

a. moderate overlap between 30 and 35 adoptions for each animal
b. slight overlap between 30 and 35 adoptions for each animal
c. no overlap between 30 and 35 adoptions for each animal
d. large overlap between 30 and 35 adoptions for each animal

Answers and Explanations for Test #2

1. D: Sarah sells 45 total sweatshirts. $\frac{1}{5}$ of the sweatshirts sold are medium. $\frac{1}{5}$ of 45 is 9. This means 9 medium sweatshirts were sold. Twice as many large sweatshirts were sold than medium sweatshirts. 18 is twice as much as 9. This means 18 large sweatshirts were sold. Subtract 9 and 18 from 45 to determine how many small sweatshirts were sold: $45 - 9 - 18 = 18$. 18 small sweatshirts were sold at $12.80 each. Multiply $18 \times \$12.80 = \$230.40$. Sarah earned $230.40 from the sales of small sweatshirts.

2. B: To find miles per hour just divide the number of miles by the number of hours. In this case 3 hours and 20 minutes is equal to $3\frac{1}{3}$ hours. 1510 divided by $3\frac{1}{3}$ is approximately 453 mph.

3. A, B, D: The net consists of 5 shapes. The area can be determined using the area formula for triangles and rectangles.

Triangles: $A = \frac{1}{2}(bh)$ which becomes $A = \frac{1}{2}(9)(6)$ and then $A = 27$. Each triangle has an area of 27 square inches. There are two of these triangles, so select "2 triangles with an area of 27 square inches".

Center rectangle: $A = bh$ becomes $A = (9)(6)$ and then $A = 54$. There is one of these rectangles, so select "1 rectangle with an area of 54 square inches".

Left and right rectangles: $A = bh$ becomes $A = (7.5)(6)$ and then $A = 45$. There are two of these rectangles, so select "2 rectangles with an area of 45 square inches".

4. C: The following proportion can be used to solve the problem: $\frac{35}{3} = \frac{x}{18}$, where x represents the number of mature trees. Solving for x gives $3x = 630$, which simplifies to $x = 210$.

5. D: The only statement that is true is statement D. The oldest visitor on Monday, represented by the furthest right dot, is approximately 77 years old. The oldest visitor on Friday is approximately 73 years old. This means that the oldest visitor on Monday is older than the oldest visitor on Friday.

Choice A is incorrect because the median age of a visitor on Monday is approximately 44. The median age of a visitor on Friday is approximately 51. 44 is not 6 more than 51.

Choice B is incorrect because the range of ages on Monday is approximately $77 - 25 = 52$. The approximate range of ages on Friday is $73 - 42 = 31$. The range of ages on Monday is larger than the range of ages on Friday.

Choice C is incorrect because the interquartile range for Friday is approximately 17. The interquartile range for Monday is approximately 24. 17 is not twice as much as 24.

6. B: The price per serving represents a unit rate. To calculate the price per one serving of cereal, divide the cost of each container by the number of servings.

Medium Box: $\$4.60 \div 10 = 0.46$ which is 46 cents per serving. Move the decimal point one place to the left when dividing by 10.

Bargain Bag: $\$3.30 \div 30 = 0.11$ which is 11 cents per serving. Dividing by 30 is the same thing as dividing by 10 and then dividing by 3. Move the decimal point one place to the left to divide by 10, 3.3 becomes 0.33. Then divide by 3. 0.33 divided by 3 is 0.11.

Family Size Bag: $\$3.80 \div 20 = 0.19$ which is 19 cents per serving. Dividing by 20 is the same thing as dividing by 10 and then dividing by 2. Move the decimal point one place to the left to divide by 10, 3.8 becomes 0.38. Then divide by 2. 0.38 divided by 2 is 0.19.

Jumbo Bag: $\$8.60 \div 20 = 0.43$ which is 43 cents per serving. Dividing by 20 is the same thing as dividing by 10 and then dividing by 2. Move the decimal point one place to the left when dividing by 10, 8.6 becomes 0.86. Then divide by 2. 0.86 divided by 2 is 0.43.

The least expensive cereal is the Bargain Bag because it has the lowest price per serving.

7. Part A: A: Since the line that divides the shaded and non-shaded region runs from corner to corner it cuts the rectangle in half. This means you can just find the area of the rectangle and divide by 2. However, there are two smaller rectangles like this. So, if you take half of each that is the same as one whole rectangle. The area of the rectangle is 5 cm times 12 cm which is 60 cm. Since you would divide by 2 to get the area of one but then multiply back by 2 to get the area of both there is no need to do either. The area of the shaded region is 60 sq cm.

Part B: B: As mentioned in Part A, since the line that divides them cuts the rectangle in half, the regions are the same size.

8. C: Start by converting both values to fraction form. 3.5 is equivalent to $3\frac{1}{2}$, or the improper fraction $\frac{7}{2}$. The problem is now $\frac{7}{2} \times \frac{1}{4}$. Multiply numerator by numerator, and denominator by denominator, then simplify if necessary. $\frac{7}{2} \times \frac{1}{4}$ becomes $\frac{7}{8}$, which is in simplest form.

9. C: The only true statement from the list of items is choice C. The least popular item in both grades was vegetable chili. $11 \times 2 = 22$, and 31 is greater than 22. $14 \times 2 = 28$, and 30 is greater than 28. This shows that calzones received twice as many votes as vegetable chili did in both 7th and 8th grade.

10. B: Based on the company's charge per half of an acre, the original charge is equal to $\$25 \times 4$, or \$100, since there are 4 half-acres in 2 acres. With the discount of 20%, the following expression can be used to determine the final charge: $x - 0.20x$, where x represents the original charge. Substitution of 100 for x gives $100 - 0.20(100)$, which equals $100 - 20$, or 80. Thus, the company will charge \$80.

11. B: The original price was \$290,600 (\$278,00 + \$12,600). To determine the percentage of reduction, the following proportion can be written: $\frac{12{,}600}{290{,}600} = \frac{x}{100}$. To solve, cross multiply to create the equation: $\$1{,}260{,}000 = \$290{,}600x$, which simplifies to $x \approx 4\%$. Thus, the percentage of reduction was approximately 4%.

12. D: The total was \$5.17 and the 4 apples cost \$3.76 since $0.94 \times 4 = 3.76$. Therefore, \$5.17-\$3.76=\$1.41 that was spent on bananas. Since there were 3 bananas, divide \$1.41 by 3 to get \$0.47 per banana. The equation $5.17 = 4(0.94) + 3b$ could also be used to solve this problem.

13. C: First, find what Melanie makes in a week. She makes \$12 an hour times 40 hours, so she makes \$480. Then take off 15% percent for her taxes ($100\% - 15\% = 85\%$) using the proportion: $\frac{x}{480} = \frac{85}{100}$. After cross multiplying and solving for x, it is determined that Melanie makes \$408 in one week. Next, find what Lynn makes in one week. She makes \$14 an hour times 40 hours, so she makes \$560. Then take 18% off for her taxes ($100\% - 18\% = 82\%$) using the proportion $\frac{x}{560} = \frac{82}{100}$. After cross multiplying and solving for x, it is determined that Lynn makes \$459.2 in one week. Then subtract what Melanie makes from what Lynn makes to find out how much more Lynn makes: \$459.20-\$408= \$51.20.

14. D: One way to find the equation is by finding the slope (m) and y-intercept (b) separately and then plugging them into the equation $y = mx + b$. Start by using the slope formula to find the slope of the linear function. Choose any two points from the table, like (1,9) and (2,11).

$$m = \frac{y_2 - y_1}{x_2 - x_1} = \frac{11 - 9}{2 - 1} = \frac{2}{1} = 2$$

Therefore, the slope of the line is 2, meaning for every increase in 1 x-value, the y-value increases by 2. Now we need to find the y-intercept, or the value of y when $x = 0$. Since the table gives us the value of y when $x = 1$, we can use the slope to work backwards. Subtract 2 from the y-value of 9, the value when $x = 1$.

$$9 - 2 = 7$$

Therefore, the value of y when $x = 0$, or the y-intercept, is 7. Finally, substitute 2 into the equation as the value for slope (m) and 7 into the equation as the value for the y-intercept (b).

$$y = 2x + 7$$

The table lists ordered pairs representing the linear equation $y = 2x + 7$. Each y-value is 7 more than twice the value of the x. If the value of x is 5, then the value of y is 17. 17 is 7 more than twice the value of 5. (5,17) is the only ordered pair that follows this rule. Every (x, y) pair in the table follows this rule.

15. D: The sum of the interior angles of a triangle is 180°. In this case, the tringle has interior angles that measure 50°, b°, and b°. This means that the equation $b° + 50° = 180°$ is true. Equation A is correct: $180° = 50° + b° + b°$.

The two b angles can be combined into $2b$. This means that equation B is also correct: $50° + 2b° = 180°$.

When 50 is subtracted from both sides of the equation $50° + 2b° = 180°$, the result is $180° - 50° = 2b°$. This means that equation C is also correct. Equations A, B, and C are correct.

Equation D is incorrect because the sum of the interior angles does not equal 360°.

16. C: The number of flowers Eliza can plant depends on how many minutes she is working. This means number of minutes is the independent variable, x, and the number of flowers is the dependent variable, y. Set up the constant of proportionality equation $y = kx$. In order to isolate the variable k, divide both sides of the equation by x.

$$\frac{y}{x} = k$$

Now substitute corresponding values in for x and y in order to solve for k. For example, $\frac{y}{x} = k$ becomes $\frac{12}{1} = k$ which simplifies to $12 = k$. The constant of proportionality is 12.

17. B: Point T is equal to $2\frac{2}{3}$ and S is equal to 4. Perform all of the equations to figure out which one produces a number that is not on the number line. 2T-S= $2(2\frac{2}{3})$-4= $1\frac{1}{3}$ which is not on the number line.

18. Part A: C: There are a total of 8 spaces on the spinner all of equal size. There are 6 spaces that are 12 or greater. $\frac{6}{8} = \frac{3}{4}$.

Part B: A: The first time the probability was $\frac{3}{4}$ and the second time the probability is also $\frac{3}{4}$. The probability of it happening both times though is $\frac{3}{4} \times \frac{3}{4}$ which is $\frac{9}{16}$.

19. B: If he buys each toy for \$4.10 and then has another \$1.30 in it, then he has a total of \$5.40 in each toy. He marks it up 30% to sell it (100% + 30% = 130%), so the following proportion can be used to determine the sales price: $\frac{x}{5.40} = \frac{130}{100}$. Cross multiply and solve for x, so his sales price is 7.02.

20. A: Complementary angles sum to 90 degrees. Since Angle B measures 28°, Angle A measures 90° − 28°, or 62°.

21. A: Similar polygons must have congruent corresponding angles and proportional corresponding sides. Both requirements must be fulfilled in order to declare similarity in polygons.

22. D: The only correct statement is choice D. The mode refers to the most common value. The height that is most common will have the greatest number of dots. The mode for Class A is 173 centimeters, which has 4 dots. The mode for Class B is 183 centimeters, which has 3 dots. 183 is 10 more than 173, therefore the mode in Class B is 10 more than the mode in Class A.

23. A: If it takes him $\frac{2}{5}$ of a minute to dribble $\frac{2}{3}$ of the field then divide by 2 to get $\frac{1}{5}$ of a minute for $\frac{1}{3}$ of the field. Then you can multiply by 3 to get $\frac{3}{3}$ of the field in $\frac{3}{5}$ of a minute. $\frac{3}{5}$ of a minute equals 36 seconds.

24. C: If he puts a tire on that is 2 inches thick then that adds 4 inches to the overall diameter. Now the radius is 12 inches. The formula for circumference is $2\pi r$. 2 times 12π is 24π.

25. B: If all the side lengths in the rectangle $ABCD$ are multiplied or divided by the same amount, then the new rectangle will be similar to rectangle $ABCD$. The only set of side lengths similar to rectangle $ABCD$ is 60 m, 60 m, 96 m, 96 m. In this case, all the original side lengths are multiplied by 3, resulting in a similar rectangle.

$$20 \times 3 = 60$$
$$32 \times 3 = 96$$

26. B: Company 2 charges \$50 each month plus a \$20 startup fee. The \$20 startup fee represents the graph's y-intercept. The \$50 per month charge is represented by the graph's slope of 50.

$$m = \frac{y_2 - y_1}{x_2 - x_1} = \frac{70 - 20}{1 - 0} = \frac{50}{1} = 50$$

The graphed line has a slope of 50 and a y-intercept of 20. This line is expressed as the equation $y = 50x + 20$. The pricing structure for Company 2 is graphed.

27. C: The area of a parallelogram can be calculated using the formula $A = bh$. The length of the base of the parallelogram is 18 cm, and the height is 8 cm. Thus, the area is equal to 18×8 cm^2, or 144 cm^2.

28. \$71.79: The scenario is a unit rate problem. 4 tickets cost \$287.16. A proportion can be used to find the cost of one ticket. Set two ratios equal to each other, and then use cross-multiplication to solve for the unknown price.

$$\frac{4 \text{ tickets}}{\$287.16} = \frac{1 \text{ ticket}}{\$x}$$

Cross-multiply to solve for x.

$$4x = 287.16$$

Divide both sides of the equation by 4.

$$\frac{4x}{4} = \frac{287.16}{4}$$
$$x = 71.79$$

The cost of one game ticket is \$71.79.

29. A: The box is a rectangular prism, and the amount of available space inside the box is synonymous with the volume of the box. The volume of a rectangular prism is calculated by finding the product of the length, width, and height. Thus, the volume of the box is equal to $12 \times 8 \times 6$ in^3, or 576 cubic inches.

30. D: The distance around the pothole indicates the circumference of the pothole. The circumference of a circle can be determined by using the formula $C = \pi d$, where C represents the circumference and d represents the diameter. The diameter of the pothole is 18 inches (9×2). Substituting a diameter of 18 inches and 3.14 for the value of pi gives the following: $C = 3.14(18)$, or 56.52. Thus, the distance around the pothole is equal to 56.52 inches.

31. B: The area of a trapezoid can be found by using the formula $A = \frac{1}{2}(b_1 + b_2)h$, where b_1 and b_2 represent the lengths of the bases and h represents the height of the trapezoid. Substituting the given base lengths and height reveals the following: $A = \frac{1}{2}(7 + 10)5$, which equals 42.5. Thus, the area of the trapezoid is 42.5 cm^2.

32. D: The sample space of rolling each die is 6. Thus, the sample space of rolling two dice is equal to the product of the sample spaces. $6 \times 6 = 36$; therefore, the sample space is equal to 36.

33. A: Flipping a coin one time has a sample space equal to 2, i.e., T or H. Flipping a coin 2 times has a sample space equal to 4, i.e., TT, HH, TH, HT. Flipping a coin 3 times has a sample space of 8, i.e., TTT, HHH, THT, HTH, TTH, HHT, THH, HTT.

34. B: The events are independent since the spin of a spinner does not have an effect on the outcome of the flip of a coin. The probability of two independent events can be found using the formula $P(A\ and\ B) = P(A) \cdot P(B)$. The probability of landing on a number less than 5 is $\frac{4}{8}$ since there are 4 possible numbers less than 5 (1, 2, 3, and 4). The probability of getting tails is $\frac{1}{2}$. The probability of landing on a number less than 5 and getting tails is $\frac{4}{8} \cdot \frac{1}{2}$, which equals $\frac{4}{16}$, or $\frac{1}{4}$.

35. D: The events are independent since Ann replaces the first marble drawn. The probability of two independent events can be found using the formula $P(A\ and\ B) = P(A) \cdot P(B)$. The probability of pulling out a yellow marble is $\frac{8}{18}$. The probability of pulling out a green marble after the yellow marble has been replaced is $\frac{1}{18}$. The probability that Ann pulls out a yellow marble and then a green marble is $\frac{8}{18} \cdot \frac{1}{18}$, which equals $\frac{8}{324}$, which reduces to $\frac{2}{81}$.

36. C: First, convert the length and width of the study in the blueprint to the actual dimensions using the given scale factor $\frac{4 \text{ feet}}{1 \text{ inch}}$.

$$\text{Length} = 2.5 \text{ inches} \cdot \frac{4 \text{ feet}}{1 \text{ inch}} = 2.5 \cdot 4 \text{ feet} = 10 \text{ feet}$$
$$\text{Width} = 2 \text{ inches} \cdot \frac{4 \text{ feet}}{1 \text{ inch}} = 2 \cdot 4 \text{ feet} = 8 \text{ feet}$$

Then, convert the actual dimensions of the study with the new scale of 1 inch = 2 feet using the scale factor $\frac{1\text{ inch}}{2\text{ feet}}$.

$$\text{Length} = 10\text{ feet} \cdot \frac{1\text{ inch}}{2\text{ feet}} = \frac{10}{2}\text{ inches} = 5\text{ inches}$$
$$\text{Width} = 8\text{ feet} \cdot \frac{1\text{ inch}}{2\text{ feet}} = \frac{8}{2}\text{ inches} = 4\text{ inches}$$

Therefore, the dimensions of the study in the new blueprint are 4 inches by 3 inches.

37. B, E: If the cross-section is perpendicular to the base and parallel to the 12 cm by 1 cm face of the prism, the result is a rectangle with dimensions congruent to the parallel face. Similarly, if the cross-section is perpendicular to the base and parallel to the 12 cm by 2 cm face of the prism, the result is a rectangle with dimensions congruent to the parallel face.

38. A: There is a moderate overlap between the number of apples sold daily and the number of oranges sold daily. Apples were sold on 13 days between the amounts of 20 and 30, and oranges were sold on 27 days between the amounts of 20 and 30.

39. Part A: C: He should label seven as adults with 20/20 vision and thirteen without 20/20 vision. This would give the spinner a 35% chance ($\frac{7}{20}$=0.35) of selecting an adult with 20/20 vision.

Part B: A: After labeling the spinner, he should spin the spinner five times and record the results of the five spins. He should repeat this process many times until he has enough outcomes to calculate the probability.

40. A: For a tree diagram, each set of branches represents one event. The number of branches should equal the number of possibilities for that event. There are two types of bread, so the first set of branches should have two possibilities: 6 or 12 inches. There are five types of meat, so each branch for bread type should have five branches to represent the combinations of meat that can be had with each bread. The total number of outcomes is ten since $2 \times 5 = 10$. Answer choice A is the best representation of the sample space. Answer choice B does not use different branches to represent the two different types of bread, and answer choice C does not use different branches to represent the five different types of meat. Answer choice D does not include all types of possible meat with each type of bread.

41. D: Since this is an example of SAS, it results in a unique triangle. Drawing this requires technology or a ruler and protractor, but the resulting triangle will look like the triangle below. Any orientation of the same triangle is a correct answer as long as the 45° angle and the length of each side are drawn accurately.

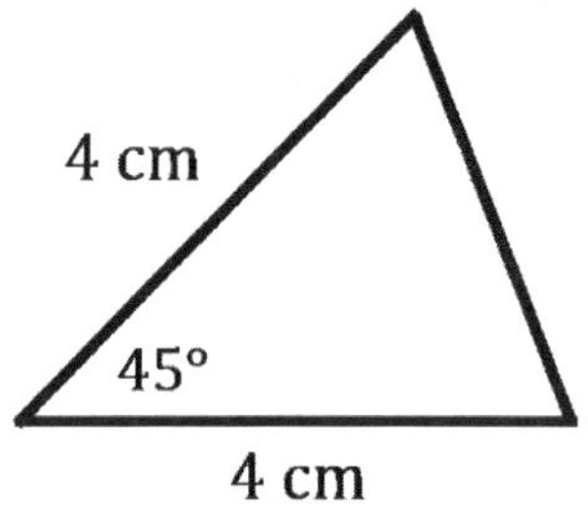

42. D: The $m\angle CAD$ is equal to 81°. Angle CAD is adjacent to angle DAB, so their sum is equal to the measure of angle CAB.

$$m\angle CAD + m\angle DAB = m\angle CAB$$
$$(3x + 12) + (2x - 10) = 117$$

$$\frac{5x + 2}{-2} = \frac{117}{-2}$$
$$\frac{5x}{5} = \frac{115}{5}$$
$$x = 23$$

Substitute $x = 23$ into $3x + 12$ to find the measure of angle CAD.

$$m\angle CAD = 3(23) + 12 = 69 + 12 = 81°$$

43. B: Since the probability of selecting a winner is 20%, the chance process of spinning a 10-sided spinner should have an outcome that has a 20% chance of occurring. 20% of ten sides is two, so two of the sides should be labeled "winners" and the other eight "losers." Then, to simulate buying 5 cards, the spinner should be spun five times, and the number of winners out of 5 should be recorded. To approximate the probability of getting 0 out of 5 winners, the simulation of five sample spins must be repeated many times to calculate the number of times out of the many simulations 0 out of 5 winners occurred. Answer choice B is the best simulation. Answer choice A does not repeat the process of 5 spins. Answer choices C and D label the spinner with an 80% chance of winning, not 20%.

44. C: The inequality will be less than or equal to 25 because she only has $25 available to spend on her purchase.

45. C: If t equals Truman's age now, and 3t equals Henry's age now, $t - 2$ equals Truman's age two years ago and $3t - 2$ equals Henry's age two years ago. Since Henry was 5 times as old as Truman two years ago, we can solve for $3t - 2 = 5(t - 2)$. Solving this gives us $3t - 2 = 5t - 10$ or$2t = 8$. Therefore, $t = 4$. Since Henry is three times as old as Truman, Henry is 12.

46. D: Start by calculating the cost of each person's mowing and edging.

Elise's cost: $0.0025(7{,}500) + 0.0015(7{,}500) = 18.75 + 11.25 = \$30$

Max's cost: $0.002(7{,}500) + 0.0015(7{,}500) = 15 + 11.25 = \$26.25$

Now we can set up an inequality, letting x be the size of the flower bed. For Elise's services to be a better deal, they must cost less than Max's.

$$30 + 0.055x < 26.25 + 0.065x$$

Solve for x by subtracting $0.055x$ from both sides.

$$30 < 26.25 + 0.01x$$

Now, subtract 26.25 from each side.

$$3.75 < 0.01x$$

We rewrite this as $0.01x > 3.75$ and divide each side by 0.01 to obtain $x > 375$. It is important to remember to reverse the inequality sign when we move the x to the left so we don't end up with $x < 375$ (answer choice B).

47. B: Since $\frac{4}{5}$ of $\frac{5}{7}$ of 35 boys were at the practice, this is $35 \times \frac{5}{7} \times \frac{4}{5} = 35 \times \frac{4}{7} = 5 \times 4 = 20$.

48. A: Absolute value is the distance a number is away from zero. Therefore, it is always a positive value, so $-6 + |-6| = -6 + 6$. Opposite values are numbers that are the same distance away from zero on a number line, but on opposite sides of zero. When adding opposite values together, the resulting value will always equal zero. Therefore, $-6 + 6 = 0$.

49. C: Raquel's total cost y equals \$12 times the number of tickets x, plus \$8. In other words, $y = 12x + 8$.

50. B: There is a slight overlap between the number of cats and dogs adopted. There were five months where 30 to 35 cats were adopted and three months where 30 to 35 dogs were adopted. For the most part, the number of dogs adopted each month was higher than the number of cats.

Online Resources

Due to our efforts to try to keep this book to a manageable length, we've created a link that will give you access to all of your online resources:

mometrix.com/resources719/terranextg7math

It's Your Moment, Let's Celebrate It!

Share your story @mometrixtestpreparation